Deploying .NET Applications
Learning MSBuild and ClickOnce

Sayed Y. Hashimi and
Sayed Ibrahim Hashimi

Apress®

Deploying .NET Applications: Learning MSBuild and ClickOnce

Copyright © 2006 by Sayed Y. Hashimi, Sayed Ibrahim Hashimi

ISBN-13 (pbk): 978-1-59059-652-4

ISBN-10 (pbk): 1-59059-652-8

Printed and bound in the United States of America 9 8 7 6 5 4 3 2 1

Lead Editor: Jonathan Hassell
Technical Reviewer: Bart De Smet
Editorial Board: Steve Anglin, Ewan Buckingham, Gary Cornell, Jason Gilmore, Jonathan Gennick, Jonathan Hassell, James Huddleston, Chris Mills, Matthew Moodie, Dominic Shakeshaft, Jim Sumser, Keir Thomas, Matt Wade
Project Manager: Richard Dal Porto
Copy Edit Manager: Nicole LeClerc
Copy Editor: Kim Wimpsett
Assistant Production Director: Kari Brooks-Copony
Production Editor: Ellie Fountain
Compositor: Kinetic Publishing Services, LLC
Proofreader: Dan Shaw
Indexer: Brenda Miller
Artist: Kinetic Publishing Services, LLC
Cover Designer: Kurt Krames
Manufacturing Director: Tom Debolski

Distributed to the book trade worldwide by Springer-Verlag New York, Inc., 233 Spring Street, 6th Floor, New York, NY 10013. Phone 1-800-SPRINGER, fax 201-348-4505, e-mail orders-ny@springer-sbm.com, or visit http://www.springeronline.com.

For information on translations, please contact Apress directly at 2560 Ninth Street, Suite 219, Berkeley, CA 94710. Phone 510-549-5930, fax 510-549-5939, e-mail info@apress.com, or visit http://www.apress.com.

The source code for this book is available to readers at http://www.apress.com in the Source Code section.

To my parents, Sayed A. and Sohayla Hashimi,
and to my wife and daughter, Farishta and Fairoza.
—Sayed Y. Hashimi

To my parents, Sayed A. and Sohayla Hashimi,
because this would have not been possible without their support and guidance.
—Sayed Ibrahim Hashimi

Contents at a Glance

Contents

About the Authors

 **SAYED Y. HASHIMI** was born in Kabul, Afghanistan, and now resides in Jacksonville, Florida. Sayed has expertise in the areas of healthcare, banking, logistics, scientific computing, and civil/structural engineering. In his professional career, Sayed has developed large-scale distributed applications with a variety of programming languages and platforms, including C++, Java, and .NET. He has published articles in major software journals and is the principal author of *Pro Service-Oriented Smart Clients with .NET 2.0* (Apress, 2005). Sayed has a master's degree in engineering from the University of Florida. You can reach Sayed by visiting http://www.sayedhashimi.com.

 **SAYED IBRAHIM HASHIMI** has a computer engineering degree from the University of Florida. He works in Jacksonville, Florida, as a developer and architect. He is an expert in the financial, education, and collection industries. His primary focus is working with .NET, but he also has extensive industrial experience with Java-based technologies. Sayed's research interests include a wide range of topics including computer graphics, peer-to-peer technologies, and lucid dreaming. You can read Sayed's blog at http://www.sedodream.com. When he's not busy creating software or dreaming, you're likely to find him at the local coffee shop.

About the Technical Reviewer

■BART DE SMET was born on February 11, 1983, in Belgium and has a master's degree in computer science from Ghent University. Since early 2000, Bart has been involved in the wonderful world of .NET and is also a Visual C# MVP. While keeping his brain busy with further university studies, he focuses on C#, the CLR, SQL Server 2005, and WinFX. Regularly you can find Bart speaking at various European Microsoft events, and if time permits, he writes articles for the local MSDN Web site. To read about his adventures in the .NET galaxy, check out Bart's blog at http://blogs.bartdesmet.net/bart.

Acknowledgments

Writing this book took effort from not only the authors but also from some of the very talented staff at Apress. Therefore, we would like to thank Jonathan Hassell, Richard Dal Porto, Ellie Fountain, and Kim Wimpsett. We would also like to acknowledge the technical reviewer, Bart De Smet, for taking the time to review the book. His corrections and commentary were invaluable.

Introduction

This book covers two important aspects of the software life cycle: build and deployment. The coverage of these crucial topics is only half the attraction of this book, though. The other half is the technologies covered: MSBuild and ClickOnce.

What Is MSBuild?

Previously the build process that Visual Studio followed was basically a black box and was difficult to customize. With the arrival of Visual Studio 2005 and .NET 2.0 comes the arrival of the Microsoft Build Engine, otherwise known as MSBuild. MSBuild is the utility that Visual Studio uses to build your managed (C#, VB .NET, and J#) projects. MSBuild is an XML-based build engine and a tool that has been developed with customizability and extensibility in mind from its conception. By using MSBuild, you can change how your projects are built, creating customizations to fit your needs.

With the advent of MSBuild, you no longer have to rely on third-party tools to handle the custom aspects of building your application. In addition, not only is this approach supported by Microsoft, but it is completely integrated with Visual Studio. If you need to tweak the settings for the C# compiler or how resources are generated, you now have this ability. The entire build process is open, and you can customize it in any way necessary. With other third-party tools this is simply unachievable.

In this book, we will start with MSBuild concepts that you need to know in order to get started, and then we will cover some advanced topics. Over the course of a few chapters we will take you from an MSBuild newbie to an MSBuild expert! For example, we will discuss how to inject custom steps into the build process, how to create custom tasks, and much more. We will cover all of the necessary topics that you need to know in order to use MSBuild in all the great ways that it was intended.

What Is ClickOnce?

For more than a decade now, technology decision makers have implemented business processes using "the disconnected Web" simply because Web applications are easy to deploy. If you perform a feature-by-feature comparison of a Web application versus a desktop application (such as a Windows Forms application), you'll be amazed to see what you bypass just to have something easily deployed (see Table 1).

Table 1. *Web Application vs. Desktop Application*

Feature	Desktop Application	Web Application
Has interactive and stateful user interface?	Yes	No
Offers offline support?	Yes	No
Uses desktop resources?	Yes	No
Is easy to deploy?	No	Yes

Organizations have repeatedly given up interactive and stateful applications just so they can easily deploy them. In addition, organizations have repeatedly given up all the benefits of having access to a workstation's local resources so they can easily deploy applications. Finally, organizations have repeatedly given up the benefits of having applications function without a server connection so they can easily deploy them. You don't have to do this anymore. Click-Once, finally, solves the complicated problem of "easily deploying a desktop application" and gives the desktop back to you.

ClickOnce enables you to deploy Windows Forms applications just like you deploy Web-based applications. In addition, ClickOnce provides automatic updates and traditional features found in a Windows Installer, without the disadvantages. For example, the ClickOnce technology can add entries to the user's Start menu and provides an icon in Add/Remove Programs for the user to uninstall the application. It does this without requiring users to be administrators on their workstation. ClickOnce provides all of this out of the box.

With ClickOnce you get the ease of deployment of a Web application along with the following additional benefits inherent in a Windows Forms application:

- Web-based installation

- Automatic and configurable updates via a URL

- Installation without administrator privileges (users don't have to be admins to install ClickOnce applications)

- Automatic rollback facilities and traditional desktop installations (such as a menu item under the user's Start menu)

These features, as a whole, have not been available to thick client applications in the past. With ClickOnce, organizations can return to offering dynamic applications that interact with the user's desktop (for example, with Microsoft Office, a printer, a network, and so on) while providing easy installation and automatic updates.

Who Should Read This Book?

This book was written for developers and deployment engineers working with .NET 2.0 on the Windows platform. Developers will benefit from reading this book because build and deployment are fundamental aspects of writing and testing software. Deployment engineers will benefit from reading this book because ClickOnce is now the recommended deployment model for Windows Forms applications and because MSBuild is now the unified build engine for the Windows platform.

What's in This Book?

This book covers build and deployment using MSBuild and ClickOnce. The book is broken up into two parts; the first part (Chapters 2–5) covers MSBuild, and the second part (Chapters 6–9) covers ClickOnce. Here is a breakdown of each chapter:

Chapter 1, "Deployment Prerequisites": Most large organizations have a team dedicated to build and deployment. Individuals on a team like this are not developers. In this chapter, we'll assume you are not a developer and give you the proper background required to do build and deployment. We'll talk about .NET, application architecture, and various types of applications. The goal of this chapter is to help you to understand what you can expect to build and deploy.

Chapter 2, "The Unified Build Engine: MSBuild": In previous versions of Visual Studio, the build process was mostly a black box; because of this, performing customizations to the build process was not very easy. With the new versions of Visual Studio and the .NET Framework, the build process is fully exposed and documented. It is easy to fine-tune the steps that will be followed when your projects are built. MSBuild is an XML-based build system; in this chapter, we'll introduce MSBuild and its fundamental concepts.

Chapter 3, "MSBuild: By Example": In Chapter 2, we'll outline the fundamentals of MSBuild. Like with many other technologies, it is easier to get a feel for MSBuild when you see it in use in different scenarios. The aim of this chapter is to provide real examples that will provide a concrete foundation to your MSBuild knowledge. Topics vary from how to use MSBuild item metadata to the difference between the @ syntax and the % notation.

Chapter 4, "Extending MSBuild": MSBuild is a system with extensibility as a focal point from its conception. Two aspects that MSBuild provides are flexible and powerful extensions: custom tasks and custom loggers. In this chapter, we present a real-world custom task from the ground up. This task and its accompanying targets file are responsible for executing any NUnit tasks that are contained in the built assemblies. As a sample of a real-world logger, we'll show how to create a custom XML logger.

Chapter 5, "Introducing Team Foundation Server and Team Build: With this version of Visual Studio, Microsoft has made some other tools available. One of these tools is the Team Foundation Server (TFS). A part of TFS is a new source control management tool. When using TFS, you can also use Team Build, which is a utility that can create, maintain, and execute public builds. For enterprise organizations, creating and verifying a public build is a critical component of projects. With TFS and Team Build, you can achieve this. In this chapter, we'll introduce the necessary concepts to use TFS and Team Build to create and customize your public build.

Chapter 6, "Deploying Smart Clients with ClickOnce": This chapter opens the second part of the book—deploying Windows Forms applications with ClickOnce. This chapter is an overview of what ClickOnce is. We'll start by building the case for why ClickOnce is important. We'll talk about some of the technologies that tried to do the same thing but failed. We'll give short introductions to how ClickOnce supports automatic updates. We'll also cover how to handle the sensitive issue of giving an application the proper privileges to do what it needs on the client.

Chapter 7, "ClickOnce Updates, Security, and the Bootstrapper": This chapter tells you everything you need to know about ClickOnce updates, security, and the generic bootstrapper. We'll start by dissecting the deployment and application manifest files. We'll then jump into how an application is configured for updates and when and how an application is updated in the background. After you understand the details of ClickOnce updates, we'll talk about ClickOnce security. Historically, thick client applications that have a client-side footprint have always been restricted to a security sandbox. This sandbox either was not configurable at all or was configurable in a way that was not practical. After reading this chapter, you'll see how ClickOnce solves this problem in a practical manner. The last topic we'll talk about in this chapter concerns getting application prerequisites deployed with your ClickOnce applications, which will prep you for the next chapter.

Chapter 8, "The ClickOnce Data Directory and Deploying Prerequisites": Nontrivial business applications today need a way to store application data. Storing application state is not something new and is easily accomplished if you have a connection to your database. But what if your application is a smart client and has to support offline capabilities? In other words, where do you store application state if you don't have a connection to your database on the network? ClickOnce provides the ClickOnce data directory for you to store application state. The ClickOnce data directory is something special and is managed as you move from one version of your application to the next. This chapter talks about the data directory, offline support, and how to migrate data as your application gets updated. The second portion of this chapter is about deploying custom prerequisites. Visual Studio 2005 comes with a short list of popular packages that you can deploy with your application, but what if you have your own prerequisites that you built or one that is not in the list? How do you deploy your own prerequisites? This chapter will tell you how to do that.

Chapter 9, "ClickOnce Tools and Scenarios": This chapter will talk about three tools that will help in deploying ClickOnce applications and some common ClickOnce scenarios. The tools discussed include the Bootstrapper Manifest Generator (BMG), the Manifest Generation and Editing (MAGE) tool, and MSBuild. The BMG is a Windows Forms application that provides a user interface for building the package and product manifest files that are required to deploy a custom prerequisite. The MAGE tool is a Windows Forms application that helps you build the deployment and application manifest files for your ClickOnce applications. We'll also talk about how you can automate a ClickOnce deployment—of course, you do this using MSBuild tasks. Finally, we'll present some common ClickOnce scenarios, covering practical ClickOnce problems and offering possible solutions.

After reading this book, you'll have a good understanding of the fundamentals of MSBuild and ClickOnce. You'll also understand how to use the two technologies to establish a build and deployment process in your organization.

CHAPTER 1

Deployment Prerequisites

Build and deployment are engineering problems, and in most big organizations, these are delegated to an entire team. The members of these teams aren't necessarily developers, yet they are experts on build and deployment processes and engineering. That is, you do not need to know how to code or know how something was created to be able to build and/or deploy it. And you should not have to know this!

Having said that, as a build and deployment engineer, you should have a fundamental understanding of the various types of applications and application architectures. You should, for example, know the types of components in a Web application versus a Windows Forms application. Similarly, you should know the differences between client-server architecture and n-tier architecture. Why is this important? It is important for a deployment and build engineer to be familiar with the various types of applications and application architectures for two reasons. The first and obvious reason is that in order to build an application or deploy it, you need to know what components it contains. For example, with a Web application, it helps to know it has a configuration file and you may have to modify this file when you write a build script for it. With a client-server application, it helps to know it has a client-side deployment and a server-side deployment. Having this knowledge helps you do your job better. The second important reason is that often deployment engineers have to perform a basic level of testing after deploying an application. Having some basic knowledge about the type of application and its architecture can go along way to resolving some fundamental problems.

In this chapter, we will define the various types of applications and briefly describe commonly used application architectures. We will also define the .NET Framework and describe methods of deploying the .NET runtime.

Types of Applications

With the .NET Framework, you can build Windows Forms applications, Web applications, Web services, smart device applications, Windows services, console applications, and hosted applications:

> *Windows Forms applications*: Windows Forms applications are applications with a graphical user interface (GUI) front end, and they run on desktops. Examples of this type of application include Microsoft Word, Microsoft Excel, and so on.

Web applications: Web applications are applications built with ASP.NET. These applications have a server-side component and a client-side component. The server-side contains the business logic, and the client-side contains the view (GUI) that is displayed in a browser. Web applications are accessed via a uniform resource locator (URL)—for example, `http://www.sayedhashimi.com`.

Web services: Web services are standards-based systems accessible over a network such as the Internet. Web services are generally employed to connect disparate systems. Web services are sometimes called XML Web Services.

Smart device applications: Smart device applications are applications that target mobile devices (for example, Smartphone devices). Smart device applications are built with the .NET Compact Framework, a subset of the .NET Framework.

Windows services: Windows services are executables that run in the background. The special feature of Windows services is that they don't require an interactive user. That is, Windows services can run while no one is logged on to the system. An example of a Windows service is a device driver or an application that performs background tasks based on a timer.

Console applications: Console applications are executables that are run from the Windows command prompt. Functionally, console applications are similar to Windows Forms applications; the difference is that console applications don't have a Windows Forms user interface and are text oriented.

Hosted applications: Last but not least, you can build hosted applications with the .NET Framework. Hosted applications are applications that allow the hosting of managed code inside an application. Hosted applications provide the facility for you to allow your customers (clients) to extend your application. Hosted applications are built with something called Visual Studio Tools for Applications (VSTA). Microsoft also has a variation of VSTA for the Microsoft Office suite called Visual Studio Tools for the Microsoft Office System (VSTO). The idea behind VSTO is to leverage the power of Office, Visual Studio, and managed code to build more feature-rich applications. Historically, VSTO came before VSTA; Microsoft extended the idea in VSTA to allow third parties to benefit from managed code extensibility in its own products.

That's the quick, five-minute tour. We'll now cover these types of applications individually so you can better understand them and the components they contain.

Windows Forms (Smart Client) Applications

Windows Forms applications are desktop applications that have rich user interfaces. For example, the Visual Studio integrated development environment (IDE) is an example of a Windows Forms application.[1] Windows Forms applications are built using the .NET Framework class libraries and have the following features:

---

1. Visual Studio 2005 was not actually written using Windows Forms, although part of it is managed code. The user interface is an example of a Windows Forms application.

- They possess a dynamic user interface with rich controls (for example, DataGrids).

- Users generally have the ability to do sophisticated actions quickly (for example, dragging and dropping).

- The application is installed on desktops and thus uses desktop resources. For example, the application can use the printer, the hard drive, and so on. The application can also communicate with running applications on the machine or spawn new processes and threads.

Recently, Microsoft decided to label Windows Forms applications as *smart clients* (see Figure 1-1).

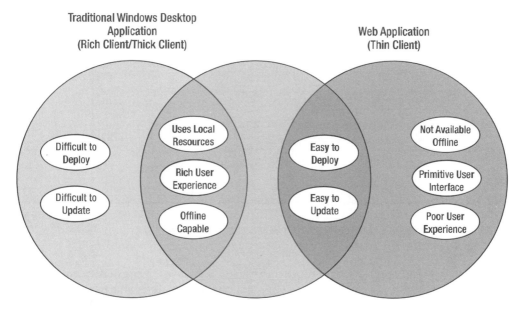

Figure 1-1. *Features of a thick[2] client, a thin client, and a smart client*

Smart client applications are Windows Forms applications with several additional features to those listed previously. For instance, a smart client has the following features:

- It supports offline capabilities. That is, the application doesn't require a network connection and is intelligent about detecting network connectivity automatically. So, for example, if you run a smart client application on your laptop and decide to go talk to a client in an area where you can't access your network (or the Internet), the smart client will still work even though your database is not accessible.

- It is easy to deploy and update.

---

2. *Thick client, rich client,* and *fat client* are synonyms.

In Visual Studio 2005, you create Windows Forms/smart client applications by choosing Windows Application in the New Project dialog box, under Visual C# or Visual Basic (see Figure 1-2).

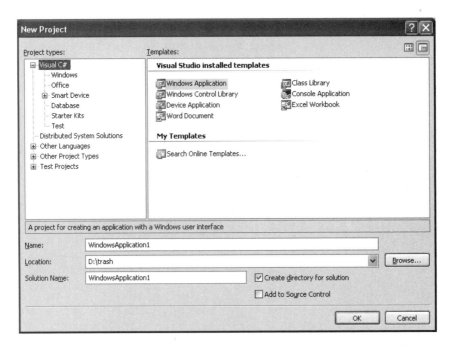

Figure 1-2. *New Windows Forms application in Visual Studio 2005*

Windows Forms applications comprise an executable, zero or more dependent assemblies, resource files,[3] and an application configuration file. The executable has an `.exe` extension, and the dependent assemblies typically have a `.dll` extension. In .NET, these DLLs are called *assemblies*. The dependent assemblies are generally placed in a folder named `bin` or directly next to the executable.[4] Often the application will also use shared

---

3. You can also embed resource files, such as images, data files, and so on, within assemblies.

4. Strictly speaking, putting dependent assemblies within the `bin` directory is a Visual Studio convention. The common language runtime (CLR) assembly loader uses a concept known as *probing* to locate assemblies. The `bin` directory happens to be one of the directories that is "probed" when the CLR looks to load an assembly. For more details about this, see `http://msdn.microsoft.com/library/ default.asp?url=/library/en-us/cpguide/html/cpconassemblies.asp`.

assemblies from the global assembly cache (GAC). The GAC contains assemblies that are shared among the applications installed on the machine. You can see the contents of the GAC by going to %windir%\assembly.

A deployment of a Windows Forms application looks like Figure 1-3.

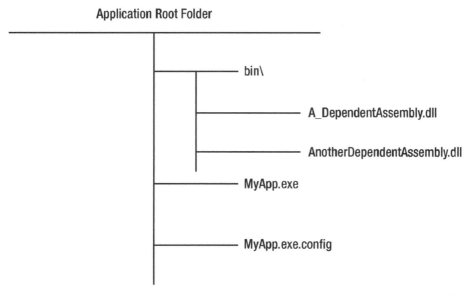

Figure 1-3. *Typical Windows Forms deployment*

You can deploy Windows Forms applications using ClickOnce.[5] You can use ClickOnce to deploy a rich client application using a Web-based deployment model. That is, you can deploy Windows Forms applications over the Web.

Other deployment options exist, such as Windows Installer (MSI), but ClickOnce is the new recommended method of deploying Windows Forms applications. Visual Studio 2005 has built-in support for deploying Windows Forms applications. Figure 1-4 shows the Publish dialog box used to configure the deployment of a Windows Forms application. We will talk about this in great detail in later chapters.

---

5. ClickOnce is new deployment technology built into the .NET runtime 1.0.

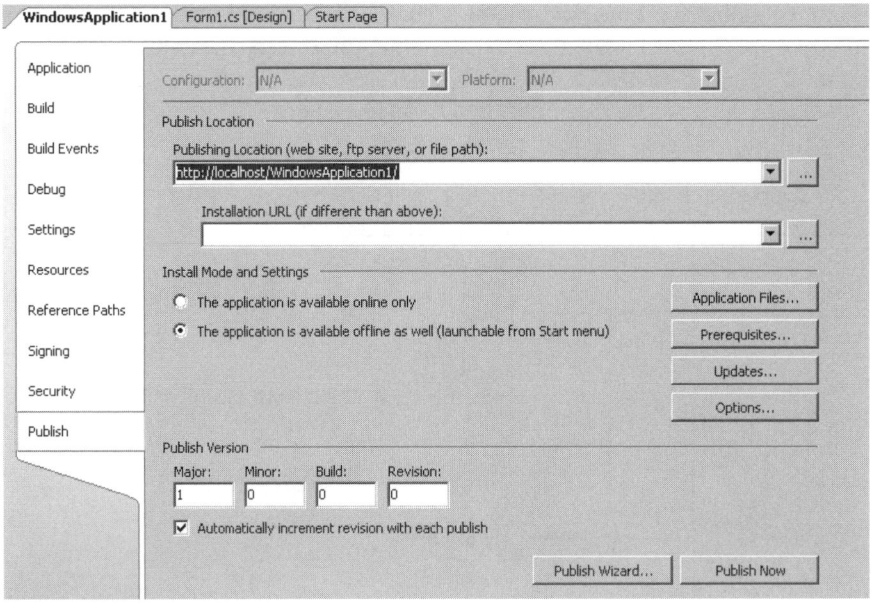

Figure 1-4. *The deployment of a smart client application using Visual Studio 2005*

Web Applications

A Web application is an application that is targeted to render in a browser. With the .NET Framework, you build Web applications using ASP.NET. To build a new Web application using Visual Studio 2005, you choose File ➤ New ➤ Web Site.

Figure 1-5 shows the New Web Site dialog box in Visual Studio 2005. An ASP.NET application consists of dynamic pages, static pages, configuration files, resources, and dependent assemblies. From a deployment perspective, it is important to know that a Web application's dependent assemblies are located in a folder named bin.[6] Moreover, the configuration of a Web application is stored in a file called web.config. The web.config file is an Extensible Markup Language (XML) file. Application authors generally put environment-specific settings (for example, a database connection string) in this file. Therefore, during deployment, the file will likely need to be modified to reflect the environment in which the application is being deployed. In the past, this task was either done by hand or done by an automated script. With Visual Studio 2005, you can use a Web-based administration console to modify the web.config file of an application (see Figure 1-6).

---

6. ASP.NET requires Web applications to have a bin folder; with Windows Forms applications, the bin folder is just one place where the probing process looks for assemblies.

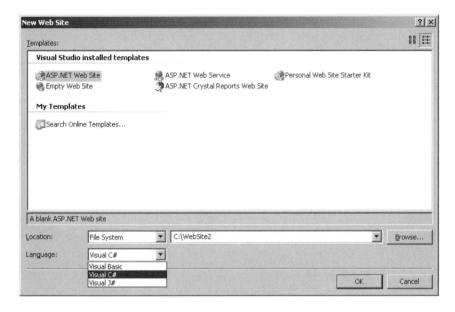

Figure 1-5. *New Web Site dialog box in Visual Studio 2005*

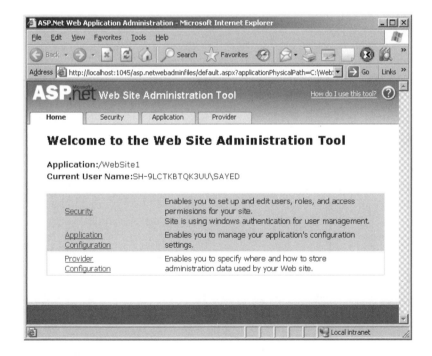

Figure 1-6. *Web Site Administration Tool console*

You can access the administration console from the Website ➤ ASP.NET Configuration menu item in Visual Studio 2005. As shown in Figure 1-6, the administration console is a Web-based tool. From the URL, you can conclude that when Visual Studio was installed, it created an application called asp.netwebadminfiles whose default.aspx file takes the path to a Web application. With this path, the application knows which application's configuration file to display in the administration console. Note that you can also get to the administration console from Visual Studio 2005 by clicking the ASP.NET Configuration button in the Solution Explorer (see Figure 1-7).

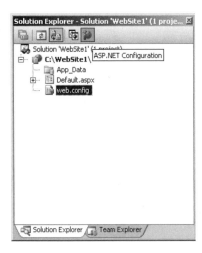

Figure 1-7. *ASP.NET configuration via the Solution Explorer in Visual Studio 2005*

A typical deployment of a Web application looks like Figure 1-8.

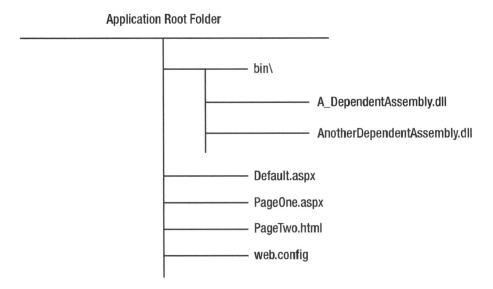

Figure 1-8. *A typical deployment of a Web application*

Web applications are deployed simply by copying files to the Web server.[7] Visual Studio 2005 has a built-in Web deployment tool that helps with this (see Figure 1-9). You can access this tool via Web Site ➤ Copy Web Site menu item.

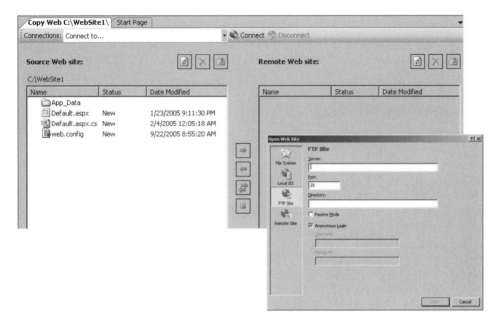

Figure 1-9. *Web site deployment tool in Visual Studio 2005*

With the deployment tool in Visual Studio 2005, you can deploy your Web applications to a Web server, to a File Transfer Protocol (FTP) site, or to a folder somewhere.

Web Services

Web services in .NET have an .asmx file extension. The .asmx file provides the means for clients to call Web services over Hypertext Transfer Protocol (HTTP). The actual Web service implementation is embedded within an assembly. On a Windows platform, Web services are typically hosted under Internet Information Services (IIS).[8] Therefore, from a deployment perspective, deploying Web services is no different than deploying Web applications. A Web service, in fact, can reside by itself under its own Web application, or it can reside under a Web application that has the usual ASPX and HTML files. Because Web services are packaged as part of a Web application, Web services have a web.config file that they use for storing and retrieving application configuration.

---

7. This is commonly called *xcopy* deployment.

8. You can also host Web services outside of IIS. For example, you can host Web services outside of IIS using Web Services Enhancements (WSE).

Smart Device Applications

Smart device applications run on smart devices. Visual Studio 2005 has project templates that target three types of smart devices: Pocket PC 2003, Smartphone 2003, and Windows CE 5.0. The Pocket PC and Smartphone projects target these specific devices; the Windows CE project type does not target any specific device. (In other words, it does not reference any device-specific functionality.) Figure 1-10 shows the New Project dialog box for smart device applications. The dialog box allows you to create graphical applications, console applications, and support assemblies that all target smart devices.

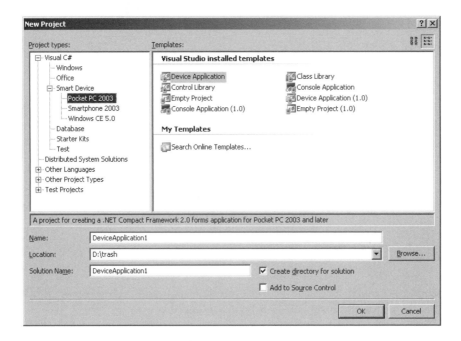

Figure 1-10. *New smart device application in Visual Studio 2005*

Smart device applications are built on top of the .NET Compact Framework (.NET CF). The .NET CF is a subset of the .NET Framework. This means the .NET CF doesn't have all the functionality that is available in the .NET Framework.

You can build Web applications, console applications, Windows Forms applications, and so on, that target devices that are not smart devices (that is, desktops). Similarly, you can build a Web application or a Windows Forms application that targets smart devices. Therefore, deploying Web applications that target smart devices is no different because Web pages are still deployed to an actual server and rendered to the smart device. Note that you cannot use a smart device as a Web server, however. With Windows Forms and console applications, you have to install the applications on the smart device. This turns out to be different from what you do for desktop applications. That is, you use ClickOnce to deploy Windows Forms applications to desktops. You don't, however, have this luxury to deploy to smart devices. Instead, you have to package these applications using CAB files.

Windows Services

Windows services are executables that run in the background and have no user interface. You can create a Windows Service using Visual Studio 2005 by selecting Windows Service in the New Project dialog box (see Figure 1-11). Windows services are supported on Windows NT, Windows 2000, Windows XP, Windows Server 2003, and future versions of the operating system. These versions of Windows are multiuser systems. This means multiple users can be logged on to the system simultaneously. In addition, generally there is no one logged on to the main console (the server itself). Therefore, having a UI for these services is a bit useless.

■**Note** You can manage and configure Windows services through a console called Service Control Manager (SCM).[9]

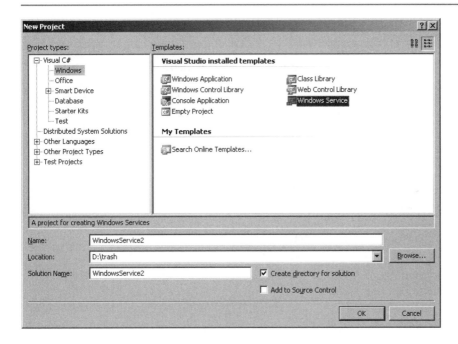

Figure 1-11. *New Windows service project and service configuration*

Having said that, you can still have a service that has a UI. For almost all cases, Windows services don't have UIs, but Windows still allows you to have one if you need one. Services that have a UI need a special flag enabled. You can set the special flag by right-clicking the service from the Services list in the Microsoft Management Console (MMC) and choosing Properties ➤ Log On tab (see Figure 1-12). Then check the Allow Service to Interact with Desktop box.

---

9. Refer to http://www.microsoft.com/technet/prodtechnol/windows2000serv/howto/mmcsteps.mspx for more details.

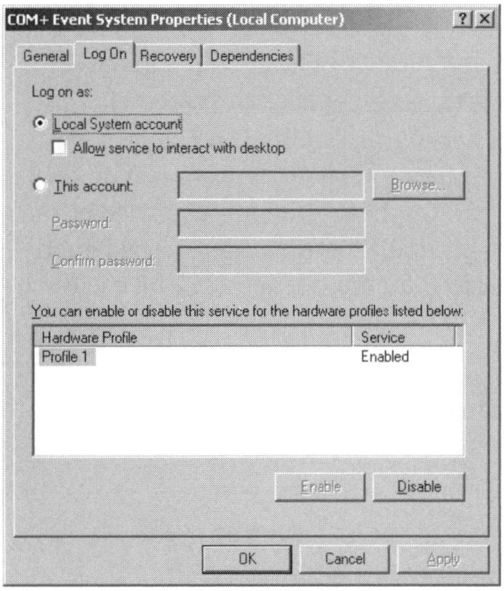

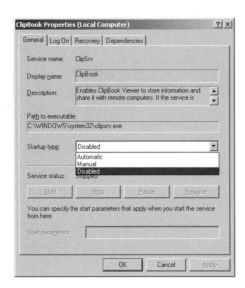

Figure 1-12. *Configuring a Windows service to interact with the desktop[10]*

Windows services comprise an executable, zero or more dependent assemblies, resources, and a configuration file. The executable contains service-level event methods (for example, OnStart), which are fired when a service is started, stopped, and so on, through the SCM (see Figure 1-13).[11]

Figure 1-13. *Start-up configuration of a Windows service[12]*

---

10. This feature is likely to be dropped in future versions of Windows.

11. For a complete list of events, see http://msdn.microsoft.com/library/default.asp?url=/library/en-us/vbcon/html/vbconserviceapplicationprogrammingarchitecture.asp.

12. You can view the services on Windows XP by right-clicking My Computer and then selecting Manage. From there, choose Services under Services and Applications.

Console Applications

Console applications are text-oriented applications that run from the Windows command prompt. You can create a console application by selecting Console Application in the New Project dialog box (see Figure 1-14).

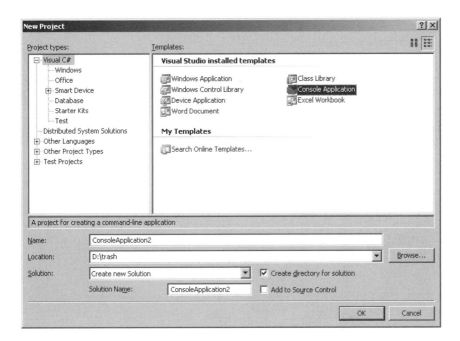

Figure 1-14. *New console applications in the New Project dialog box*

Similar to Windows Forms applications, console applications comprise an executable, dependent assemblies (DLLs), resource files, and an application configuration file. The executable generally has zero or more dependent assemblies. The dependent assemblies are placed in a folder named `bin`, which is directly next to the application's executable. The application configuration file is placed next to the application executable and uses the following naming convention: `executableAssemblyName.exe.config`. Note that this configuration file generally contains environment-specific settings, among other things. Therefore, this configuration file is something you have to be aware of and know how to modify.

Hosted Applications

Hosted applications "host" a scripting engine within the application to provide an extensibility feature. In effect, by hosting a scripting engine, they provide a means for customers to extend the functionality of the application to better meet their needs. In the past, organizations used Windows Script or Visual Basic for Applications (VBA) as a scripting engine. With .NET, you use VSTA instead. VSTA is an improvement over the other technologies because it relies on, and benefits from, the use of managed code.

Hosted applications are no different from the other application types. There is nothing more special about how you deploy an application just because it's hosting a scripting engine.

Application Architectures

It is important for a build and deployment engineer to have a foundational understanding of some of the common application architectures in order to effectively do their job. We will now discuss a few of the common application architectures in use today. Specifically, we will discuss the client-server, *n*-tier, and service-oriented architectures. We'll start with client-server.

Client-Server Architecture

Mainframe architecture was popular in the late 70s and most of the 80s. With mainframes, users sat in front of a terminal, and as they typed, keystrokes were sent to the host for processing. This architecture had some limitations: it didn't support GUIs, and users couldn't access multiple databases from geographically remote places. These limitations popularized the client-server architecture.

Figure 1-15 shows that within a client-server architecture, applications are divided into three layers: the presentation layer, the business logic layer (BLL), and the data access layer (DAL). Each layer has specific responsibilities. The presentation layer is responsible for managing the user interface interaction with the user, the business logic layer provides business services, and the data layer handles storing and retrieving data. The presentation layer usually resides on the client, and the business logic layer and data layer sit on the server(s). This, however, is not always true. To differentiate this, you need to understand the differences between thin, thick, and smart clients.

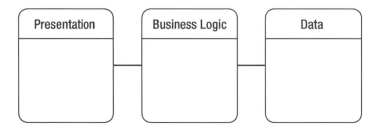

Figure 1-15. *Layers within a client-server architecture*

Thin Client

An ASP.NET Web application is an example of a thin client. A *thin client* application renders the view to the client, and almost all the processing takes place on the server(s). In the context of a client-server architecture, the presentation is rendered to the client (for example, Hypertext Markup Language [HTML] to a browser), and both the business layer and the data layer are distributed across one or more servers. Thin clients are always rendered in the browser and are easy to develop, update, and maintain. They do, however, have several disadvantages: subpar user experiences, compelling security restrictions, and a network connection requirement (in other words, no offline capability). This type of application, however, has been a popular choice in the past decade because it is easy to deploy and can reach users at a global level. Although the disadvantages seem to outweigh the advantages here, quite a bit of improvements have been made to thin client technologies over the past few years. Specifically, the release of .NET introduced ASP.NET, and future improvements are on the way (such as Atlas[13]).

Thick Client

A *thick client* is the opposite of a thin client. Sometimes this type of application houses all three layers on the client desktop. Thick clients are dynamic and offer users a rich experience. The disadvantages to this type of application include more difficult deployments and poor maintenance and versioning options. Note that the difficulties in deployment and updates led technology decision makers to choose thin clients in the past decade. The tables are turning, however. With the release of Visual Studio 2005, you have a technology that allows you to deploy rich client applications using a thin client deployment model (ClickOnce).

Smart Client

Smart clients offer the benefits of both a thin client and a thick client (refer to Figure 1-1). Essentially, if you take all of the advantages of having a thin client and combine them with the benefits of a thick client while throwing away their disadvantages, you end up with a smart client.

N-Tier Architecture

In the previous discussion, we talked about the three layers of an application. To reiterate, an application has a presentation layer, a business logic layer, and a data access layer (refer to Figure 1-15). Generally, these layers are separate and run on different machines. For example, you usually see the presentation on a Web server and the business logic and data access layers on an application server. But you sometimes have applications where all three layers are bundled together. When this is the case, you have a *one-tier* architecture. Similarly, when the presentation is separate from the business logic and data access layers, you have a *two-tier* architecture. When each of the layers lies on different machines, you have a *three-tier* architecture (see Figure 1-16).

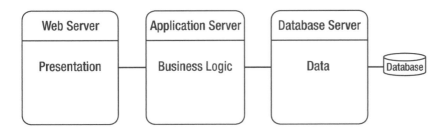

Figure 1-16. *Three-tier architecture*

For scalability, performance, and maintainability reasons, an application is broken up into layers. This allows what's known as *n*-tier architecture. With *n*-tier architecture, you can

---

13. Find out more about the Atlas project at http://www.asp.net/default.aspx?tabindex=9&tabid=47.

have the business logic and data access logic running on many machines, as shown in Figure 1-17. In fact, all three layers can be spread across multiple machines. It's not uncommon to use Web farms, load balancers, and database clusters to achieve optimal performance.

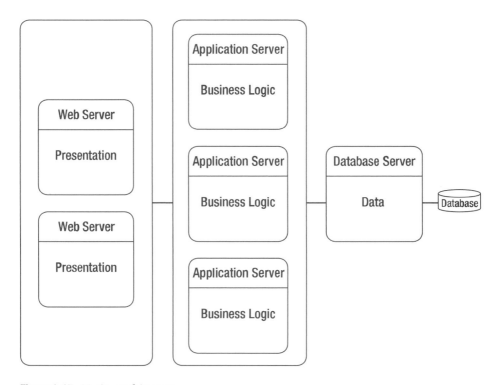

Figure 1-17. N-*tier architecture*

Service-Oriented Architecture

Service-oriented architecture (SOA) has become a buzzword of late. Although the concepts behind SOA have been around for more than a decade now, SOA has gained extreme popularity lately because of Web services. The fundamental idea behind SOA is that organizations have a host of services that they provide, and we should try to align Web services to these real-world services.[14] Doing so will then mitigate the risk when changes are required. Moreover, the Web services that align to the real-world services are built upon XML-based standards, which means you have cross-platform interoperability. Figure 1-18 shows a typical SOA.

---

14. Web services should implement the "real-world" services provided by the organization.

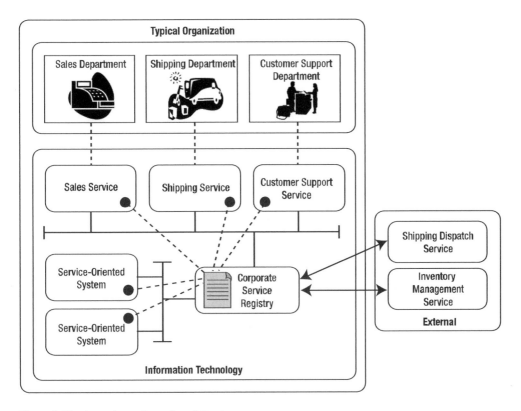

Figure 1-18. *A service-oriented architecture*

Strategies for Deploying the .NET Framework

Applications built with the .NET Framework require the .NET redistributable package (the .NET runtime) in order to run. As it stands now, the .NET runtime is not distributed with the supported versions of Windows operating systems. This means you are responsible for getting the .NET runtime to your clients. Depending on your deployment method, you either package the .NET redistributable with your deployment or require that users have the .NET runtime prior to running your installer. If you are going to require that your clients already have the.NET runtime installed, you can have them download it from `http://msdn.microsoft.com/netframework/downloads`. The download page provides a link to download the .NET redistributable software development kit (SDK) along with the service packs. In an enterprise environment, you also have other options. For example, large organizations often use Microsoft Systems Management Server (SMS) to handle the automatic distribution of the .NET runtime (among others deployments).

Where Do You Need the .NET Runtime?

We started this chapter by talking about the types of applications you can expect to deploy and the architectures of these applications. We talked about the layered client-server application and how these layers are generally distributed over several machines. Now we will discuss where you need to install the .NET runtime. We'll explain the typical deployments of a thin client and a smart client, since these are the types of applications you can expect to see.

Typical Deployment of a Smart Client

Figure 1-19 shows a typical three-tier deployment of a smart client and where the .NET runtime is required.

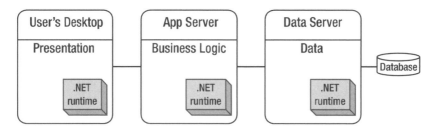

Figure 1-19. *Typical smart client and .NET runtime requirements*

With a traditional three-tier deployment of a smart client, the presentation is implemented using Windows Forms. This requires that the .NET runtime is installed wherever the presentation layer is going to run, which is a user's desktop. The business logic usually resides on an application server and can be implemented using COM+ components. Thus, the machine where the business logic is going to run requires the .NET runtime. The data access layer can be on the same machine where the business logic is deployed; however, it's not uncommon to see the data access layer on a separate machine. The data access layer is implemented using ADO.NET, so you need to have the .NET runtime installed on this machine as well.

Typical Deployment of a Thin Client

Figure 1-20 shows a typical deployment of a thin client application.

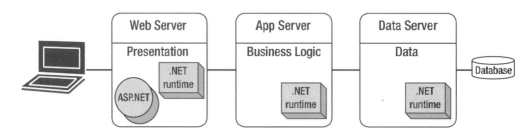

Figure 1-20. *Typical deployment of a thin client*

With a thin client, the presentation layer serves HTML to clients over HTTP. The presentation is usually implemented using ASP.NET. This means you need to have the .NET runtime on the Web server. What about the client's browser that receives HTML? Since the client is receiving HTML, it does not require the .NET runtime[15] (which is a big advantage of building thin clients).

The business logic and data access layers both require the .NET runtime if they are implemented using managed code.

Summary

In this chapter, we talked about the various types of applications and application architectures. It is important for build and deployment engineers to be familiar with what they are going to be building and deploying. This knowledge comes in handy after you do a build or a deployment and have to verify that it was successful.

We also talked about distributing the .NET runtime. In the next chapter, we will start the multichapter coverage of Microsoft's new build engine (MSBuild).

---

15. You can host Windows Forms components within a browser, which requires the .NET runtime on the client.

CHAPTER 2

■■■

The Unified Build Engine: MSBuild

Software systems have moved from stand-alone applications installed on single machines to large, distributed applications hosted over a network of machines. To create executables of stand-alone applications, you opened a command prompt and executed a few commands to convert the source code into executables. To deploy these applications, you took the generated executables and stored them on floppy disks and "sneakernetted" the application to the clients. The distributed systems of today are considerably more complex; they are much larger and so are their user bases. To build and deploy these systems, you must use predefined processes, along with automated build and deployment tools, to ensure reliability and repeatability. For example, most organizations define what are known as *pipelines*, and applications are built and deployed automatically to a pipeline for testing and verification. An application starts in an integration environment, then moves to a staging environment, and finally moves to production. At each point, tests are automatically executed in an attempt to ensure quality.

At the heart of a build and deployment process is a build and release tool. That is, one tool is responsible for getting, building, and then deploying these applications automatically. Moreover, it is the same tool that is used to migrate the applications from one environment (for example, staging) to another (for example, production).

Just as software development tools have evolved, so have the tools that are used to build and deploy them. Why do you need build tools? Why aren't scripts or batch files sufficient? Well, build tools are a necessary component of application development now because the steps for building software have increased in complexity. Previously, builds required simpler steps, such as copying and moving files, in order to perform the build. Now many applications are using third-party libraries and require more complex tasks, such as file signing and incremental building (more on this in Chapter 4). This increase in complexity has given rise to the need for build-specific tools. In other words, people started by building their software, somewhat manually, and realized they needed a repeatable process. Tools such as Make, NMake, Ant/NAnt, and Jam (among others) can create a repeatable process.

In this chapter, we will discuss MSBuild, but we will also highlight some of the most popular build tools and build systems used in the recent past. Note that a *build tool* is a component or application whose sole responsibility is to take source code and produce binaries (for example, machine code, Java bytecode, Microsoft Intermediate Language [MSIL], and so on). A *build system* is a collection of build-related tools that together offer facilities to build, deploy, configure, and test solutions. Build tools and build systems are often packaged as part of popular software development systems.

Introducing Build Tools and Systems

In the following sections, we will describe some of the popular build tools and build systems.

Make-Style Build Tools

Several build tools are extensions of the original BSD Make. The most popular of the extensions include GNU Make, NMake, OPus Make, Jam, and Cook. With all of these tools, you place a file, usually called a *makefile*, near the source code that describes what needs to be built. To do a build, users usually enter make in a Unix shell or Windows Command window.

GNU Make

GNU Make is probably the most popular build tool on the Unix platform. GNU Make obtained its popularity because of the vast number of extensions it made to BSD Make. GNU Make is a part of the GNU toolset and, thus, is still alive and supported. This build tool is distributed under the GNU open source license.

NMake

NMake was originally developed by AT&T Laboratories as an open source project. Recently it has been extended by Lucent Technologies and is packaged as part of a commercial product called Lucent nmake Product Builder. Microsoft also has a version it calls Microsoft Program Maintenance Utility (NMAKE.EXE). The versions produced by AT&T and Lucent are compatible with the original BSD Make; the version produced by Microsoft is not.

OPus Make

OPus Make was a popular build tool in the 90s. This tool became popular for its multiplatform support and rather lengthy list of features, including support for logical operators in conditional expressions, regular expression substitutions, a rich set of directives, and more.

Jam and Cook

GNU Make, NMake, and OPus Make were all extensions of Make but use the same style used by the original BSD Make. For example, they all relied on the makefile and added features (such as macros). Jam and Cook are variants of Make that don't rely on the makefile but use another variation of a text file to define what needs to be built. The interesting feature of these two products is that they support parallel builds while avoiding recursion.

GBS

The GNU Build System (GBS) is a suite of build tools that, together, provide facilities to build, configure, and release software systems. GBS is popular in the open source community because it provides a feature that places an abstraction layer over the build platform. GBS is mostly used within the open source community.

CMake and QMake

Cross Platform Make (CMake) and Qtopia Build System (QMake) are build systems, not build tools, that decided to piggyback on the popularity of Make. These build systems have a lot of similarities in that they both market their portability features and support various build tools. CMake offers a GUI and a command-line interface; QMake supports only a command-line interface.

Ant/NAnt

The build tools described in the previous sections all use a build description file (for example, a makefile). Most rely on either cryptic commands or full-blown programming languages to describe what needs to be built. The problem with describing builds using commands and/or languages is obviously that the builds are difficult to create and maintain.

Ant is a cross-platform build tool popular in the Java community. Ant discarded the idea of using commands or programming languages to describe builds and instead uses XML-based configuration files. Build steps are described using something called *tasks*, which are implemented with the Java programming language (rather than by writing scripts) and are grouped under a *target*. This is an example Ant file:

```
<project>
    <target name="compile">
        <mkdir dir="build/classes"/>
        <javac srcdir="src" destdir="build/classes"/>
    </target>

    <target name="jar">
        <mkdir dir="build/jar"/>
        <jar destfile="build/jar/HelloWorld.jar" basedir="build/classes">
            <manifest>
                <attribute name="Main-Class" value="sayed.HelloWorld"/>
            </manifest>
        </jar>
    </target>

    <target name="run">
        <java jar="build/jar/HelloWorld.jar" fork="true"/>
    </target>
</project>
```

To perform a build using Ant, you place a file named build.xml next to your source tree and enter ant at the command prompt. Ant is command-line driven; however, several popular extensions offer GUIs for Ant.

As far as NAnt goes, NAnt is a port of Ant to the .NET platform. NAnt maintains the same concepts of Ant. That is, NAnt also uses an XML-based build file and defines features such as targets, tasks, and so on.

We'll now begin discussing the next-generation build tool: MSBuild.

Introducing MSBuild

MSBuild is Microsoft's solution to the automated build problem. MSBuild allows you to perform all the necessary steps to properly build your .NET applications. MSBuild provides this functionality transparently.

In prior versions of Visual Studio, the build process was, for the most part, hidden to the user. You could, for example, supplement your build with pre- and post-events, but you could not change *how* the build occurred. In Visual Studio 2005, you have this feature! Visual Studio 2005 uses MSBuild to build your solutions. Microsoft has exposed and defined this build process as part of the MSBuild schema.

Visual Studio uses your project file as input to MSBuild. In this example, we will show how to create a simple project file using Visual Studio. You can use this file to understand some of the key elements of MSBuild. It will also serve as a point of extension to explore some of the other features of MSBuild. Although MSBuild supports many application types, we will show how to create a simple Windows Forms application.

To create this simple project, follow these steps:

1. Start Visual Studio, and create a new C# Windows application named **MSBuild1**.

2. Accept the defaults, and click OK.

3. In the Form Designer, drag and drop a new label onto the form.

4. Set the text of the label to **MSBuild demo**.

The form should look like Figure 2-1.

Figure 2-1. *Sample Windows application*

Open the project file (`MSBuild1.csproj`) in your favorite XML or text editor. You'll notice that the root element is the `Project` element. Beneath this you'll see three element types in this file:

- `PropertyGroup`

- `ItemGroup`

- `Import`

A few other elements could be present at this level, but we will discuss those elements as you get to them. You'll see an element that is commented out as well: the `Target` element. We will discuss this important piece of the MSBuild file later in this chapter. The `PropertyGroup` element is a container for defined properties. Similarly, the `ItemGroup` element is a container for defined items. The `Import` tag allows you to import other MSBuild files into the current project. We will examine how this will affect your files later in this chapter.

An MSBuild file has four main elements: properties, items, targets, and tasks. A *property* defines a value associated with a name. Simply put, it is a key/value pair. In this project file, you'll find many properties defined:

```
<DebugSymbols>true</DebugSymbols>
<DebugType>full</DebugType>
<Optimize>false</Optimize>
<OutputPath>bin\Debug\</OutputPath>
```

You'll find these defined under the `<PropertyGroup Condition=" '$(Configuration)` `|$(Platform)' == 'Debug|AnyCPU' ">` tag. You can change these values directly from Visual Studio by using the Configuration drop-down list.

Items are another crucial part of the MSBuild project file. When performing a build, many steps must reference a file or a set of files. In MSBuild this is usually accomplished through items. An *item* is a named reference to a file or to many files. These items contain associated metadata, such as the full path or filename. Throughout the discussion of MSBuild, we will discuss items in more depth.

A *target* is a container for related tasks that will be executed sequentially. Besides containing tasks, a target can be given a set of dependent targets and a list of inputs and outputs. *Incremental building*, which is discussed in more detail in Chapter 4, is the process of skipping unnecessary steps. This is driven completely by the associated input and output files for a target. When you invoke MSBuild, you must specify a target that is to be executed; after that, MSBuild will perform a dependency analysis to determine exactly what other targets need to be executed as well.

A *task* is a unit of work in MSBuild. For example, `Copy` or `LocateRequiredAssemblies` could be defined as a task. In this sample, you will not find any tasks defined. This is because this sample utilizes predefined tasks to complete the build. (We will cover the predefined task later in this chapter in the "Predefined Tasks" section.) Tasks must be located within a `Target` element. A `Target` element consists of a group of related tasks that are executed sequentially. Possible targets are `PrepareForDeployment` and `CopyToServers`.

As mentioned, this project uses predefined tasks to accomplish the build. You may be wondering where these tasks are actually defined. To answer that question, scroll toward the bottom of the project file, and you'll find the following declaration: `<Import Project="$(MSBuildBinPath)\` `Microsoft.CSharp.targets" />`. This import statement is using a property, `MSBuildBinPath`, to specify where to find the `Microsoft.CSharp.targets` file, which contains many predefined tasks. The `Microsoft.CSharp.targets` file is located in the `%windir%\Microsoft.NET\Framework\` `v2.0.50727\` directory. By using the `$()` syntax, the property `MSBuildBinPath` is evaluated, and its value replaces the reference. This property is a reserved property whose value is the location of `msbuild.exe`. A few other reserved properties exist, which we will discuss in the next section.

Properties

As stated, a property is a simple key/value pair. Let's examine another property definition from the `MSBuild.csproj` file: `<RootNamespace>MSBuild1</RootNamespace>`. This property is defined in the first `PropertyGroup` element. If you needed to reference this property somewhere else in the MSBuild file, you would simply use the `$()` notation. For instance, you would use `$(RootNamespace)`.

Refer to the property declaration again: `<PropertyGroup Condition=" '$(Configuration) |$(Platform)' == 'Debug|AnyCPU' ">`. Notice the `Condition` attribute; every MSBuild element has an optional `Condition` attribute. If this condition evaluates to `true`, then the element is processed; otherwise, it is ignored. Table 2-1 summarizes the basic condition syntax.

Table 2-1. *Property Conditions*

Symbol	Description
`==`	Checks for equality; returns `true` if both have the same value.
`!=`	Checks for inequality; returns `true` if both don't have the same value.
`Exists`	Checks for existence of a file. You provide the file path as an argument, such as in `Exists(MSBuildDemo.txt)`. This will return `true` if `MSBuildDemo.txt` is present.
`!Exists`	Checks for the nonexistence of a file. You use this condition in a similar manner as the `Exists` condition.

The `<Configuration Condition=" '$(Configuration)' == '' ">Debug</Configuration>` property will not be executed unless the `Configuration` property has not already been set. In the next section, you'll see how you can use these properties in tasks that you create. You may find a number of reserved properties helpful in your MSBuild project. Table 2-2 lists their names, their descriptions, and the values that are returned for the project you will start shortly. In the "Targets" section, you will create a target to print the values for these properties.

Table 2-2. *Reserved Properties*

Name	Description	Example
`MSBuildBinPath`	Full path of the .NET Framework MSBuild bin directory.	`%windir%\Microsoft.NET\ Framework\v2.0.50727`
`MSBuildExtensionsPath`	Full path to the `MSBuild` folder located in the `Program Files` directory. This is a nice location to keep other MSBuild files that the current file references.	`C:\Program Files\MSBuild`
`MSBuildProjectDefaultTargets`	The value for the `DefaultTargets` attribute that is in the `Project` element.	`Build`
`MSBuildProjectDirectory`	Full path to the location of project file.	`C:\MSBuild\MSBuild1\MSBuild1`
`MSBuildProjectExtension`	Extension of the project filename, including the initial dot.	`.csproj`

Name	Description	Example
MSBuildProjectFile	Filename of the project file, including extension.	MSBuild1.csproj
MSBuildProjectFullPath	Full path to the project file, including the filename.	C:\MSBuild\MSBuild1\ MSBuild1\MSBuild1.csproj
MSBuildProjectName	Name of the MSBuild project file, excluding the file extension.	MSBuild1

Targets

As mentioned, *targets* are containers for related tasks that will be executed sequentially. Some example targets are Build, Deploy, and SetupEnvironment. Let's examine the parts of a target:

```
<Target
    Name="SampleTarget"
    Inputs="SampleInput"
    Outputs="SampleOutput"
    DependsOnTargets="DependentTarget"
>
    <Message Text="SampleTarget executed, SampleInput: @(SampleInput)" />
</Target>
<Target Name="DependentTarget">
    <Message Text="DependentTarget executed" />
</Target>
```

Each target has a Name attribute that is required to be a nonempty string. This name is how you will refer to the target. Additionally, a target can have inputs; if you declare a target to have inputs, then it must have outputs as well. The purpose of the inputs/outputs is to facilitate incremental builds. That is, if a portion of your build does not need to be reexecuted, then it will not be. In a build process, if you had a Target defined as CopyResources, it may take as an input a list of files containing the location on disk of all external resources. The corresponding output may be the desired location of these resources. When MSBuild encounters this target, it will compare the time stamps of these files to each other. If it is not necessary to reexecute that CopyResources target, then it will be skipped.

The DependsOnTarget parameter is a list of targets, separated by semicolons, that are required to be run before this target executes. It is important to note at this time that during a build a target will be executed only once. So, if you had two targets that both depended on a common target, that one target will not be executed twice but only once. Now you will examine how you can get started executing some targets that employ some of the predefined tasks.

Executing and Creating Targets

In this section, we will discuss the process involved in executing and creating targets. You can utilize many predefined targets in your builds. (Many predefined tasks also exist; we will wait to cover those in the "Predefined Tasks" section.) To emphasize the detachment of MSBuild from Visual Studio, we will be executing the targets strictly from the command line. The first step you'll want to perform is to open the previously created project file in your favorite text editor. Then, open the Visual Studio 2005 command prompt from the Start menu. From the command prompt, navigate to the directory in which your `MSBuild1.csproj` file is located. (Note that MSBuild is also capable of processing solution files, despite that solutions files are not in MSBuild format.) From there, execute the following command: `>msbuild`. This will execute the default target on the only project file residing in that directory. Your output should look something like Figure 2-2.

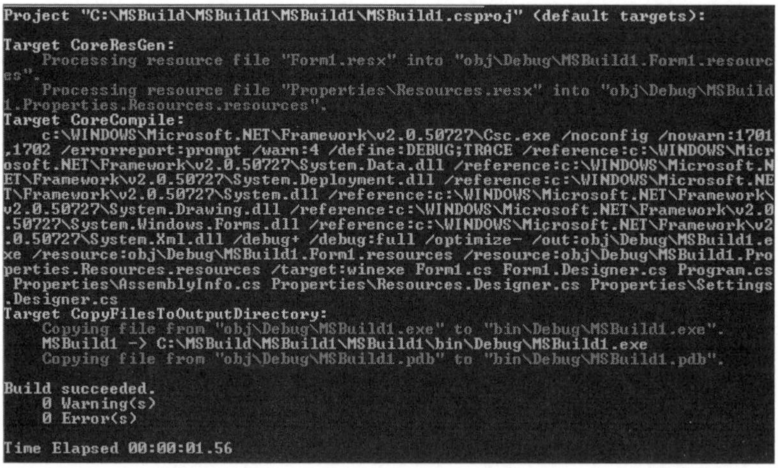

```
Project "C:\MSBuild\MSBuild1\MSBuild1\MSBuild1.csproj" (default targets):

Target CoreResGen:
    Processing resource file "Form1.resx" into "obj\Debug\MSBuild1.Form1.resourc
es".
    Processing resource file "Properties\Resources.resx" into "obj\Debug\MSBuild
1.Properties.Resources.resources".
Target CoreCompile:
    c:\WINDOWS\Microsoft.NET\Framework\v2.0.50727\Csc.exe /noconfig /nowarn:1701
,1702 /errorreport:prompt /warn:4 /define:DEBUG;TRACE /reference:c:\WINDOWS\Micr
osoft.NET\Framework\v2.0.50727\System.Data.dll /reference:c:\WINDOWS\Microsoft.N
ET\Framework\v2.0.50727\System.Deployment.dll /reference:c:\WINDOWS\Microsoft.NE
T\Framework\v2.0.50727\System.dll /reference:c:\WINDOWS\Microsoft.NET\Framework\
v2.0.50727\System.Drawing.dll /reference:c:\WINDOWS\Microsoft.NET\Framework\v2.0
.50727\System.Windows.Forms.dll /reference:c:\WINDOWS\Microsoft.NET\Framework\v2
.0.50727\System.Xml.dll /debug+ /debug:full /optimize- /out:obj\Debug\MSBuild1.e
xe /resource:obj\Debug\MSBuild1.Form1.resources /resource:obj\Debug\MSBuild1.Pro
perties.Resources.resources /target:winexe Form1.cs Form1.Designer.cs Program.cs
 Properties\AssemblyInfo.cs Properties\Resources.Designer.cs Properties\Settings
.Designer.cs
Target CopyFilesToOutputDirectory:
    Copying file from "obj\Debug\MSBuild1.exe" to "bin\Debug\MSBuild1.exe".
    MSBuild1 -> C:\MSBuild\MSBuild1\MSBuild1\bin\Debug\MSBuild1.exe
    Copying file from "obj\Debug\MSBuild1.pdb" to "bin\Debug\MSBuild1.pdb".

Build succeeded.
    0 Warning(s)
    0 Error(s)

Time Elapsed 00:00:01.56
```

Figure 2-2. *Output from* `msbuild.exe` *on the default target*

You specify the default target in the root `Project` element of the project file. In this case, you have `<Project DefaultTargets="Build" xmlns="http://schemas.microsoft.com/developer/msbuild/2003">`. If you invoke MSBuild on this project file without specifying the target, then the `Build` project will be executed. This target is a predefined target and is not included in your project file. Actually, no targets are defined in this file. This file has an import statement that imports `Microsoft.CSharp.targets`, and that file imports `Microsoft.Common.targets`. These two files define many targets, and these are the predefined targets. We will discuss this in more detail in the "Predefined Targets" section.

Now let's inject the two targets discussed earlier into this project file. You can place them anywhere in the file as long as they are defined as child elements of the `Project` tag. As a reminder, the two targets are as follows:

```
<Target
    Name="SampleTarget"
    Inputs="SampleInput"
    Outputs="SampleOutput"
    DependsOnTargets="DependentTarget"
>
    <Message Text="SampleTarget executed, SampleInput: @(SampleInput) " />
</Target>
<Target Name="DependentTarget">

    <Message Text="DependentTarget executed" />
</Target>
```

At this point, save this file as MSBuild1_rev2.csproj so you have a backup of the project file in the same directory. The previous example executed the only project in the directory. If two or more project files exist, then you must specify which one to execute. To do this, you can supply the name of the project to build as a command-line parameter. To build this project, execute the following command: >msbuild MSBuild1_rev2.csproj. Following this, you may see similar output as you did when you built the previous project, or you will see that many targets were skipped. This depends on whether your source files have changed since your last build. Skipping up-to-date targets is called *incremental building* and is a core aspect of MSBuild; we will discuss this in the "Predefined Targets" section and in more depth in Chapter 4. If you'd like to see it build again, you can invoke >msbuild MSBuild1_rev2.csproj /t:Clean;build. This will clean out the previously built files and then build the project. Notice that the target names are case-insensitive. To execute the target, you simply execute >msbuild MSBuild1_rev2.csproj /t:SampleTarget. Figure 2-3 shows the output.

```
Project "C:\MSBuild\MSBuild1\MSBuild1\MSBuild1_rev2.csproj" (SampleTarget target
(s)):

Target DependentTarget:
    DependentTarget executed
Target SampleTarget:
    SampleTarget executed, SampleInput:

Build succeeded.
    0 Warning(s)
    0 Error(s)

Time Elapsed 00:00:00.03
```

Figure 2-3. *Output from the execution of* SampleTarget

Now that you have started specifying some parameters for msbuild.exe, you may be interested in what other options are available. Table 2-3 summarizes those options.

Table 2-3. msbuild.exe *Command-Line Parameters*

Switch	Short	Description
/help	/?	Displays usage for msbuild.exe.
/nologo		Inhibits the copyright message when msbuild.exe is executed.
/version	/ver	Displays the version of msbuild.exe.
@file		Allows you to pass command-line parameters to msbuild.exe from the file specified.
/noautoresponse	/noautorsp	Allows you to specify to not automatically include the msbuild.rsp file. This file can specify command-line arguments for MSBuild. If it is present, it will be consumed, unless you set this flag. If you have long command-line arguments, this is the suggested manner to pass them to MSBuild.

Continued

Table 2-3. *Continued*

Switch	Short	Description
/target:<target>	/t	Specifies which targets should be executed. Targets are declared in a semicolon-separated list.
/property:<n>=<v>	/p	Allows you to set properties for the build. If a property is specified that exists in the project file, then this value will take precedence.
/logger:<logger>		Specifies the logger used to capture and records MSBuild events as they occur.
/verbosity:<level>	/v	Sets the type of information MSBuild will output. Possible values include d (detailed), diag (diagnostic), m (minimal), q (quiet), and n (normal).
/consoleloggerparameters <parameters>	/clp	Passes parameters to the console logger for MSBuild.
/noconsolelogger	/noconlog	Turns off logging to the console.
/validate	/val	Validates the MSBuild project file with the MSBuild schema file in use.
/validate:<schema>	/val	Validates the MSBuild project file with the MSBuild schema file specified.

From the output of the previous example in Figure 2-3, did you notice that the dependent target executed first? As mentioned, a target will execute only once during the build process. To demonstrate this, add the following target to your MSBuild project file:

```
<Target
    Name="DependsAgain"
    DependsOnTargets="DependentTarget"
>
    <Message Text="DependsAgain has executed"/>
</Target>
```

Now invoke MSBuild with the following command: C:\MSBuild\MSBuild1\MSBuild1> msbuild MSBuild1_rev2.csproj /t:SampleTarget;DependsAgain. Figure 2-4 shows the output.

```
Project "C:\MSBuild\MSBuild1\MSBuild1\MSBuild1_rev2.csproj" (SampleTarget;Depend
sAgain target(s)):

Target DependentTarget:
    DependentTarget executed
Target SampleTarget:
    SampleTarget executed. SampleInput:
Target DependsAgain:
    DependsAgain has executed

Build succeeded.
    0 Warning(s)
    0 Error(s)

Time Elapsed 00:00:00.01
```

Figure 2-4. msbuild.exe *output for the target* SampleTarget;DependsAgain

As you can see, DependentTarget seems to have executed only once, before the execution of SampleTarget. The output presented in Figure 2-4 does not make it obvious that this target was skipped the second time. If you use the command-line parameter /v:d or /v:diag, it will explicitly state that this target was indeed skipped. Previously it was mentioned that a Target will be described to print the values for the reserved properties; the specification for that target is as follows:

```
<Target Name="PrintReservedProperties">
    <Message Text="MSBuildProjectDirectory        : ➡
$(MSBuildProjectDirectory)" />
    <Message Text="MSBuildProjectFile             : ➡
$(MSBuildProjectFile)" />
    <Message Text="MSBuildProjectExtension        : ➡
$(MSBuildProjectExtension)" />
    <Message Text="MSBuildProjectFullPath         : ➡
$(MSBuildProjectFullPath)" />
    <Message Text="MSBuildProjectName             : ➡
$(MSBuildProjectName)" />
    <Message Text="MSBuildBinPath                 : ➡
$(MSBuildBinPath)" />
    <Message Text="MSBuildProjectDefaultTargets : ➡
$(MSBuildProjectDefaultTargets)" />
    <Message Text="MSBuildExtensionsPath          : ➡
$(MSBuildExtensionsPath)" />
</Target>
```

After you add this to the project file, you can invoke it with the following command: >msbuild MSBuild1.csproj /t:PrintReservedProperties. Note this was added to the original version of the project file, not the MSBuild1_rev2.csproj file.

In Figure 2-5, you can see the values for the reserved properties that are available with MSBuild. Now we will explain some predefined targets.

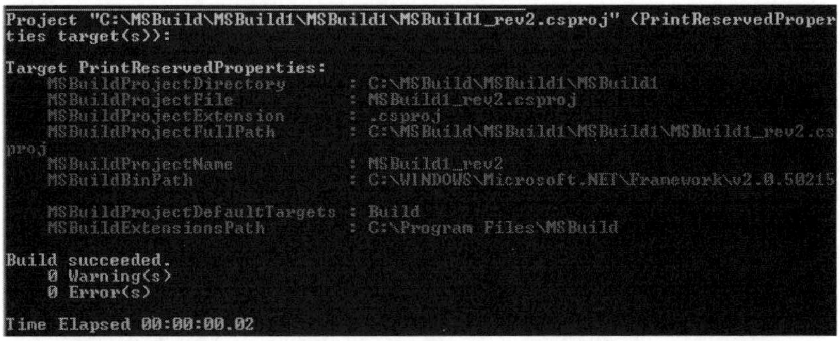

Figure 2-5. *Output for reserved properties*

Predefined Targets

Previously you saw the predefined Build target execute. You may be wondering what other predefined targets are available and where they are located. Predefined targets are housed in either the Microsoft.CSharp.targets file (if your project is a C# project; otherwise, see the import statement in your project file) or the Microsoft.Common.targets file. The Microsoft.CSharp.targets file is imported into your project with the Import element. That file then imports the Microsoft.Common.targets file. As you examine these predefined targets, keep in mind that you may override them to declare your own behavior. For example, if you wanted to copy resources to another location during the build process, then you could change the Build target. You will examine a target that changes how your C# files are built later in this section. Table 2-4 lists some predefined targets; this is not an exhaustive list because many targets exist simply as support for other targets.

Table 2-4. *Some Predefined Targets*

Name	Description
BeforeBuild	Empty target that will be called before the build process begins. You can use this to augment the build with your own steps. For example, you can use this to clean items or stop running services.
AfterBuild	Empty target that will be called after the build process is complete. You can use this if you want to augment the build process with your own build steps. For example, you can use this to copy output to specific directories or restart a service.
CoreBuild	This is the target that actually builds your project.
BeforeCompile	Empty target that will be called before your project gets compiled. If you need to augment the compile with preprocessing, override this task.
AfterCompile	Empty target that will be called after your project has been compiled. If you need to perform steps after project compilation, you can override this task.
Compile	Target responsible for compiling your project.
CoreCompile	Target that will actually make the call to the underlying compiler for your files.
BeforeRebuild	Empty target that will be executed before Rebuild starts.
AfterRebuild	Empty target that will be executed after Rebuild has completed.
Rebuild	Target that rebuilds your project.
BeforeClean	Empty target that is executed before Clean is performed.
AfterClean	Empty target that is invoked after the Clean target has completed.
Clean	Target that will perform a clean on your project. All intermediate and built files will be removed.
PostBuildEvent	Target that will be specified through Visual Studio to run after a successful/unsuccessful build.
PreBuildEvent	Target that will be created through Visual Studio to run before a build.
Run	Target used to start your application, if it is an executable project.
BeforePublish	Empty target that will be called before Publish has started.

Name	Description
AfterPublish	Empty target that will be executed after Publish has completed.
Publish	Use this to replicate the ClickOnce Publish behavior from outside Visual Studio. Note: This is not the target that Visual Studio will invoke when using ClickOnce, but it is the suggested means to replicate the functionality.
PublishOnly	Publish target used by ClickOnce. Note: If you override BuildPublish and AfterPublish, those targets will also be invoked by this target.
SignClickOnceDeployment	Target that will sign the deployment files created by ClickOnce.
BeforeResolveReferences	Empty target that is executed before ResolveReferences is invoked.
AfterResolveReferences	Empty target that is called after the ResolveReferences target has completed.
ResolveReferences	Target that is responsible for resolving the project references.
BeforeResGen	Empty target that is invoked before ResGen is run.
AfterResGen	Empty target that is called after ResGen has completed.
ResGen	Target that will generate resources for your project.
GenerateBootstrapper	Target that will create the bootstrapper setup.exe file.
CreateSatelliteAssemblies	Target that will create all the assemblies for all the cultures your project has defined.
GenerateApplicationManifest	Target that will create an application manifest for your project.
ComputeClickOnceManifestInfo	Target that will gather the information necessary to create a ClickOnce manifest.
GenerateDeploymentManifest	Target that will create a deployment manifest for your project.

Now that you know many of the existing targets, how can you change how these steps are executed? Well, keep in mind that the C# targets, properties, and tasks can be overridden with custom versions. The version defined last will be chosen (more on this later in this section). One method of changing these existing targets is to completely override the entire target. This will likely not be the mechanism you'll want to use. A better alternative is to create a target you'd like to have performed. Then inject that target in the DependsOnTargets list at the location at which you'd like it to be executed. To clarify this, you will learn how to change the way your projects are built.

To change how your project is built, you have a few options. You can create targets BeforeBuild and AfterBuild, and those will be executed at the appropriate time. You could define PreBuildEvent or PostBuildEvent. These options provide a simple and convenient means for customizing the build process, but what if you need more control? Previously we mentioned that you can redefine the build target, but this is not a good idea. We'll show how a build is performed, and then we will show a better method. From the Microsoft.Common.targets file, the Build target, and its required property, is defined as follows:

```
<PropertyGroup>
    <BuildDependsOn>
        BeforeBuild;
        CoreBuild;
```

```
            PostBuildEvent;
            AfterBuild
        </BuildDependsOn>
    </PropertyGroup>
    <Target
        Name="Build"
        Condition=" '$(InvalidConfigurationWarning)' != 'true' "
        Outputs="$(TargetPath)"
        DependsOnTargets="$(BuildDependsOn)"/>
```

From this excerpt you can see that the Build target itself doesn't actually do anything; it simply calls other targets to do all the work. Also notice that the DependsOnTargets attribute is a property instead of simply containing the list itself. This is because if you wanted to add a step to the build, you could just override the BuildDependsOn property with your target name injected in there. For example, if you had a target defined as RecoredBuildCompletion that you wanted to execute after your build completed, you would simply insert the following property definition into your project file:

```
<PropertyGroup>
    <BuildDependsOn>
        BeforeBuild;
        CoreBuild;
        PostBuildEvent;
        AfterBuild
        RecordBuildCompletion;
    </BuildDependsOn>
</PropertyGroup>
```

Now when your project gets built, MSBuild will ignore the BuildDependsOn property that is defined in the Microsoft.Common.targets file, because this BuildDependsOn property overrides its definition. When MSBuild evaluates properties and items, the last definition provided will be used. So, the placement of these declarations is important; in this case, this declaration must be after the import declaration for Microsoft.Common.targets. Because of this statement, your RecordBuildCompletion target will be executed at the end. For this simple example, this is the same as overriding the AfterBuild target.

Continuing with how projects are built, you'll notice that CoreBuild is a dependent target for the Build target. Let's examine its definition from the Microsoft.Common.targets file:

```
<PropertyGroup>
    <CoreBuildDependsOn>
        BuildOnlySettings;
        PrepareForBuild;
        PreBuildEvent;
        UnmanagedUnregistration;
        ResolveReferences;
        PrepareResources;
        ResolveKeySource;
        Compile;
        SGen;
```

```
        CreateSatelliteAssemblies;
        GenerateManifests;
        PrepareForRun;
        ObjectRelationalValidator;
        UnmanagedRegistration;
        IncrementalClean
    </CoreBuildDependsOn>
</PropertyGroup>
<Target
    Name="CoreBuild"
    DependsOnTargets="$(CoreBuildDependsOn)">

    <OnError Condition="'$(RunPostBuildEvent)'=='Always' or➥
 '$(RunPostBuildEvent)'=='OnOutputUpdated'" ➥
 ExecuteTargets="TimeStampAfterCompile;PostBuildEvent"/>
    <OnError ExecuteTargets="RecordFileWrites"/>

</Target>
```

Here you can see how the build process is broken down. You'll want to look at the CoreBuildDependsOn property. The items in that list are targets that will be executed, in order, when your project is built. If you need more fine-grained control over the build, typically you'll create a new target and override the CoreBuildDependsOn property with it included in the list. So let's do just that; we will show how to create a target, PrintIntermediateAssemblyName, and place this target after the Compile step in the build process. For this target, you'll also print the value for the CoreBuildDependsOn property. You just need to modify the CoreBuildDependsOn property and define the required target. Add the following to the project file:

```
<PropertyGroup>
    <CoreBuildDependsOn>
        BuildOnlySettings;
        PrepareForBuild;
        PreBuildEvent;
        UnmanagedUnregistration;
        ResolveReferences;
        PrepareResources;
        ResolveKeySource;
        Compile;
        PrintIntermediateAssemblyName;
        SGen;
        CreateSatelliteAssemblies;
        GenerateManifests;
        PrepareForRun;
        ObjectRelationalValidator;
        UnmanagedRegistration;
        IncrementalClean
    </CoreBuildDependsOn>
</PropertyGroup>
```

```
<Target Name="PrintIntermediateAssemblyName" DependsOnTargets="Compile">
    <Message Text="Intermediate assembly name: @(IntermediateAssembly)" />
    <Message Text="Int assm full path:
$(MSBuildProjectDirectory)\@(IntermediateAssembly)"/>

    <Message Text="---------CoreBuildDependsOn--------------"/>
    <Message Text="$(CoreBuildDependsOn)"/>
    <Message Text="---------------------------------------"/>
</Target>
```

The property `IntermediateAssembly` is an output item of the `Compile` target. You can just print its value to the console using the `Message` task. Note: when you access items, you always use the @() syntax, and when accessing properties, you use the $() syntax. You'll find more about this in Chapter 3.

Following this, you will invoke the `Build` target and watch its output. Since the `DefaultTarget` is `Build`, you can call MSBuild on this project without specifying a file, and `Build` will execute. Use this command to invoke it: >msbuild MSBuild1_rev2.csproj /v:detailed /t:Clean;Build. We chose to execute `Clean` and then `Build` to make sure that all targets are reexecuted for the build. Figure 2-6 shows the result of this build.

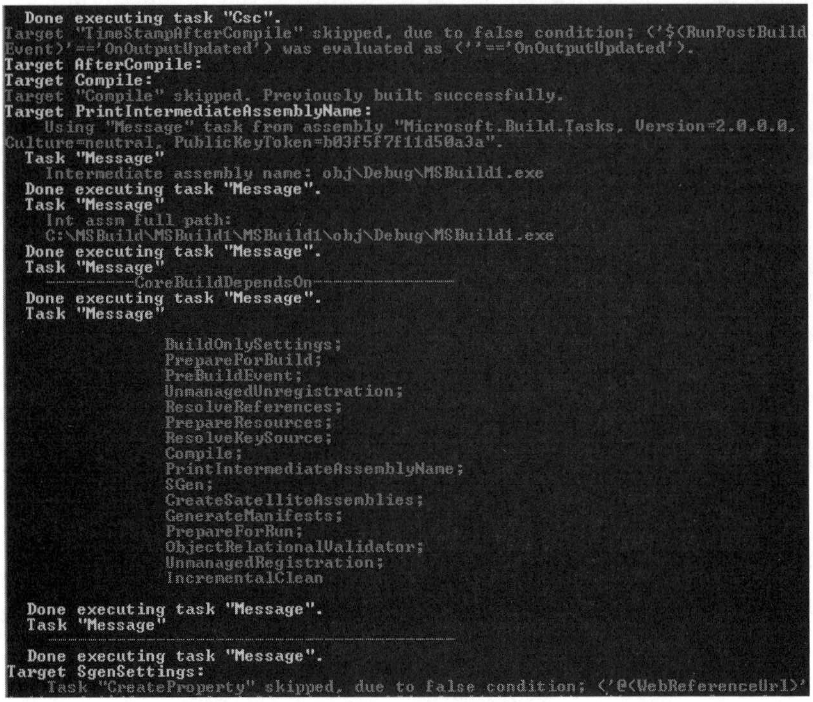

Figure 2-6. *Output from customized build*

From Figure 2-6 you can see that the task was indeed executed immediately after the `Compile` target completed. In previous versions of Visual Studio, this was basically impossible, but it took you only a few minutes to complete it! Now that you know how to execute targets, you can move on to creating some new tasks.

Tasks

As stated, a *task* is a unit of work. You'll want to create generic and simple tasks. If you need to adhere to a flow of execution, such as locate ➤ copy ➤ delete, you'll want to create each of those as tasks; actually, you will most likely have to write only the locate task because the copy and delete are predefined. The components that will model the flow of execution will be targets. Tasks are usually declared within targets, but it is possible to have them outside as well.

Predefined Tasks

Many predefined tasks are available to you out of the box. These tasks are declared in the `Microsoft.Common.Tasks` file and are contained in the `Microsoft.Build.Tasks` assembly. Table 2-5 summarizes the predefined tasks that are available.

Table 2-5. *Predefined Tasks*

Name	Description
AL	Assembly linker. Creates one assembly from many other components.
AspNetCompiler	Precompiles ASP.NET files.
AssignCulture	Given a list of files whose filenames contain a culture identifier, creates items that contain this culture as metadata, instead of being embedded in the filename.
Copy	Copies files from one location to another.
CreateItem	Creates a new item. You can also use this to copy an item.
CreateProperty	Creates a property, similarly to CreateItem; you can use this to copy properties.
Csc	Invokes the C# compiler.
Delete	Deletes files.
Error	Raises an MSBuild error.
Exec	Invokes the specified application.
FindUnderPath	Determines whether specified items exist under the specified path.
GenerateApplicationManifest	Creates an application manifest that can include such things as globally unique identifiers (GUIDs), assemblies, and files. Note: You can use this to create a ClickOnce manifest.
GenerateBootstrapper	Creates an application that can download your application and all of its dependencies.
GenerateDeploymentManifest	Creates a ClickOnce manifest.
GenerateResource	Creates resources; this is functionally similar to the resgen.exe application.
GetAssemblyIdentity	Given a list of files that contain assemblies, gets all the IDs of contained assemblies.

Continued

Table 2-5. *Continued*

Name	Description
GetFrameworkPath	Returns the full path of the location where the .NET Framework assemblies are installed.
GetFrameworkSdkPath	Returns the full path of the .NET Framework SDK.
LC	Creates license files for applications.
MakeDir	Creates directories.
Message	Outputs messages.
MSBuild	Invokes a build on another MSBuild project file.
ReadLinesFromFile	Reads lines from a specified file.
RegisterAssembly	Used in a similar way as the Assembly Registration tool (regasm.exe).
RemoveDir	Removes directories and their contents.
RemoveDuplicates	Removes duplicates from the given item collection.
ResGen	Wrapper for the resgen.exe application that can be used to create binary .resource files.
ResolveAssemblyReference	Given a list of assemblies, determines what other assemblies depend on assemblies in that list.
ResolveComReference	Given either a list of library names or a .tlb file, discovers the location on disk.
ResolveKeySource	Resolves the strong name key source.
ResolveNativeReference	Resolves native references.
SGen	Creates an XML serialization for specified assemblies.
SignFile	Given a certificate, signs files.
Touch	Updates the file access/modified date.
UnregisterAssembly	Unregisters the specified assembly. This is the inverse operation of the RegisterAssembly task.
Vbc	Wrapper for the Visual Basic compiler.
VCBuild	Wrapper for the Visual C++ compiler.
Warning	Raises an MSBuild warning.
WriteLinesToFile	Writes lines to text files.

Before you begin to write a task, or a target for that matter, you should always double-check to make sure you're not reinventing the wheel. We will show how to create a simple task: HelloTask.

Creating a Task

By this point you probably have a general feeling for what a task is, but you most likely still have many questions regarding them. For example, how can new tasks be implemented? Tasks actually are implemented in code, so whatever you are able to do in code you are able to accomplish in a task. This even includes showing dialog boxes and launching external applications. In the build process, you probably will not want to show dialog boxes, but you have the option if you desire.

■Note Before we discuss tasks, we will briefly discuss metadata, which is used in the task samples. Items can have metadata associated with them. Items actually have two classes of metadata: well-known metadata and custom metadata. We will provide more details about metadata in later chapters. An example of the well-known metadata is `FullPath`; you can get the full path to an item by simply getting the value of this metadata item. To access metadata, you use the `%()` operator. To get the full path for an item, use the syntax `@(ItemName->'%(FullPath)')`.

In this section, you will learn how to create a simple task, including invoking it from your project file. This simple task will be `HelloTask`. The `HelloTask` task will accept an assembly name as its input, prepend *HelloTask:*, and return it to the target that called it. To do this, your task must be able to accept an input and be able to create an output. Generally, creating a task involves three general steps:

1. Specify the task in your project file.

2. Write the .NET class behind the task.

3. Specify in the project file where the task can be found.

Now you will dissect these steps and create your first custom task! You first need to specify the task in your project file. Since you know you will pass in the assembly name, it should depend on the `Compile` target, and you want to print the result to the console. Insert the following target into the project file:

```
<Target Name="DoHelloTask" DependsOnTargets="Compile">
    <HelloTask
        TheAssembly="@(IntermediateAssembly->'%(FullPath)') "
    >
        <Output TaskParameter="HelloOutput" PropertyName="HelloTaskString" />
    </HelloTask>
    <!-- Now print out the task output -->
    <Message Text="$(HelloTaskString)"/>
</Target>
```

You have just created a new target, `DoHelloTarget`, that depends on the `Compile` target and calls a custom task, the `HelloTask` task. This task has one input, `TheAssembly`. `TheAssembly` has been passed the value of `"@(IntermediateAssembly->'%(FullPath)')"`. Previously we used `IntermediateAssembly`, but this time you have specified you would like `FullPath` to be passed into the task. (We will discuss other operations that can be performed in later chapters.) The output for the `HelloTask` task is defined by the `<Output TaskParameter="HelloOutput" PropertyName="HelloTaskString" />` line. Since tasks are implemented in code, MSBuild must have a mechanism to determine what the inputs and outputs are. Inputs and outputs are properties of those classes. The inputs of your task are attributes of the task element. The names of these attributes must be the same as their corresponding properties in the implementing class. The outputs must be specified inside an `Output` tag, and the value of its `PropertyName` attribute must be the same as the name of the corresponding class. The `TaskParameter` attribute of the `Output` element is the name used to refer to this value in the MSBuild project file(s). You are finished with the first step, so now you will move on to the next one.

Now you have to write the code that lies behind the task. For this you will need to perform the following steps:

1. Launch a new instance of Visual Studio.

2. Create a new class library project.

3. For the name, specify **SampleTasks1**.

4. Click Finish, and rename the class to **HelloTask**.

5. Add a reference for `Microsoft.Build.Framework` and `Microsoft.Build.Utilities`.

6. Add the using statements for both namespaces, namely, `using Microsoft.Build.Framework;` and `using Microsoft.Build.Utilities;`.

At this point, you'll have an empty class with a few references included. This is a good time to make sure you haven't mistyped anything, so you should build the project. After you confirm your build, you need to make this class a task. To do this, you'll need to inherit from the base class `Microsoft.Build.Utilities.Task`. This class has the `public bool Execute()` method that you will need to override. This method is automatically called when it is time to execute the task. Also, you'll need to specify the properties for the task. MSBuild will set the input properties, and you'll want them to be of the `Microsoft.Build.Framework.ITaskItem` type. The following is the class that represents this task:

```
public class HelloTask : Task
{
    private ITaskItem _theAssembly;
    private string _helloOutput;

    //This is the parameter for the input. Place Required
    //attribute to ensure that is has been specified before you continue
    [Required]
    public ITaskItem TheAssembly
    {
        get
        {
            return this._theAssembly;
        }
        set
        {
            this._theAssembly = value;
        }
    }
    //This is your output.
    //Place the Output attribute so MSBuild can find it.
    [Output]
    public string HelloOutput
    {
```

```
        get
        {
            return this._helloOutput;
        }
        set
        {
            this._helloOutput = value;
        }
    }
    /// <summary>
    /// This is the method that will automatically be called
    /// by MSBuild to execute your task.
    /// </summary>
    /// <returns>true if task succeeded false otherwise</returns>
    public override bool Execute()
    {
        this.HelloOutput = "HelloTask: " + this.TheAssembly;
        return true;
    }
}
```

You should note a few things about this class file. The inputs and outputs are defined as properties, and both have get() and set() methods. Also, for outputs you should place the Output attribute on the property, and for required properties you should use the Required attribute. As mentioned, the Execute() method is the method that will automatically be called by MSBuild when it is time to execute your task. For properties that are Required, those are promised to be set before Execute() is invoked. Your task can perform whatever steps you require, but the only way it can interact with other tasks in your MSBuild file(s) will be through your properties.

Now that you have defined how this task will be performed, it is time to finish the integration. Following these three steps will conclude creating the task:

1. Build the assembly that contains the task.

2. Place the assembly in a known and accessible location.

3. Declare the task in your project file and the location of the assembly that contains it.

Build the assembly as you normally do through Visual Studio. You can also use MSBuild now that you know how. After this, a .dll file is created that you can place in a new TaskAssemblies folder in the same directory as your project. In a large build scenario, you may have a specific location, or the GAC, in which all task assemblies are automatically placed upon build. So, now you need to add the following statement to the project file:

```
<UsingTask TaskName="HelloTask" ➥
AssemblyFile="C:\MSBuild\MSBuild1\MSBuild1\TaskAssemblies\SampleTasks1.dll" />
```

This statement can appear anywhere in the project file. The AssemblyFile attribute of UsingTask specifies where the assembly is located, and TaskName specifies which task is declared inside that assembly. A Condition attribute exists, as it does for every MSBuild element. The last element that can be present is the AssemblyName attribute. The AssemblyName specifies the name of the assembly that contains the required task implementation. You must choose between using the AssemblyFile or AssemblyName attribute; you cannot use both, but at least one must be present. If you use AssemblyFile, then the class will be loaded by the System.Reflection.LoadFrom method; if you use AssemblyName, then it will be loaded using System.Reflection.Load.

Now that you are finished, you should invoke it and see whether it works. At this point, you should have the SampleTasks1.dll file in the TaskAssemblies folder, which is in the same directory in which your project file resides. Your project file must contain the following statements:

```
<UsingTask TaskName="HelloTask" ➥
AssemblyFile="C:\MSBuild\MSBuild1\MSBuild1\TaskAssemblies\SampleTasks1.dll"/>
<Target Name="DoHelloTask" DependsOnTargets="Compile">
    <HelloTask
        TheAssembly="@(IntermediateAssembly->'%(FullPath)')"
    >
        <Output TaskParameter="HelloOutput" PropertyName="HelloTaskString" />
    </HelloTask>
    <!-- Now print out the task output -->
    <Message Text="$(HelloTaskString)"/>
</Target>
```

To invoke this task, execute the following command: >msbuild MSBuild1_rev2.csproj /t: DoHelloTask. If you get some errors, usually they are descriptive, and you may need to modify your project file. If all goes well, your output should look like Figure 2-7.

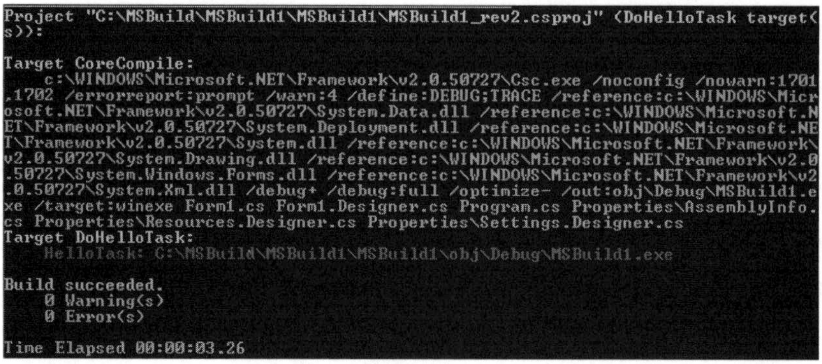

Figure 2-7. *Output from* HelloTask *execution*

From Figure 2-7, you can see that HelloTask successfully completed and printed the path of the intermediate assembly to the console. Notice that this target also caused the Compile target to be executed. This is the expected behavior because it is in the DependsOnTargets list. From this simple example, you can imagine how your projects can use MSBuild to automate and streamline your build and deploy methods. In later chapters, we will discuss in further detail how to use MSBuild.

Summary

In this chapter, we discussed what build tools are and why they are now a required component in the software development life cycle. We also introduced Microsoft's new build tool, MSBuild. We covered all of the key elements that you need to start customizing your builds using MSBuild. For the next few chapters, we will build on this foundation so you can extend your build process to suit your needs. In the next chapter, for example, we will show MSBuild in action. You will see many examples of using MSBuild to help you comprehend some of the difficult-to-understand features and to provide more of a concrete basis on which to further build.

■■■

MSBuild: By Example

Even if you have experience using an XML task-based build tool, such as Ant or NAnt, MSBuild is significantly different. In fact, MSBuild is different not only in execution but also in syntax. Therefore, to really get a feel for MSBuild, you must get your hands dirty using the tool. As you begin to explore what MSBuild has to offer to your projects, you will naturally seek more knowledge of MSBuild. This chapter will help you get your hands dirty by showing you several examples of how you can use MSBuild. Also, this chapter will present some important techniques for using MSBuild effectively. We will provide a variety of tips, covering topics such as integrating MSBuild into Visual Studio and formatting your output.

These samples are set up to be mostly independent. This is because each sample expresses a set of specific ideas, so you will be able to examine and try each concept on its own. After this chapter, you should have a much greater feel for building your applications with MSBuild. Following this chapter, we will continue the coverage of MSBuild by showing how to use some of its more advanced features.

Introducing Well-Known Metadata

When using MSBuild, you have two primary ways to pass data to tasks and targets; those are through properties and through items. A *property* is a key/value pair, and an *item* is typically a reference to a file. For example, when your project is compiled, the Compile item is evaluated to determine which files should be included. Using items for files over properties has some advantages; one of these advantages is that items can have metadata attached to them. The following is a sample of an item declaration from the Microsoft.Common.targets file:

```
<ItemGroup>
    <AppConfigFileDestination Include="$(OutDir)$(TargetFileName).config"/>
</ItemGroup>
```

In the previous declaration, the item AppConfigFileDestination is being defined, and its value is specified in the Include attribute. This attribute is using two properties, OutDir and TargetFileName, to create the name of the config file. An example of its value is bin\debug\WindowsApplication1.exe.config.

When you specify which files are included in the item declaration, you can include multiple files by separating them with semicolons. Another way to include multiple files is to use expressions that include wildcards. You can use three wildcard elements with MSBuild: ?, *, and **. You can use ? to replace a single character with any character. For example, the include declaration `Include="c?r.cs"` would include the files `car.cs`, `cbr.cs`, `ccr.cs`, and so on. The * element can replace any location with zero or more characters. To change the previous example, `Include="c*r.cs"` would include `car.cs`, `caar.cs`, `cr.cs`, `colorer.cs`, and so on. The ** notation tells MSBuild to search the directories recursively for the pattern. For example, `Include="src\**\*.cs"` would include all the files under the `src` directory with `.cs` extensions.

When you include an item in your MSBuild project file, it may seem you are simply adding a text entry, but what you don't see is what's happening behind the scenes. When you add an item, you're adding a rich object to your project, and you get some information for free!

For this example, we will use `MetaDataEx.csproj`. This is a simple Windows Forms application, similar to the one contained in Chapter 2. Table 3-1 describes the metadata that is automatically set when your project file is loaded; this is *well-known* metadata.

Table 3-1. *An Item's Well-Known Metadata*

Metadata Name	Description
Identity	A unique value for each item in the item collection.
Filename	Filename for this item, not including the extension.
Extension	File extension for this item.
FullPath	Full path of this item including the filename.
RelativeDir	Path to this item relative to the current working directory.
RootDir	Root directory to which this item belongs.
RecursiveDir	Used for items that were created using wildcards. This would be the directory that replaces the wildcard(s) statements that determine the directory.
Directory	The directory of this item.
AccessedTime	Last time this item was accessed.
CreatedTime	Time the item was created.
ModifiedTime	Time this item was modified.

The following is a target that demonstrates how to use well-known metadata:

```
<ItemGroup>
    <MDForm Include="MetaDataFrm.cs">
        <Author>
            <Name>Sayed Ibrahim Hashimi</Name>
            <Email>sayed.hashimi@gmail.com</Email>
        </Author>
    </MDForm>
```

```xml
    <MDFormOther Include="..\..\**\MSBuild1\*.cs">
        <Author>
            <Name>Sayed Y. Hashimi</Name>
            <Email>hashimi_sayed@gmail.com</Email>
        </Author>
    </MDFormOther>
</ItemGroup>
<Target Name="ShowWellKnownMD">
    <Message Text="Normal: @(MDForm)" />
    <Message Text="FullPath: @(MDForm->'%(FullPath)') " />
    <Message Text="RootDir: @(MDForm->'%(RootDir)')" />
    <Message Text="Filename: @(MDForm->'%(Filename)')" />
    <Message Text="Extension: @(MDForm->'%(Extension)')" />
    <Message Text="RelativeDir: @(MDForm->'%(RelativeDir)')" />
    <Message Text="Directory: @(MDForm->'%(Directory)')" />
    <Message Text="RecusriveDir: @(MDForm->'%(RecursiveDir)')" />
    <Message Text="Identity: @(MDForm->'%(Identity)')" />
    <Message Text="ModifiedTime: @(MDForm->'%(ModifiedTime)')" />
    <Message Text="CreatedTime: @(MDForm->'%(CreatedTime)')" />
    <Message Text="AccessedTime: @(MDForm->'%(AccessedTime)')" />

    <Message Text="%0D%0A;--------------"/>
    <Message Text="Recursive dir [MDFormOther]: "/>
    <Message Text="%09@(MDFormOther->'%(Filename)➥
            %09%(RecursiveDir)', '%0D%0A%09;')"/>

    <Message Text="%0D%0A;Relative dir [MDFormOther]: "/>
    <Message Text="%09;@(MDFormOther->'%(Filename)➥
            %09;%(RelativeDir)', '%0D%0A%09;')"/>
</Target>
```

In this snippet from the MetaDataEx project file, an ItemGroup contains the item declarations upon which this target will act. This ItemGroup defines two items. One of these items, MDForm, includes only a single file and is explicitly defined. This item will provide the results of many of the metadata queries in this sample. The other item contains many files and has been defined using wildcards. This item will demonstrate how to use the RecursiveDir and RelativeDir metadata values. This file also includes some formatting of the output; for further information regarding formatting, see the "Formatting Your Output" section. To invoke this target on your project, you will invoke MSBuild by executing the following at the command line: >msbuild MetaDataEx.csproj /t:ShowWellKnownMD. Figure 3-1 shows the output from this target.

```
Project "C:\MSBuild\MSBuildExamples\MetaDataEx\MetaDataEx.csproj" (ShowWellKnown
MD target(s)):

Target ShowWellKnownMD:
    Normal: MetaDataFrm.cs
    FullPath: C:\MSBuild\MSBuildExamples\MetaDataEx\MetaDataFrm.cs
    RootDir: C:\
    Filename: MetaDataFrm
    Extension: .cs
    RelativeDir:
    Directory: MSBuild\MSBuildExamples\MetaDataEx\
    RecusriveDir:
    Identity: MetaDataFrm.cs
    ModifiedTime: 2005-10-05 23:25:00.8320256
    CreatedTime: 2005-10-05 23:20:01.4114800
    AccessedTime: 2005-10-06 01:05:40.5266800


    Recursive dir [MDFormOther]:
        Form1    MSBuild1\MSBuild1\
        Form1.Designer  MSBuild1\MSBuild1\
        Program MSBuild1\MSBuild1\

    Relative dir [MDFormOther]:
        Form1    ..\..\MSBuild1\MSBuild1\
        Form1.Designer  ..\..\MSBuild1\MSBuild1\
        Program ..\..\MSBuild1\MSBuild1\

Build succeeded.
    0 Warning(s)
    0 Error(s)

Time Elapsed 00:00:00.03
```

Figure 3-1. *Well-known metadata output*

In Figure 3-1 you can see that MSBuild was able to resolve the items to the actual files on disk. If you are creating a new task that acts upon a file, you most likely will want to pass the task the FullPath value of the item. This will ensure that your task is dealing with the same file as your MSBuild project file. For example, if you want to copy IntermediateAssembly to another location, then you can use a declaration similar to the following one:

```
<Copy SourceFiles="@(IntermediateAssembly->'%(FullPath)')"
    DestinationFiles=➡
"@(IntermediateAssembly->'$(Destination)\%(Filename)%(Extension)')"/>
```

This will copy the IntermediateAssembly to the Destination location and preserve the filename and extension. It is a best practice to use the FullPath for items as inputs to the tasks to ensure that no other file can be used in its place. When you are creating your MSBuild targets and tasks, it is helpful to remember what metadata is available to you out of the box and to remember how you can use it effectively.

Formatting Your Output

As you use MSBuild to build your projects, you may want to format your output for increased readability or for other reasons. MSBuild uses the % character to show the beginning of an escaped character. The % character is followed by the ASCII character code for the desired character. You can find a complete reference for these codes in the MSDN Help documentation. For example, if you would like to place a carriage return line feed (\r\n) in your text, use the %0D%0A code. For example, consider the following FormatNewLine target, which is in the MSBuildEx.csproj file:

```
<Target Name="FormatNewline">
    <Message Text="FirstLine%0D%0ASecondLine" />
</Target>
```

To execute this target, you call MSBuild with the following at the command line:
>msbuild MetaDataEx.csproj /t:FormatNewLine. Figure 3-2 shows the output from this target.

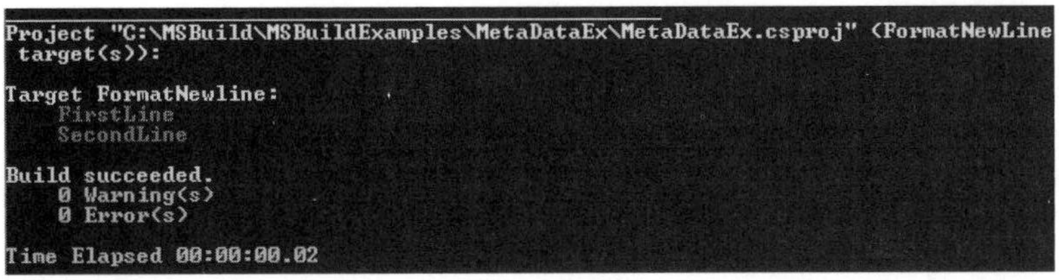

```
Project "C:\MSBuild\MSBuildExamples\MetaDataEx\MetaDataEx.csproj" (FormatNewLine
 target(s)):

Target FormatNewline:
    FirstLine
    SecondLine

Build succeeded.
    0 Warning(s)
    0 Error(s)

Time Elapsed 00:00:00.02
```

Figure 3-2. *MSBuild-formatted output*

From Figure 3-2 you can see that the new line was successfully inserted into the output for this text. Table 3-2 lists some ASCII character codes that you may find useful when creating your project files.

Table 3-2. *Useful ASCII Character Code Escape Values*

Character	ASCII Escape Value
Carriage return	%0D
Line feed	%0A
New line	%0D%0A
Tab	%09
Space	%20
Quotes (")	%22
Apostrophe (')	%27
Ampersand (&)	%26
Percent sign (%)	%25

In some circumstances when you are using a vector value, you may want to change the delimiter when using the Message task. Refer to the following target:

```
<Target Name="ShowFiles">
    <Message Text="MDFormOther files:" />
    <!-- Uses standard ; delimiter -->
    <Message Text="@(MDFormOther->'%(Filename)')" />
    <!-- Uses , delimiter instead-->
    <Message Text="@(MDFormOther->'%(Filename)', ',')" />
</Target>
```

The <Message Text="@(MDFormOther->'%(Filename)')" /> call will print the values for the files included with the default delimiter, which is a semicolon. If you want a different delimiter, you can specify it as an argument. For example, the <Message Text="@(MDFormOther->'%(Filename)', ',')" /> call changes the delimiter to a comma. You can also use this feature to format your output! For example, if you want to align all the filenames, you can specify the delimiter to be a new line. Add the following message invocation to the target:

```
<Message Text="@(MDFormOther->'%(Filename)', '%0D%0A')" />
```

This invocation is specifying that a new line should delimit all the entries that will be included in the list. The target will look like the following snippet now:

```
<Target Name="ShowFiles">
    <Message Text="MDFormOther files:" />
    <!-- Uses standard ; delimiter -->
    <Message Text="Default delimiter" />
    <Message Text="@(MDFormOther->'%(Filename)')" />
    <!-- Uses , delimiter instead-->
    <Message Text="Comma delimiter" />
    <Message Text="@(MDFormOther->'%(Filename)', ',')" />
    <!-- This lines up the filenames -->
    <Message Text="Align on new lines"/>
    <Message Text="@(MDFormOther->'%(Filename)', '%0D%0A')" />
</Target>
```

When you execute this task, you will get the result shown in Figure 3-3.

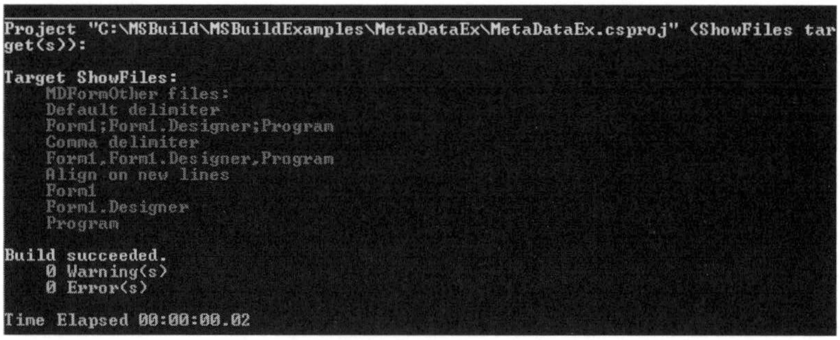

Figure 3-3. *Output from* ShowFiles *with custom delimiter*

I'm sure you noticed that this output is still not very readable. Now you'll add a few features to make it better. First, we will show how to add new lines to separate the sections of this output. To add a new line, insert `<Message Text="%0D%0A"/>` where desired. Second, we'll show how to align all the elements under their headings with tabs. To do this, you can add a tab before the result for the first two targets. But for the last target, you will also have to add a tab to the delimiter. The final target should look like the following:

```
<Target Name="ShowFilesFinal">
    <Message Text="MDFormOther files:%0D%0A" />
    <!-- Uses standard ; delimiter -->
    <Message Text="Default delimiter" />
    <Message Text="%09@(MDFormOther->'%(Filename)')" />
    <Message Text="%0D%0A"/>
```

```
    <!-- Uses , delimiter instead-->
    <Message Text="Comma delimiter" />
    <Message Text="%09@(MDFormOther->'%(Filename)', ',')" />
    <Message Text="%0D%0A"/>
    <!-- This lines up the filenames -->
    <Message Text="Align on new lines"/>
    <Message Text="%09@(MDFormOther->'%(Filename)', '%0D%0A%09;')" />
    <Message Text="%0D%0A"/>
</Target>
```

Figure 3-4 shows the output from executing this new target.

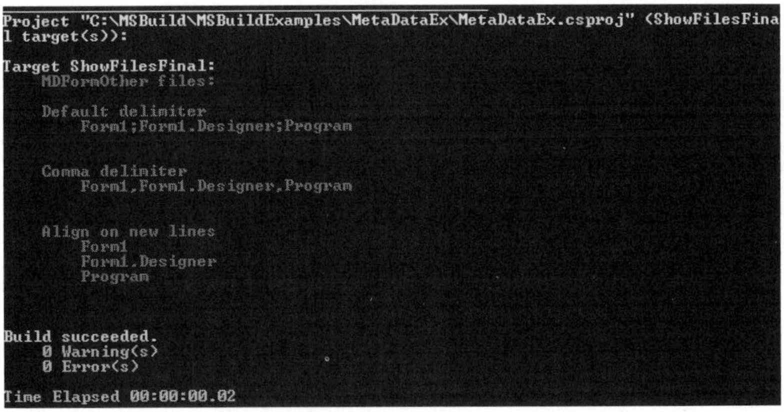

Figure 3-4. *Output from message with formatting*

You can see that the output from this target execution is much more readable than the previous invocations.

Now you have successfully made the output much easier to read, but what have you done to the readability of the build file itself? Sifting through all the ASCII values is not only nonintuitive but is distracting. What can you do to avoid this problem? You may have guessed—you can keep these values inside properties. In a few cases, this method doesn't work as expected, such as when you are placing whitespace-related items inside the properties. But you can get around that. We will skip covering those issues for now, however, in order to examine the other issues first. Refer to the following properties:

```
<PropertyGroup>
    <AT_SIGN>%40</AT_SIGN>
    <PERCENT_SIGN>%25</PERCENT_SIGN>
    <DOUBLE_QUOTE>%22</DOUBLE_QUOTE>
    <SINGLE_QUOTE>%27</SINGLE_QUOTE>
    <CR>%0D</CR>
    <LF>%0A</LF>
    <!-- New line items removed -->
</PropertyGroup>
```

From these properties you can see that the ASCII values for each character in the previous table have been supplied in the appropriate property. Now you will examine how you can use these properties in your build files. Refer to the following target:

```
<Target Name="ShowAsciiProps">
    <Message Text="At sign: $(AT_SIGN)" />
    <Message Text="Percent: $(PERCENT_SIGN)"/>
    <Message Text="Double $(DOUBLE_QUOTE)Quote$(DOUBLE_QUOTE)" />
    <Message Text="Single $(SINGLE_QUOTE)Quote$(SINGLE_QUOTE)"/>
</Target>
```

You can execute this target at the command line with `>msbuild MetaDataEx.csproj /t:ShowAsciiProps`. Figure 3-5 shows the output from this target.

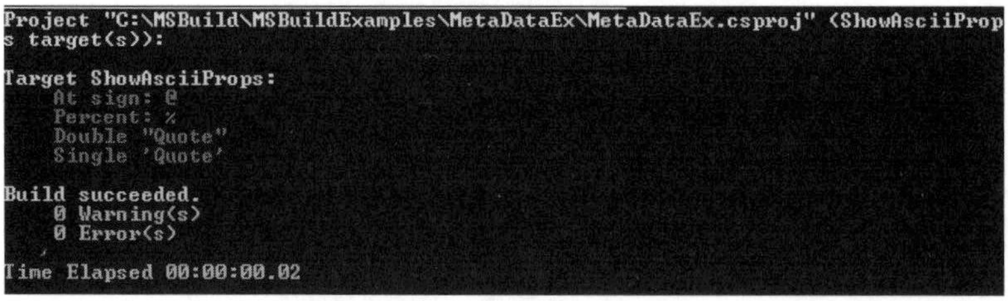

Figure 3-5. *Output from the* ShowUnicodeProps *target*

So, now you can embed ASCII values inside the project file while maintaining its readability. Now we'll cover the tricky situations. Since you have seen how to use escaped characters, we will show how you can align MSBuild output using them.

In the previous example where you placed the ASCII values inside properties, we skipped over how to deal with the whitespace characters. Here is the remainder of PropertyGroup that was truncated previously and that contains working versions of the values:

```
<PropertyGroup>
    <TAB>%09</TAB>
    <HARD_NEW_LINE>%0A%0D%0C%08</HARD_NEW_LINE>
    <SOFT_NEW_LINE>%0A%20%08</SOFT_NEW_LINE>
</PropertyGroup>
```

If you look at the definition for TAB, you'll see that the %09 character is the ASCII character code value for the tab character. This defines two variations for the new line: a HARD_NEW_LINE and a SOFT_NEW_LINE. The SOFT_NEW_LINE is the one that acts as a new line embedded inside your text as ASCII. The SOFT_NEW_LINE will drop down a line and start at the same horizontal position as the start of the previous line. The HARD_NEW_LINE will drop down a line and start at the beginning of the next line. Let's see what they look like. Here is a target to test these new values:

```
<Target Name="ShowAsciiWhiteSpaceProps">
    <Message Text="Space$(SPACE)Here"/>
    <Message Text="Space Here"/>

    <Message Text=" "/>

    <Message Text="A Tab$(TAB)Example"/>
    <Message Text="A Tab%09Example"/>

    <Message Text=" "/>
    <Message Text="(soft)New$(SOFT_NEW_LINE)Line"/>
    <Message Text=" "/>
    <Message Text="(hard)New$(HARD_NEW_LINE)Line"/>
    <Message Text=" "/>

    <Message Text="New%0D%0A;Line"/>
</Target>
```

In the ShowAsciiWhiteSpaceProps target, first the test messages are displayed, and the last message contains the ASCII code embedded within the text. You can invoke this target by executing the following at the command line: >msbuild MetaDataEx.csproj /t:ShowAsciiWhiteSpaceProps. Figure 3-6 shows the result of this execution.

Figure 3-6. *Output from the* ShowUnicodeWhiteSpaceProps *target*

Make a note of the difference between a SOFT_NEW_LINE and a HARD_NEW_LINE before you choose to use either. You'll most likely want to stick to the SOFT_NEW_LINE.

With these tricks you should be able to format your output for simple situations. If you need more fine-grained control over how the output is being returned, you may have to implement your own task to conduct the formatting for you. Because creating a task is a fairly simple process, if you are not able to format your output after a few minutes of trying, just create a new task to do it for you! Another option is to write a custom logger to perform this for you, which is covered in detail in Chapter 4.

Editing MSBuild Files with IntelliSense

You can edit your MSBuild files in any way you'd like. You can use any text/XML editor that you desire. If you use a simple tool, such as Notepad, this will work, but it will not provide you with any assistance as your create your project files. Some XML editors use the XML Schema Document (XSD) to give you some assistance. One such tool is Visual Studio! If you open your project file inside Visual Studio, then IntelliSense will be enabled, and you will be able to create your MSBuild files much more quickly.

Visual Studio's IntelliSense is particularly useful when you know what you want to do but don't remember all the details. For instance, if you are creating a target to copy all your source files that need to call the Copy task, you may not remember what all of its attributes are. If you open the file in Visual Studio, then as you create the new target, you will be given the list of options available to you. For example, as you are creating the call to the Copy task, you will be provided with a list like the one shown in Figure 3-7 that tells you the names of the attributes.

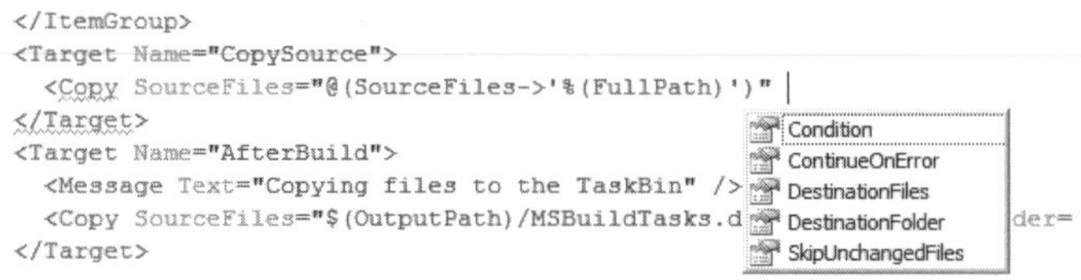

```
  </ItemGroup>
  <Target Name="CopySource">
    <Copy SourceFiles="@(SourceFiles->'%(FullPath)')" |
  </Target>
  <Target Name="AfterBuild">                    Condition
    <Message Text="Copying files to the TaskBin" />  ContinueOnError
    <Copy SourceFiles="$(OutputPath)/MSBuildTasks.d    DestinationFiles          der=
  </Target>                                             DestinationFolder
                                                        SkipUnchangedFiles
```

Figure 3-7. *Visual Studio IntelliSense for MSBuild files*

In Figure 3-7 you can see how you will spend less time if you create your MSBuild files using Visual Studio. This will also decrease the amount of errors you create as your write your targets. If you are developing your project using Visual Studio and you want to edit the project file concurrently, then you have two options for using Visual Studio as your editor:

- Open a new instance of Visual Studio, and load your project file there.

- Unload your project, edit your project file, and then reload your project.

You can employ the option of opening your project file in a new instance of Visual Studio. If you'd like to have only a single instance of Visual Studio, then you can follow these steps:

1. Unload the project. You can do this in the Solution Explorer by right-clicking the project and then selecting Unload Project. If you have a file from that project open, you can select Project ➤ Unload Project.

2. Open the project file for editing. To do this, select File ➤ Open ➤ File.

Note You cannot drag and drop the project file into Visual Studio.

---

3. Select your project file, and click Open.

4. Edit your project file, and then save the changes.

5. Close the project file.

6. Reload the project.

Integrating MSBuild into Visual Studio

Throughout this chapter you have been using MSBuild at the command line. We have a few reasons for giving these instructions: to emphasize the separation of MSBuild from Visual Studio and because complex builds are more easily executed from the command line. However, you can integrate MSBuild into Visual Studio in a simple way. In Visual Studio, you can add menu items to the Tools menu to invoke any executable. This is the method you will employ to integrate MSBuild into Visual Studio. To do this, follow these simple steps:

1. Open the External Tools dialog box by selecting Tools ➤ External Tools.

2. Add a new tool by clicking Add.

3. Enter **MSBuild** (or anything you'd like to call it) for the title.

4. For the command, provide the full path to the msbuild.exe file.

5. For the arguments, you need to provide the full path to the project file. First add the project directory, as shown in Figure 3-8.

Figure 3-8. *MSBuild project directory specification*

6. Then, add a backward slash (\) followed by the project filename. Specify the project filename in a similar way as you specified the project directory.

7. Following this, you can specify any arguments for MSBuild in the same text box.

8. Set Initial Directory to be Project Directory, just like in Figure 3-8.

9. Also check the Use Output Window and Prompt for Arguments boxes.

10. The resultant dialog box should look similar to Figure 3-9. Click OK to finish.

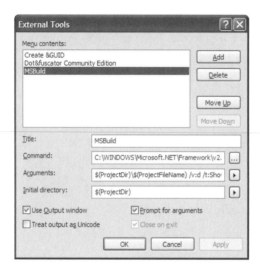

Figure 3-9. *MSBuild integration into Visual Studio*

As you can see in Figure 3-9, the verbosity of MSBuild has been specified to be detailed (d), and a target has also been specified. Since you have checked the Prompt for Arguments radio button, you can change these default arguments for each execution of MSBuild if you choose.

After you close the dialog box, make sure one of your project files is open. Invoke MSBuild by selecting Tools ➤ MSBuild (or whatever you set as the value for the title). At this point, you will see a dialog box similar to Figure 3-10.

Figure 3-10. *MSBuild dialog box in Visual Studio*

As mentioned, this specifies a default verbosity and the target that you want to have executed, but you can change this before every invocation if you choose. Also, if you'd like to change the default values, use the External Tools dialog box to modify the MSBuild external tool definition. As you specify these values, keep in mind that this will be the same for every instance of Visual Studio. Because of this, many times it is inappropriate to specify a default target, unless it is a common one such as Build. After you have decided what arguments to specify, click the OK button, and your build will begin. Since you checked the Use Output Window box, all of the output from MSBuild will be redirected to the Output window inside Visual Studio. After executing this task, you will see the Output window shown in Figure 3-11.

Note This view of the Output window shows only the end of the MSBuild output.

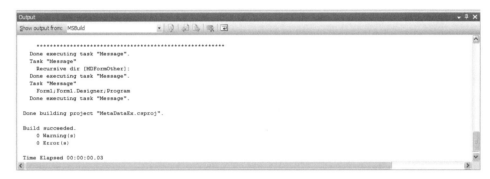

Figure 3-11. *Output window from MSBuild execution inside Visual Studio*

As we have shown, it is simple to integrate MSBuild into Visual Studio by using the External Tools dialog box in Visual Studio. This is particularly useful for targets that you find yourself frequently executing.

Introducing Custom Metadata

Metadata, the data that describes data, seems to be becoming just as important as the data itself. It seems that every new technology has metadata incorporated into its plan. MSBuild is certainly no different! In fact, MSBuild heavily relies on metadata. Earlier we showed how to access and use well-known metadata. *Well-known* metadata is "automagically" generated for your items. Some examples of well-known metadata in MSBuild are the full path of the file and its directory. You are not limited only to the well-known metadata, though. You can add custom metadata to items as well. Refer to the following ItemGroup:

```
<ItemGroup>
    <MDForm Include="MetaDataFrm.cs">
        <Name>Sayed Ibrahim Hashimi</Name>
        <Email>sayed.hashimi@gmail.com</Email>
    </MDForm>
    <MDFormOther Include="..\..\**\MSBuild1\*.cs">
        <Name>Sayed Y. Hashimi</Name>
        <Email>hashimi_sayed@gmail.com</Email>
```

```
    </MDFormOther>
</ItemGroup>
```

This item group has two items defined: MDForm and MDFormOther. With the files that are included in the items, the author information is provided in the Name and Email elements. The name and e-mail address are provided for those responsible for the classes included. How can you use this information in your MSBuild project files? Refer to the following target that prints the author information for these items:

```
<Target Name="PrintAuthorInfo">
    <Message Text="@(MDForm->'%(Filename)%(Extension)')" />
    <Message Text="%09Name:%09@(MDForm->'%(Name)')"/>
    <Message Text="%09Email:%09@(MDForm->'%(Email)')"/>

    <Message Text="%0D%0A"/>  <!--New line -->
    <Message Text="@(MDFormOther->'%(Filename)%(Extension)', '  ')" />

    <Message Text="%09Name:%09%(MDFormOther.Name)"/>
    <Message Text="%09Email:%09%(MDFormOther.Email)"/>
    <!-- Don't use this will print name/e-mail
         once for each file included in the item
    <Message Text="%09Name:%09@(MDFormOther->'%(Name)')"/>
    <Message Text="%09Email:%09@(MDFormOther->'%(Email)')"/>
    -->
</Target>
```

This target will first print the name and e-mail address for the MDForm author. The Message item that prints the name and e-mail is `<Message Text="%09Name:%09@(MDForm->'%(Name)')"/>`. This Message item contains some formatting to make it more readable (which is covered in the "Formatting Your Output" section if you are wondering about all the weird characters). If you strip away the formatting, you are left with `<Message Text="Name: @(MDForm->'%(Name)')"/>`. So, you just learned how to access the Name metadata element. It is just like how you access well-known metadata.

Did you notice that the name/e-mail is printed differently in the MDFormOther item as opposed to the technique used in the MDForm item? Here are the different ways the name is printed, minus the formatting:

```
<Message Text="Name: @(MDForm->'%(Name)')"/>
<Message Text="Name: %(MDFormOther.Name)"/>
```

In the MDForm item, you are accessing the name as a vector value, and in MDFormOther you are accessing it as a scalar value. We discuss the difference between scalar and vector values in further detail in the "Understanding the Difference Between @ and %" section. We will briefly review the concepts here for completeness. When you use the % syntax, you are saying you are expecting a vector-valued result. That is, if three items are included, you want each to be processed separately. So, if there is another item in the MDForm include list, then you will see the name printed one time for each include. With the @ and -> syntax, you are requesting the result in a single string. In this scenario, the MDFormOther technique is the correct approach.

The difference between vector and scalar values can be confusing; if you need more information, see the next section.

Understanding the Difference Between @ and %

When using MSBuild, you have three ways to evaluate an item/property expression to a value, as described in Table 3-3.

Table 3-3. *Methods to Access Item/Property Values*

Syntax	Description
$()	Extracts the value of a property
@()	Extracts the value of an item as a list, that is, vector
%()	Extracts value of an item as a single string, that is, scalar

The simplest of these methods is the $() syntax. You will use this syntax when referencing properties and only for properties.

Now we will discuss the two methods to retrieve item values. Why is there one method to access a property and two methods to access an item? As mentioned, a property is a simple key/value pair. So, for every key, there is only a single value. In other words, a property has a one-to-one relationship between the key and value. An item, on the other hand, has a one-to-many relationship. An item can contain many values inside it, but it can also contain just one. Examine the following item definition:

```
<ItemGroup>
    <MDForm Include="MetaDataFrm.cs">
        <Name>Sayed Ibrahim Hashimi</Name>
        <Email>sayed.hashimi@gmail.com</Email>
    </MDForm>
    <!-- Remainder truncated to conserve space -->
</ItemGroup>
```

The MDForm item here contains one value inside it, which is MetaDataFrm.cs. Now you will see what happens when you use both methods to access the value for this item and compare the results. The following is a simple target to demonstrate this:

```
<Target Name="VectorScalar1">
    <Message Text="%40(MDForm->'% (Filename)'):  @(MDForm->'%(Filename)')" />
    <Message Text="%25(MDForm.Filename): %(MDForm.Filename)" />
</Target>
```

This target will simply print the value for the filename of this item. Note the use of %40, which is the escape code for the at (@) character; similarly, the % character is escaped with %25. Figure 3-12 shows the output from this target.

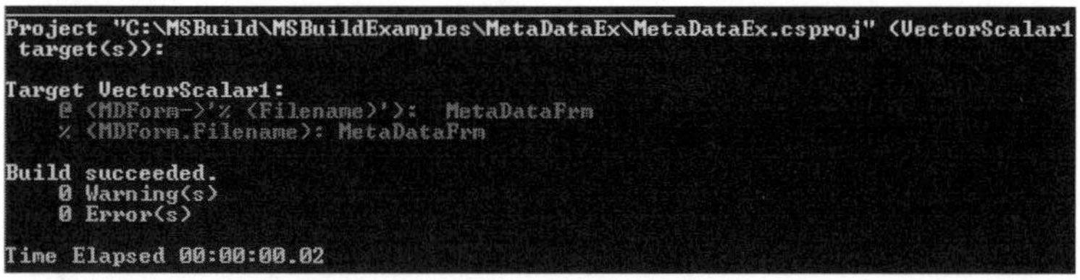

Figure 3-12. *Output from the target* VectorScalar1

As you can see, the results of both reference methods are the same! Well, now you will see another target that is similar and see whether there is any difference. The following is the definition of the target and the property that it references:

```
<Target Name="VectorScalar2">
    <Message Text="%40(Compile->'% (Filename)'):  @(Compile->'%(Filename)')"/>

    <Message Text=" "/>    <!-- Empty line for readability -->

    <Message Text="%25(Compile.Filename): %(Compile.Filename)"/>
</Target>

<ItemGroup>
    <Compile Include="MetaDataFrm.cs">
        <SubType>Form</SubType>
    </Compile>
    <Compile Include="MetaDataFrm.Designer.cs">
        <DependentUpon>MetaDataFrm.cs</DependentUpon>
    </Compile>
    <Compile Include="Program.cs" />
    <Compile Include="Properties\AssemblyInfo.cs" />
    <EmbeddedResource Include="Properties\Resources.resx">
        <Generator>ResXFileCodeGenerator</Generator>
        <LastGenOutput>Resources.Designer.cs</LastGenOutput>
        <SubType>Designer</SubType>
    </EmbeddedResource>
    <Compile Include="Properties\Resources.Designer.cs">
        <AutoGen>True</AutoGen>
        <DependentUpon>Resources.resx</DependentUpon>
    </Compile>
    <None Include="Properties\Settings.settings">
        <Generator>SettingsSingleFileGenerator</Generator>
        <LastGenOutput>Settings.Designer.cs</LastGenOutput>
    </None>
    <Compile Include="Properties\Settings.Designer.cs">
        <AutoGen>True</AutoGen>
        <DependentUpon>Settings.settings</DependentUpon>
        <DesignTimeSharedInput>True</DesignTimeSharedInput>
    </Compile>
</ItemGroup>
```

This target is almost identical to the previous target, with the exception that there is a blank line printed to increase readability, and you'll see why. Execute this target with the following command: >msbuild MetaDataEx.csproj /t:VectorScalar2. Figure 3-13 shows the output from this execution.

```
Project "C:\MSBuild\MSBuildExamples\MetaDataEx\MetaDataEx.csproj" (VectorScalar2
 target(s)):

Target VectorScalar2:
    @ (Compile->'% (Filename)'):  MetaDataFrm;MetaDataFrm.Designer;Program;Assem
blyInfo;Resources.Designer;Settings.Designer

    % (Compile.Filename): MetaDataFrm
    % (Compile.Filename): MetaDataFrm.Designer
    % (Compile.Filename): Program
    % (Compile.Filename): AssemblyInfo
    % (Compile.Filename): Resources.Designer
    % (Compile.Filename): Settings.Designer

Build succeeded.
    0 Warning(s)
    0 Error(s)

Time Elapsed 00:00:00.03
```

Figure 3-13. *Output from the* `VectorScalar2` *target*

In this target, you can see that the output for both syntaxes certainly differs. Now let's examine it a bit closer. The task call that generated the first section is `<Message Text="@ (Compile->'% (Filename)'): @(Compile->'%(Filename)')"/>`. This call generated a single string to be output to the console. That was all of the names of the `Compile` files separated by the default semicolon delimiter. This is the behavior of the `@` syntax. You specify the item that you are acting upon, and then you pass the optional metadata name that you want returned. The `Filename` metadata reference name is not defined in the project file; it is well-known metadata. (We discussed well-known metadata earlier in the chapter.) No matter what item you pass in, the result will act upon the group, not the individual items.

Contrast this to the behavior of using the `%` syntax; for each item in the `Compile` list, the last `Message` task is executed. Thinking in terms of typical build steps, you will most likely be using the `%` syntax when dealing with files. On the other hand, if you are passing the item to a custom task, you will most likely send the entire item as a list. The task will then decompose the list and act upon the individual items if necessary.

The `@` notation signifies you are acting upon an array of items and that you would like to process each item in the list individually. The `->` notation is called a *transform*. A transform is a one-to-one mapping from one item into another. In this sample, you transformed the element to provide the filename of the included file. You can also perform multiple transformations at once. For instance, how could you get the filename and extension into your lists? Let's create a new target from a modified version of the previous target. This target, `VectorScalar3`, is as follows. Also, you will see an added call to the `Message` task to further clarify the use of these transformations.

```
<Target Name="VectorScalar3">
    <Message Text="%40(Compile->'%25(Filename)%25(Extension)'):➥
  @(Compile->'%(Filename)%(Extension)')"/>

    <Message Text=" "/> <!-- Empty line for readability -->

    <Message Text="%25(Compile.Filename)%25(Extension):➥
 %(Compile.Filename)%(Extension)"/>

    <Message Text=" "/> <!-- Empty line for readability -->
```

```
    <!-- Most likely not what you want to do -->
    <Message Text="%40(Compile->'%25(Filename)')%25(Extension):➡
  @(Compile->'%(Filename)')%(Extension)"/>
</Target>
```

In the first message, you are passing the value @(Compile->'%(Filename)%(Extension)').
The @ character says you are acting upon the list items of the Compile item, and the % character
determines which transformations are to be executed. In this case, you have %(Filename)%
(Extension). Figure 3-14 shows the output from this message task and for the remainder of
the target. We will explain the other items in this target shortly.

Figure 3-14. *Output from the* VectorScalar3 *target*

As you can see from Figure 3-14, the extensions of the files, which all happen to be .cs,
were appended to the text sent to the Message task. As mentioned, the %(Extension) transformation is within the @ reference. You will examine the behavior when this is not the case in a bit.
For now you will proceed to the individual transformations.

The next call to the Message task is provided %(Compile.Filename)%(Extension) for the text
value. For each item in the Compile list, a message task will be executed as before, but this time
the filename followed by the extension is sent to the Message task. Imagine that you iterate over
the Compile item list and that inside this loop you build a string with the filename and extension
from the current Compile item list. Notice in the %(Extension) transformation, the item name
was not specified. This is OK because this information is gathered from the Compile reference.

You may not find the last example to be too useful; instead, it further clarifies the distinction
between these two methods. In the last call, the Message task is provided with @(Compile->'%
(Filename)')%(Extension). Notice the difference between this text and the text from the first
invocation of the Message task. The key difference here is that the %(Extension) is outside the
@() reference. So in the output, instead of being included in the array output, %(Extension)
was simply appended to the output from the array output. Now you should be prepared to use
these mechanisms in your MSBuild files without getting tripped up.

Using Environment Variables in Your Project

In Chapter 2, you were exposed to what properties are and how to use them. Properties are similar to something you may already be familiar with—environment variables. The main difference is that a property is defined within the scope of an MSBuild execution, whereas an environment variable is available throughout the machine. In your builds, you may want to reference these environment variables, and doing so is easy! To use the value of an environment variable, you simply refer to that just as you would if it were a property. Refer to the following target, which prints the value for the `Path` environment variable:

```
<Target Name="PrintSystemPath">
    <Message Text="Path: $(Path)"/>
 </Target>
```

To invoke this target at the command line, execute `>msbuild MetaDataEx.csproj /t:PrintSystemPath`. Figure 3-15 shows the output from this invocation.

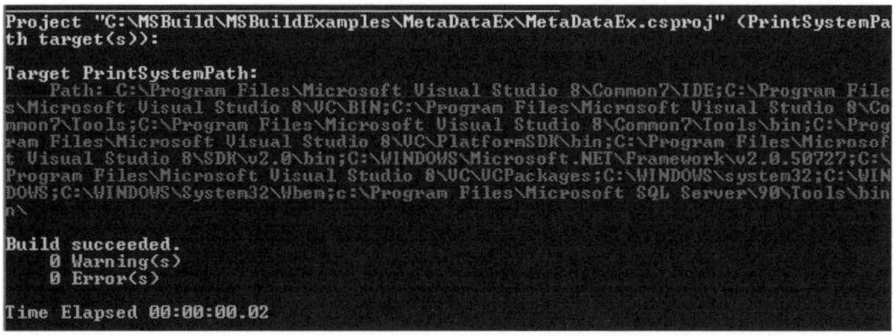

Figure 3-15. *Output from the* `PrintSystemPath` *target*

In Figure 3-15 you can see the system path's value output to the console. As you can see, using a property is just as easy as using a property that is defined in your MSBuild project file. All environment variables are available to be used just as properties are in your MSBuild project files.

Reusing MSBuild Project Elements

As you create MSBuild project files, you will want to reuse some of the elements that you defined previously. For instance, let's say you have created a new target that deploys your application to a set of servers. You will need to reuse this target in more than one project. How can you do this effectively? The most obvious answer is to copy and paste this target into every project file that needs it. This is probably the easiest solution, but it's the most difficult to maintain as well. Imagine that in your organization you have 30 projects that use this target, and you need to change the location of one of the servers. You'll have to search for all these project files and update them. Consolidating this functionality in a single place would be much better. With MSBuild you can achieve this. The element that you will need is the `Import` project element.

So, we'll now show a simple example of using the Import element. This sample will include the Import1.proj file, which is as follows:

```
<Project xmlns="http://schemas.microsoft.com/developer/msbuild/2003">
    <PropertyGroup>
        <FtpServer1URL>ftp.sedodream.com</FtpServer1URL>
        <FtpServer2URL>ftp.apress.old.com</FtpServer2URL>
    </PropertyGroup>
</Project>
```

In this project file you can see that two properties are defined that point to FTP sites. These may be two servers that applications need to be deployed in. The file that uses this, which is named ImportEx1.proj, is as follows:

```
<Project xmlns="http://schemas.microsoft.com/developer/msbuild/2003">
    <Import Project="Import1.proj"/>

    <Target Name="PropertyImport1">
        <Message Text="FtpServer1URL: $(FtpServer1URL)"/>
        <Message Text="FtpServer2URL: $(FtpServer2URL)"/>
    </Target>

</Project>
```

In this project file you are importing the Import1.proj file with the <Import Project= "Import1.proj"/> statement. Typically when you create files that are to be imported into other projects, you'll want to store them in a special location. This is because you want to avoid copying these files to many different locations. This project file has a single target that simply prints the values for the properties defined in the imported project file. You can execute the PropertyImport1 target as follows: >msbuild ImportEx1.proj /t:PropertyImport1. Figure 3-16 shows the result of this execution.

Figure 3-16. *Output from the* PropertyImport1 *target*

In Figure 3-16 you can see that the properties defined in the Import1.proj file were successfully imported into the current project. Before you explore this feature in more detail, let's examine a related issue. When you are creating MSBuild project files, what happens if there is a conflict of the properties, items, or targets? When two or more MSBuild elements have the same name, the last one defined takes precedence. You can see this in action very clearly in the following simple project file:

```
<Project xmlns="http://schemas.microsoft.com/developer/msbuild/2003">
    <PropertyGroup>
        <FtpServer1URL>files.sedodream.com</FtpServer1URL>
    </PropertyGroup>

    <Target Name="PrintFtp">
        <Message Text="FtpServer1URL: $(FtpServer1URL)"/>
    </Target>

    <PropertyGroup>
        <FtpServer1URL>ftp.sedodream.com</FtpServer1URL>
    </PropertyGroup>
</Project>
```

This project file has the property FtpServer1URL being defined twice and a target, PrintFtp, that will print its value. Based on what was stated previously, what value do you expect to be printed? To find out, invoke this target by executing the following at the command line: >msbuild OverrideEx1.proj /t:PrintFtp. Figure 3-17 shows the result of this execution.

Figure 3-17. *Output from the* PrintFtp *target*

From the execution of this target you can see that the last defined FtpServer1URL, ftp.sedodream.com, was taken as the value of that property. As you can see, there was no error or warning issued to notify you about this naming conflict. This is an expected behavior of MSBuild files. Similar to the idea of overriding methods in object-oriented programming, it is not an error if you override the value of a previously defined property.

Now we'll show what happens if you override a target. Does it have the same behavior? To determine this, refer to the following simple MSBuild project file:

```
<Project xmlns="http://schemas.microsoft.com/developer/msbuild/2003">
    <PropertyGroup>
        <Email>sayed.hashimi@gmail.com</Email>
    </PropertyGroup>

    <Target Name="EmailAdmin">
        <Message Text="Emailing: $(Email)"/>
    </Target>
```

```
<Target Name="EmailAdmin">
    <Message Text="Email sent to : $(Email)"/>
</Target>
```

`</Project>`

The previous target has a property defined, Email, and a target, EmailAdmin, defined twice. According to what we stated previously, the last EmailAdmin target defined should be executed. You can check this by invoking this target with >msbuild OverrideEx2.proj /t:EmailAdmin. Figure 3-18 shows the output from this.

Figure 3-18. *Output from the* EmailAdmin *target*

In Figure 3-18 it is clear that indeed the last EmailAdmin target was executed. Before returning to the main point of this section, we'll mention one more aspect of this. Let's modify the previous project file a bit; refer to the following:

```
<Project xmlns="http://schemas.microsoft.com/developer/msbuild/2003">
    <PropertyGroup>
        <Email>sayed.hashimi@gmail.com</Email>
    </PropertyGroup>
    <PropertyGroup>
        <Email>Sayed I. Hashimi [$(Email)]</Email>
    </PropertyGroup>
    <Target Name="EmailAdmin">
        <Message Text="Emailing: $(Email)"/>
    </Target>

    <Target Name="EmailAdmin">
        <Message Text="Email sent to : $(Email)"/>
    </Target>

</Project>
```

This is almost the same project file as you saw previously, but the second definition of the Email property is <Email>Sayed I. Hashimi [$(Email)]</Email>. This property looks like it is referencing itself! Think of the Email property as a property defined as a class member, such as in C#. When MSBuild loads this file, it will process the first Email property and set its value. When the second definition is encountered, it gets the current Email property value and adds to it. To execute this target, specify >msbuild OverrideEx3.proj /t:EmailAdmin at the command line. Figure 3-19 shows the result from this execution.

```
Project "C:\MSBuild\MSBuildExamples\ImportExamples\OverrideEx3.proj" (EmailAdmin
 target(s)):

Target EmailAdmin:
    Email sent to : Sayed I. Hashim [sayed.hashimi@gmail.com]

Build succeeded.
    0 Warning(s)
    0 Error(s)

Time Elapsed 00:00:00.03
```

Figure 3-19. *Output from the* EmailAdmin *target*

As you can see from Figure 3-19, overriding targets has the same behavior as overriding properties. When a target is defined, it will take precedence over any previously defined target with the same name. Now, you are not likely to override a property or target within the same file, so you are probably wondering why we are discussing this. The reason is that you may run into this situation when your project imports other MSBuild project files.

Let's talk about what happens when you import another MSBuild project file into yours. When MSBuild starts processing a project file, it will do this in a node-by-node manner, from the top of your project file to the bottom. When an Import element is encountered, these steps then take place:

1. The working directory is changed to that of the imported project file.

2. Project element attributes are processed.

3. Project element nodes are processed.

4. The working directory returns to importing the previous value.

The first step is to change the working directory to that of the imported project file— assuming that it has a different working directory from the current project file, that is. This is necessary to properly handle any relatively defined import statements, or to resolve locations of assemblies when the UsingTask element is inserted, within that project file. This change is not used for item declarations. Let's move on to the following step.

The next thing after that is for the Project element attributes to be processed. Possible attributes are DefaultTargets and InitialTargets. If a value is already assigned to DefaultTargets, then this is ignored; otherwise, it becomes the value of DefaultTargets. If the InitialTargets attribute is present, then that list of targets will be appended to the current list of InitialTargets. As mentioned, the DefaultTargets attribute is a list of targets to execute if no target is specified; this can be valued from only one project file. The InitialTargets attribute is a list of targets to be executed before any other targets. The value from InitialTargets can be from many different source project files.

Following the Project element attribute processing, the child nodes are processed. The same processing is performed if those nodes were immediate children in the importing file. Finally, for the last step after processing the child nodes, the directory is changed to its previous value, and processing on the original file continues. When you import a project file, it is as if you actually took that file and injected its contents inside of the file that was importing it. This is true with the exception of the Project element itself, which was previously discussed, and with issues related to the working directory, which also were previously discussed. How does this affect reusing elements across project files?

When you reuse elements in project files, you have to be aware of what happens in the case of a naming conflict. We have discussed the behavior of values overridden in the same file. Now that you know how project files are imported, we can discuss what happens when project elements are overridden across project files. The behavior of both is the same; all you have to remember is that the last element defined is the one that gives the value. Let's clear this up with a simple example. The following is the OverrideEx5.proj project file on which you will invoke MSBuild:

```
<Project xmlns="http://schemas.microsoft.com/developer/msbuild/2003">

    <PropertyGroup>
        <DeployURL>http://www.sayedhashimi.com</DeployURL>
    </PropertyGroup>

    <Import Project="ImportOverride1.targets"/>

    <Target Name="PrintDeployURL">
        <Message Text="Deployment URL: $(DeployURL)"/>
    </Target>
</Project>
```

This file contains one property, DeployURL, and one target, PrintDeployURL. This file imports the simple ImportOverride1.targets file, which is as follows:

```
<Project xmlns="http://schemas.microsoft.com/developer/msbuild/2003">
    <PropertyGroup>
        <DeployURL>http://www.sedodream.com</DeployURL>
    </PropertyGroup>
</Project>
```

This file simply defines the DeployURL property—the same one defined in the importing project file. You can find the value of this property by executing the PrintDeployURL target. What value do you expect to be printed? Let's find out by executing the PrintDeployURL target by using >msbuild OverrideEx5.proj /t:PrintDeployURL at the Visual Studio command prompt. Figure 3-20 shows the output from this execution.

```
Project "C:\MSBuild\MSBuildExamples\ImportExamples\OverrideEx5.proj" (PrintDeplo
yURL target(s)):

Target PrintDeployURL:
    Deployment URL: http://www.sedodream.com

Build succeeded.
    0 Warning(s)
    0 Error(s)

Time Elapsed 00:00:00.03
```

Figure 3-20. *Output from the* PrintDeployURL *target*

As you can see, the value from the `ImportOverride1.target` file was used instead of the value defined inside the `OverrideEx5.proj` file. Is this what you expected? This value is used because it was encountered after the first value of `DeployURL`. Essentially, a project file was processed with the following contents:

```
<Project xmlns="http://schemas.microsoft.com/developer/msbuild/2003">
    <PropertyGroup>
        <DeployURL>http://www.sayedhashimi.com</DeployURL>
    </PropertyGroup>

    <PropertyGroup>
        <DeployURL>http://www.sedodream.com</DeployURL>
    </PropertyGroup>
    <Target Name="PrintDeployURL">
        <Message Text="Deployment URL: $(DeployURL)"/>
    </Target>
</Project>
```

In the previous snippet, the import statement was replaced with the contents of `ImportOverride1.target`, stripping away the `Project` element, of course. This is exactly how MSBuild will treat your imported files. If the import statement had been before the `DeployURL` declaration, then the value `http://www.sayedhashimi.com` would have been used instead. This behavior is the same for targets that are overridden. You can give it a shot on your own to verify this. If you are importing files and you have properties or targets that you must ensure are defined as is, then you should place them after all import statements. When you execute targets on that file, then you can be sure you are using the definition that you intend. If that file is imported into other files, then you can't be so sure, but you could throw an error if that condition exists.

To summarize, when you share project files, be careful where you place your import statements, and always be aware of how MSBuild will treat them. A good method to mitigate the risk of wrongfully overridden targets is to place hooks into your targets to be overridden instead of overriding the target itself. For instance, Visual Studio provides the `BeforeBuild` and `AfterBuild` targets that are empty. Their sole purpose is to be overridden by you. You can employ a similar strategy at your organization. Another method is to use naming conventions; for instance, targets that exist for the sole purpose of being overridden could start with an underscore (_) character.

Dealing with MSBuild Errors

As you create new MSBuild targets, you are bound to encounter situations where errors occur. How should you deal with errors, and more important, how can you protect the integrity of the build when one occurs? MSBuild has two elements related to errors: the `OnError` element and the `Error` element. `OnError` specifies what to do in the case of an error, that is, what targets to execute. The `Error` call actually throws an error and calls any registered error-handling mechanisms. Let's examine the simple case of handling an error. Refer to the following `SimpleError.proj` file:

```
<Project xmlns="http://schemas.microsoft.com/developer/msbuild/2003">
    <Target Name="ThrowError">
        <Error Text="Error in ThrowError target"/>
        <OnError ExecuteTargets="MessageErrorHandler"/>
    </Target>

    <Target Name="MessageErrorHandler">
        <Message Text="An error has occurred, build will be halted"/>
    </Target>
</Project>
```

In this project file, you have two targets: one that throws the error, ThrowError, and one that handles errors, MessageErrorHandler. Previously we mentioned that targets can have error handlers associated with them. The OnError element creates this association. This element has only two possible attributes: ExecuteTargets and Condition. The ExecuteTargets attribute is a semicolon-separated list of targets to execute in the case of an error. These targets will be executed in the order they are defined. The Condition attribute is the same here as it is for every other MSBuild element. If the condition is true, then the error handler listed in ExecuteTargets will be registered; if not, then they won't. Now we'll demonstrate the execution of the ThrowError target by invoking it with >msbuild SimpleError.proj /t:ThrowError. Figure 3-21 shows the output from executing this target.

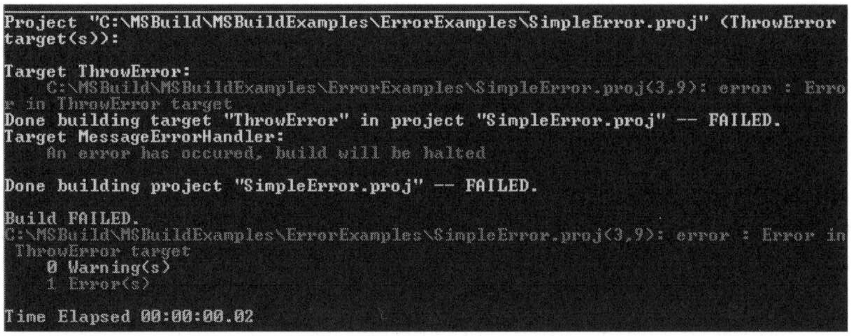

Figure 3-21. *Output from the* ThrowError *target*

From Figure 3-21 you can see that the ThrowError target was invoked and an error was thrown. Following this, the MessageErrorHandler was invoked to deal with the error. From the output you can see the following line: C:\MSBuild\MSBuildExamples\ErrorExamples\ SimpleError.proj(3,9): error : Error in ThrowError target. This tells you four facts:

The file that the error occurred in: SimpleError.proj

Where in that file it occurred: (3,9) = Line 3, position 9

What type of error it was: error (more on this in a bit)

The error message: Error in ThrowError target

When the error is logged, you can use this information to determine what caused it and how to resolve it. Let's quickly examine the full syntax for the Error element before proceeding. The Error element has five attributes, as summarized in Table 3-4.

Table 3-4. Error *Element Attributes*

Name	Description
Text	Text that is sent to the error handler. If this is not present, then there will be no location information attached with the error; that is, you won't know where in the project file to start looking.
Code	This determines the type of error and will be sent to the logger. See the following example.
Condition	Condition to determine whether to raise the error.
ContinueOnError	If this is true, then the error will be converted to a warning, and the build will continue.
HelpKeyword	A help keyword that will be sent to the logger.

We will demonstrate how to use the Code attribute in the next error-handling example. The previous example was simple but also usable for small projects. For larger, team-based applications, you may want to have a more flexible approach to error handling. For a better example, see the following Error1.proj project:

```
<Project xmlns="http://schemas.microsoft.com/developer/msbuild/2003">

    <Import Project="ErrorHandler.targets"/>
    <PropertyGroup>
        <ErrorEmails>$(ErrorEmails);deployError@sedodream.com</ErrorEmails>
    </PropertyGroup>
    <!-- Uncomment for normal execution
    <PropertyGroup>
        <WebURL>sedodream.com</WebURL>
    </PropertyGroup>
    -->

    <Target Name="DeployToWebServer">

        <Error Text="Unable to connect to webserver" Code="Deploy" ➥
Condition=" '$(WebURL)' == '' "/>
        <!--
            contents to deploy to your Web server here
        -->
        <Message Text="Deployed project to Project $(MSBuildProjectName) ➥
to webserver at: $(WebURL)"/>

        <OnError ExecuteTargets="$(ErrorHandlers)"/>
    </Target>
```

```
    <Target Name="ProjectErrorHandler">
        <Message Text="An error has occurred, build stopped."/>
    </Target>

</Project>
```

This project has two targets, one property, and one import statement. As for the two targets, one is for execution, and the other is for error handling. The property defines the ErrorEmails value. The idea of the imported file is that you could have a project file, or set of files, that every project in your organization will import. These imported files could contain the standard error-handling mechanisms. The ErrorHandler.targets file is as follows:

```
<Project xmlns="http://schemas.microsoft.com/developer/msbuild/2003">
    <PropertyGroup>
        <ErrorHandlers>
            ProjectErrorHandler;
            SolutionErrorHandler;
            ErrorLogger;
            ErrorMailer;
        </ErrorHandlers>
        <ErrorEmails>errorHandler@sayedhashimi.com</ErrorEmails>
    </PropertyGroup>

    <Target Name="SolutionErrorHandler">
        <Message Text="An error has occurred in the solution; build failed"/>
    </Target>
    <Target Name="ErrorLogger">
        <Message Text="A build error has occurred and has been logged"/>
    </Target>
    <Target Name="ErrorMailer">
        <Message Text="An error has occurred and has been emailed ➥
to: $(ErrorEmails)"/>
    </Target>
</Project>
```

The ErrorHandler.targets file has three targets that relate to the error handling defined and two properties. The targets don't do anything interesting, so we will not discuss them. Let's look at the properties defined here and see how they provide the flexibility for which you are looking. The two properties defined here are ErrorHandlers and ErrorEmails. The ErrorHandlers property contains a semicolon-separated list of targets. This property is used in the OnError element to specify which targets to execute in the case of an error. From the four targets in that property, three are defined in the ErrorHandler.targets file; the other is implemented in the Error1.proj file. Because of this technique, you can completely change the way errors are handled across the organization without actually changing a single source project. Now you will move on to the remaining property.

The ErrorEmails property defined in the ErrorHandler.targets file provides an e-mail address that should be notified when an error occurs. Now let's look at how the Error1.proj file adds to this; the snippet is as follows:

```
<PropertyGroup>
    <ErrorEmails>$(ErrorEmails);deployError@sedodream.com</ErrorEmails>
</PropertyGroup>
```

In this file, you are redefining the ErrorEmails property based on the previous definition of it. You are actually appending the e-mail deployError@sedodream.com to the list of e-mails to be notified in case of errors. Once again, if your organization needed to change who received e-mail notifications of errors, this could happen in one place as opposed to inside every project. To demonstrate the error handling, execute the DeployToWebServer target on the Error1.proj project file using the following command: >msbuild Error1.proj /t:DeployToWebServer. Figure 3-22 shows the output.

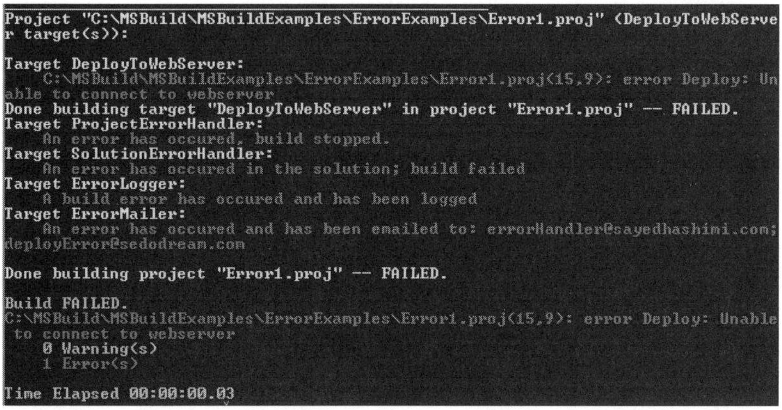

Figure 3-22. *Output from* DeployToWebServer *target*

From this output you can see that the error was raised inside DeployToWebServer. This was raised from the <Error Text="Unable to connect to webserver" Code="Deploy" Condition=" '$(WebURL)' == '' "/> element. This error was raised because the WebURL property has not been initialized. From this error you can see that the targets ProjectErrorHandler, SolutionErrorHandler, ErrorLogger, and ErrorMailer were executed in that order. This is the order in which they were defined in the ErrorHandler.targets file. Notice in this element the use of the Code attribute; once used, this information is passed to the loggers and may assist with determining how the error occurred. In the output the error type is error Deploy. Many organizations will use only integer values for this field, but you can use any string, as shown here.

When you approach a build, you must be careful to avoid errors and to easily detect when errors have occurred. You can use the MSBuild error-handling mechanisms to assist in this critical task. The previous target simply exposed the MSBuild error-handling mechanisms. This sample has shown how your organization can approach MSBuild error handling to increase flexibility and simplicity.

Summary

In the previous chapter, we introduced some fundamental concepts of MSBuild and showed some examples of how you can use MSBuild. In this chapter, we expanded on that knowledge extensively by showing a series of examples. The aim of this chapter was to clarify the topics discussed previously and to introduce many new ideas. As is the case with many other technologies, MSBuild is best learned by trying the concepts as you learn them.

CHAPTER 4

■■■

Extending MSBuild

In the previous chapters, we presented the features of MSBuild that enable you to write your own MSBuild project files. In this chapter, we will build on that knowledge by providing practical samples that you can reuse in your projects. MSBuild has two main extensibility points: custom loggers and custom tasks. We will cover these two points in great detail in this chapter. We will explain what it takes to create your own new logger and plug it into your build. Following this, we will show how to create a custom task to execute NUnit test cases contained in your built assemblies.

The XML logger will demonstrate how easy it is to truly customize MSBuild logging to suit the needs of your applications. Creating a new logger for MSBuild is actually a simple task but can be very useful. With the creation of the XML logger, it is now easy to load the contents of the log and allow an application to examine how the build is executed. If you are developing applications in larger teams with complicated build requirements, you may want to create a logger that will log build information directly into a database, as opposed to logging to a file.

The task, NUnitTask, provided in this chapter will examine the assemblies for the project being built and execute any test cases contained within them. With this task we will demonstrate how to write custom tasks and targets for use in your build process. When creating these, you must allow for easy integration and incremental building. This task will demonstrate both of these very important ideas.

Logging with MSBuild

In recent years, runtime logging has received much attention. This is because of its recognition as an invaluable resource to determine what happened during the course of execution. When an error occurs, an automated build is similar in many ways to an error occurring when an application is in use. Namely, it is difficult to determine what went wrong without a record of events. In this chapter's build, this record will be your build log. In contrast to a deployed application, a log for a successful build is helpful as well. This raises the question, how should you log with MSBuild?

MSBuild ships with two standard loggers, the console logger and the file logger; the former simply logs messages to the console, and the latter logs messages to a file you specify. By default, only the console logger will be used unless explicitly disabled with the /noconsolelogger command-line parameter (the short version is /noconlog). To specify any additional loggers, you use the /logger switch (the short form for this is /l). Let's see how you can use the file logger. This sample uses the DotNetFreeCell project that is available on Gotdotnet.com. This is a VB .NET version of the popular Windows FreeCell game. This solution, DotNetFreeCell, is composed of two projects. Those projects are DotNetFreeCell and its dependent CardLib project. To build this project, let MSBuild consume the solution file with >msbuild DotNetFreeCell\ DotNetFreeCell.sln /t:Build; alternatively, you can omit the target specification, and Build will still execute. For this to work correctly, you need to execute this command from the folder that contains the DotNetFreeCell directory. Upon executing this build, you will see that a lot of information is being passed to the console. How can you redirect this to a file as well?

As previously mentioned, to add loggers, you use the /logger parameter. The syntax for the /logger switch is as follows:

```
[<Logger class>,]<logger assembly>[;<logger parameters>]
```

where Logger class is FileLogger and is contained in the Microsoft.Build.Engine assembly. We will discuss the parameters in a bit. The full syntax in this case is as follows:

```
>msbuild DotNetFreeCell\DotNetFreeCell.sln ➡
 /l:FileLogger,Microsoft.Build.Engine;verbosity=detailed;append=true; ➡
logfile=FreeCell-Build.log
```

From these arguments you can see that you are using the Microsoft.Build.Engine. FileLogger class. The logger parameters part is an optional list of key/value pairs to be sent to the logger. This is a generic construct and is determined by the logging class being used. In this case, the example is using the FileLogger, so what are the possible parameters for it? Table 4-1 lists the available parameters.

Table 4-1. FileLogger *Parameters*

Parameter Name	Default	Description
Append	false	When true, if the file exists, it will be appended to instead of overwritten
Encoding	System dependent	Specifies how the log file will be encoded
Logfile	msbuild.log	Specifies the file to which the log contents will be written
Verbosity	Normal	Determines the verbosity for this logger

Table 4-1 includes the name of the parameter, its description, and what the default value is; in this case, you do not specify a value for it. For example, if you do not specify the value for Logfile, then the value msbuild.log is used in its place. This logger specification will append to any existing file named FreeCell-Build.log with the verbosity level set to detailed. The verbosity determines what kind of, and how much, content will be sent to the logger. Five verbosity levels exist, as summarized in Table 4-2. They are listed from the least amount of logging to the most.

Table 4-2. *Verbosity Levels*

Full Name	Short name
Quiet	q
Minimal	m
Normal	n
Detailed	d
Diagnostic	diag

When specifying the verbosity level, you can use either the full name or the short name. Typically, you will find the Normal verbosity level is sufficient to determine what steps were taken in the process of the build, but you may elect to decrease or increase the amount depending on your situation. Now that you know what you need in order to specify loggers at the command line, you'll learn how to write your own logger.

Writing a Logger

Writing a new MSBuild logger, and using it, is simple! In this section, we will discuss the requirements of a logger, and we will present a new XmlLogger. First we'll discuss some of the important players in the MSBuild logging game, as listed in Table 4-3.

Table 4-3. *Logger Components*

Name	Location	Description
ILogger	Microsoft.Build.Framework	The interface that all MSBuild loggers must implement.
Logger	Miscosoft.Build.Utilities	This is an abstract class that wraps up the ILogger interface. This class will handle the parameters and verbosity for you.
IEventSource	Microsoft.Build.Framework	This contains all the build events that can be raised. You will register your event handlers with this interface.
Various BuildEventArgs subclasses	Microsoft.Build.Framework	Subclasses of BuildEventArgs are the means that a build message is passed to your handlers. You will interact with these objects to gain insight into the meaning of the event.

Every MSBuild logger must implement the Microsoft.Build.Framework.ILogger interface. Logging with MSBuild is all event driven, so as events occur, the interested listeners get notified. We will discuss this in further detail in a bit. The ILogger interface is simple; it has two methods and two properties that need to be defined:

```
void Initialize(IEventSource eventSource);
void Shutdown();
string Parameters{ get; set; }
LoggerVerbosity Verbosity{ get; set; }
```

The MSBuild engine will set the `Parameters` and `Verbosity` properties before any events are fired. `Parameters` is a string that captures any text parameter passed in to the logger at the command line. It is left up to the writer of the class what this string looks like and how to parse it. We will provide you with an abstract base class later in this section that you can use to do this for you.

The `Initialize` method will be called before any events have occurred. In this method you will tell MSBuild which events you are interested in responding. You will do this by registering event handlers with the `eventSource` argument. In this method you could also perform any other steps to properly initialize your logger. The `Shutdown` method will be called after the build has completed. Here is where you would free any resources that you are consuming and finish any necessary processing to properly close down your logger. For instance, if you were writing a database logger, in `Initialize` you may ensure that you have a connection to the database and create some records. In `Shutdown` you will record all the remaining entries to the database and close your connection to it. You can register any of the 14 different events that you would like to handle. Table 4-4 summarizes those events.

Table 4-4. *Logger Events*

Name	Description
AnyEventRaised	Raised when any type of build event occurs.
BuildFinished	Raised when the build has completed. If you are building many projects, this will occur at the end of building all of them.
BuildStarted	This is raised before the build of any projects starts.
CustomEventRaised	Raised when a build triggers a custom event.
ErrorRaised	Raised when an error occurs during the course of the build.
MessageRaised	Raised when a message is logged.
ProjectFinished	Raised after the build for each project completes.
ProjectStarted	Raised before each project is built.
StatusEventRaised	Raised when a status event occurs.
TargetFinished	Raised after the execution of each target.
TargetStarted	Raised before the execution of each target.
TaskFinished	Raised after the execution of each task.
TaskStarted	Raised before the execution of each task.
WarningRaised	Raised when a warning event occurs.

For your loggers, you may not be interested in handling certain events; in this case, you simply don't register as an event handler for that event. Now that you are familiar with logging in MSBuild, we'll show a simple file-based logger, and then we will move on to a more complex XML logger.

To demonstrate how you accomplish logging with MSBuild, we will cover the `SimpleFileLogger` class. We present this class simply for demonstration purposes; if you need a file-based logger, the `Microsoft.Build.Engine.FileLogger` is recommended for use. Start by looking at the class signature, as shown here:

```
public class SimpleFileLogger : Logger
```

We stated previously that every MSBuild logger must implement the ILogger interface. You can see that the SimpleFileLogger does implement this interface; it does so through the Microsoft.Build.Utilities.Logger class. Another requirement is that a public parameterless constructor be available. The SimpleFileLogger class has four data members: _verbosity, _parameters, _fileName, and _messages (the buffer containing all the messages). Refer to the Initialize method, as follows:

```
public override void Initialize(IEventSource eventSource)
{
    _fileName = "simple.log";
    _messages = new StringBuilder();

    //Register for the events here
    eventSource.BuildStarted += new BuildStartedEventHandler( ➥
this.BuildStarted);
    eventSource.BuildFinished += new ➥
BuildFinishedEventHandler(this.BuildFinished);
    eventSource.ProjectStarted += new ➥
ProjectStartedEventHandler(this.ProjectStarted);
    eventSource.ProjectFinished += new ➥
ProjectFinishedEventHandler(this.ProjectFinished);
    eventSource.ErrorRaised += new BuildErrorEventHandler( ➥
this.BuildError);
    eventSource.WarningRaised += new BuildWarningEventHandler( ➥
this.BuildWarning);
    eventSource.MessageRaised += new BuildMessageEventHandler( ➥
this.BuildMessage);
}
```

This method simply sets the name of the file, initializes the message buffer, and registers for events with the event source. Notice that it did not register for every event—only the ones for which it is interested. You can register for as few or as many events as you need. Notice that each event has its own specific type of handler associated with it; this is because different events have different information associated with them. For example, when a build error occurs, you'll be sent information about the location of the error; however, when a task is started, you will not be sent any location information.

Now that you have seen the Initialize method, we will cover the Shutdown method and then move on to the event handlers. Here's Shutdown:

```
public override void Shutdown()
{
    System.IO.File.WriteAllText(_fileName, _messages.ToString());
}
```

This method simply writes the contents of the buffer to the file. This is a pretty simple logger; a much better way to store all the messages in memory would be to periodically write the messages out to the file being logged to.

Now you will examine a few of the event handlers. All of the event handlers from this class look similar; the protected method AppendLine is as follows:

```
protected void AppendLine(string line)
{
    _messages.AppendLine(line);
}
```

This method simply appends the passed-in line to the in-memory buffer containing all the messages, like so:

```
void BuildFinished(object sender, BuildFinishedEventArgs e)
{
    _messages.AppendLine("BuildFinished" + e.Message);
}
void ProjectStarted(object sender, ProjectStartedEventArgs e)
{
    _messages.AppendLine("ProjectStarted" + e.Message);
}
```

Each of these handlers is like the ones shown previously; they simply append the passed-in message to the file. The following is a sample of the output of this logger. (This sample is also using the VB DotNetFreeCell project.)

```
BuildMessage: Building target "Build" completely.
BuildMessage: No input files were specified.
ProjectFinished: Done building project "DotNetFreeCell.vbproj".
```

If you wanted to use this logger along with the FileLogger, you could accomplish this by using the following command:

```
>msbuild DotNetFreeCell\DotNetFreeCell.sln ➥
 /l:SimpleFileLogger,.\FileLoggers.dll ➥
/l:FileLogger,Microsoft.Build.Engine;logfile=test.log
```

This assumes that SimpeFileLogger is in an assembly called FileLoggers.dll located in the same directory that is invoking msbuild.exe. Notice how you can specify more than one logger to be used by using the /l switch multiple times. This logger is not very useful, because you cannot customize its output or change the name of the file to which it will write.

LOG CONTENTS

Here is a portion of the SimpleFileLogger's log file:

```
BuildMessage: Building target "CoreCompile" completely.
BuildMessage: Output file "obj\Debug\CardLib.xml" does not exist.
BuildMessage: Using "Vbc" task from assembly "Microsoft.Build.Tasks, ➥
 Version=2.0.0.0, Culture=neutral, PublicKeyToken=b03f5f7f11d50a3a".
BuildMessage: Command:
```

For a better example of a logger that you may actually write, you will examine XmlLogger. This is a logger that will log all the events to an XML file. This is particularly useful for situations when you need to programmatically determine what steps were taken during a build. Or if you wanted to place the results on a Web page, you could simply write an XSL Transformation (XSLT) to create the HTML for you.

With this XmlLogger, you'll find the base class, FileLoggerBase, that will handle many common tasks to file-based loggers. Figure 4-1 shows the class diagram as created by Visual Studio. You can view class diagrams by right-clicking the project in the Solution Explorer and selecting View Class Diagram.

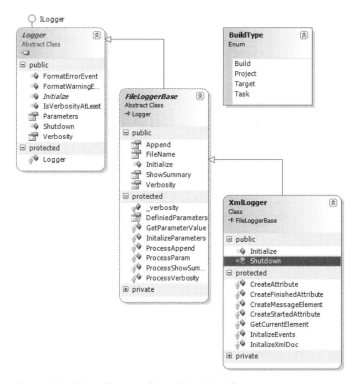

Figure 4-1. *Class diagram from Visual Studio*

From this diagram you can see that now there is an abstract class called FileLoggerBase. This class will take care of reading common parameters from the command line, and you can focus on the logging. Here is a sample of the XmlLogger's output:

```
<MSBuild>
  <Build Started="11/18/2005 9:39:44 PM" Verbosity="Normal" ➡
Finished="11/18/2005 9:39:44 PM" Succeeded="False">
    <Project Name="C:\MSBuild\DotNetFreeCell\DotNetFreeCell\ ➡
DotNetFreeCell.sln" Message="Project &quot;DotNetFreeCell.sln ➡
&quot; (default targets):" Started="11/18/2005 9:39:44 PM" ➡
Finished="11/18/2005 9:39:44 PM">
      <Target Started="11/18/2005 9:39:44 PM" Name= ➡
"ValidateSolutionConfiguration" Message="Target ➡
&quot;ValidateSolutionConfiguration&quot; in project &quot; ➡
```

```
DotNetFreeCell.sln&quot;" Finished="11/18/2005 9:39:44 PM" ➥
Succeeded="True">
        <Task Started="11/18/2005 9:39:44 PM" Name="Message" ➥
Finished="11/18/2005 9:39:44 PM" />
    </Target>
...
</MSBuild>
```

Each task appears under the target that executed it, and likewise, targets appear under their respective projects.

Now you'll learn how you can accomplish this. First you will examine the FileLoggerBase class, which is responsible for making the common tasks easy for the log writer. Its primary purpose is to handle the parameters and to parse out those that it knows. Table 4-5 lists the parameters it knows.

Table 4-5. FileLoggerBase *Known Parameters*

Full Name	Short Name	Description
Append	A	This will determine whether the file will be appended to.
Logfile	L	This will determine the file to which the log will be saved.
ShowSummary	S	This will determine whether a summary should be shown as well as normal output.
Verbosity	V	This will determine the verbosity level of the logger.

You can specify these parameters using either the full name or the short name, and they are case-insensitive. If you create a subclass of this, make sure to not conflict with these names. I'll also show you how to retrieve the values for the parameters momentarily. The first step MSBuild will take after creating your logger is to set the Verbosity property, and then it will set the Parameters value. The Parameters value is the complete string following the specification of your logger. MSBuild does not attempt to parse this string in any way; following this, the Initialize method is invoked. Knowing this, refer to the Initialize method provided in the FileLoggerBase class:

```
public override void Initialize(IEventSource eventSource)
{
    InitializeParameters();
}

protected void InitializeParameters()
{
    this._paramaterBag = new Dictionary<string, string>();
    if (this.Parameters == null || this.Parameters.Length <= 0)
        return;

    foreach (string paramString in this.Parameters.Split(';'))
    {
        string[] keyValue = paramString.Split('=');
        if (keyValue == null || keyValue.Length < 2)
            continue;
```

```
        this.ProcessParam(keyValue[0].ToLower(), keyValue[1]);
    }
}
```

The Initialize method will eventually call ProcessParam, and this method will look for the recognized parameters and set their values if they are present. In your subclasses, you can access the well-known parameters through the properties of the FileLoggerBase class, and if you have other parameters, simply call the GetParameterValue method to get the value for that parameter.

Now that you know how to use the FileLoggerBase class, you'll look at how the XmlLogger does its work. If you would like to dive into the code, it is available to you in the Source Code section of the Apress Web site (http://www.apress.com). First we will discuss the following:

- How to handle verbosity

- The important elements of different build events

- How to deal with problems

How verbosity is treated is entirely out of the hands of MSBuild and in the hands of the log writer. If a logger is registered for an event, then it will receive that event, without regard to its verbosity level. This has its benefits as well as its drawbacks. It is good because you are able to determine exactly what Detailed verbosity means to you, but it is a drawback because you are forced to implement it as well. To demonstrate this, refer to the BuildStarted event handler shown here:

```
void BuildStarted(object sender, BuildStartedEventArgs e)
{
    XmlElement buildElement = _xmlDoc.CreateElement("Build");
    _rootElement.AppendChild(buildElement);
    buildElement.Attributes.Append(CreateStartedAttribute( ➡
e.Timestamp));
    buildElement.Attributes.Append(CreateAttribute("Verbosity", ➡
this.Verbosity.ToString()));

    if (this.Parameters != null && ➡
IsVerbosityAtLeast(LoggerVerbosity.Detailed))
    {
        XmlElement paramElement = _xmlDoc.CreateElement( ➡
"LoggerParameters");
        buildElement.AppendChild(paramElement);
        foreach (string current in this.Parameters.Split( ➡
';')
        {
            XmlElement currentElement = _xmlDoc.CreateElement( ➡
"Parameter");
            currentElement.InnerText = current;
            paramElement.AppendChild(currentElement);
        }
    }
```

```
    _buildElements.Push(buildElement);
    _buildTypeList.Push(BuildType.Build);
}
```

This handler will create a new Build element and attach it to the MSBuild element. It will always add two attributes, one for the start time and one describing the current verbosity level. Following this, if the verbosity is set to at least Detailed, then an element will be created that contains all of the logger parameters and their values.

The Microsoft.Build.Utilities.Logger abstract class provides the IsVerbosityAtLeast method. You can use this to help you determine what to log. An event that happens quite frequently is a message event. The message event includes an Importance value that is associated with it. Based on this and the verbosity, you can determine whether you would like to log the message. Now let's examine the second bullet point.

What are some of the useful elements of different build event arg objects? We noted previously that each event has its own distinct class, such as BuildStartedEventArgs or BuildMessageEventArgs. Each of these classes inherits from the abstract Microsoft.Build.Framework.BuildEventArgs class. This class has five public properties: Message, Timestamp, HelpKeyword, ThreadId, and SenderName. Most of the subclasses have some important properties that you can use in your loggers, as listed in Table 4-6. The names of the properties are self-descriptive.

Table 4-6. *Some Properties from the* BuildEventArg *Subclasses*

Name	Property
BuildErrorEventArgs BuildWarningEventArgs	File Code ColumnNumber LineNumber HelpKeyword
BuildMessageEventArgs	Importance
ProjectStartedEventArgs ProjectFinishedEventArgs	ProjectFile
TargetStartedEventArgs TargetFinishedEventArgs	ProjectFile TargetFile TargetName
TaskStartedEventArgs TaskFinishedEventArgs	ProjectFile TaskName TaskFile
BuildFinishedEventArgs ProjectFinishedEventArgs TargetFinishedEventArgs TaskFinishedEventArgs	Succeeded

If you are going to create your own events, then you will use the CustomEventRaised event and pass it a subclass of CustomBuildEventArgs. In this case you will know what extra information is contained in those classes.

Now that you know how to create a new MSBuild logger, you need to know how to deal with problems when they occur. If your logger is going to throw an exception, then it will not only fail the build but will also do so in an ugly fashion. When this happens, sometimes you may not even be given details about what went wrong. These problems can sometimes be difficult to locate. The method to deal with this is to catch exceptions that may be thrown and rethrow them as a `Microsoft.Build.Framework.LoggerException`; as a best practice when rethrowing exceptions, set the inner exception to the original one. The `LoggerException` is a special exception that MSBuild will handle differently from other exceptions, and it is the preferred mechanism to signal logger failures. When a `LoggerException` is raised, the build will still fail, but you will be provided with more details about why it failed. You can even specify an error code and keyword on the exception.

This section has demonstrated how you can create your own MSBuild loggers. MSBuild loggers are easy to create and can be powerful. We have shown how to register for different event types, how to implement verbosity, and how to properly construct your loggers. If you still think that writing loggers can be difficult, all you have to do is implement one, and you'll be convinced otherwise. Now we will move forward with some other elements that are necessary for automated building. We will start with unit testing.

Using NUnit and MSBuild

Visual Studio 2005 introduced a unit testing framework. This framework allows you to create and execute unit tests for your projects. This framework is included only in certain editions of Visual Studio; for more information about specific versions, see `http://msdn.microsoft.com/vstudio/`. Because of this, we will not cover this framework; instead, we will cover the NUnit unit-testing package. NUnit is an open source unit-testing framework that is available at `http://www.nunit.org`. In this section, we will introduce NUnit, and we will provide an MSBuild task that can be used to examine assemblies and execute any NUnit test contained within them.

We will assume that most readers have heard of unit testing and have even created some unit tests previously. Because of this, we will only briefly introduce unit testing and NUnit before we begin discussing how you can integrate it into your build process. Unit testing is a means to test a small component, or *unit*, of code. The idea behind a unit test is to write the test case and execute the tests alongside the build. Once you write a unit test that passes, it should continue to pass. Should it fail, you need to examine your changes, or perhaps the test case, for any harmful content.

Introducing NUnit

To write and execute NUnit test cases, you must download and install the NUnit framework. The remainder of this section will assume that this step has been completed. Before we get to integrating MSBuild with NUnit, let's first see how you can write some NUnit test cases. Follow these steps to create a simple NUnit solution that you can write some unit tests within:

1. Create a new project named **NUnitEx1** with Visual Studio.

2. Add `nunit.framework` as a reference to this project.

3. Change the name of the class to **NUnitEx1.cs**.

Now you should have something in the Solution Explorer that looks like Figure 4-2.

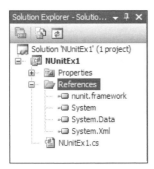

Figure 4-2. NUnitEx1 *Solution Explorer*

If NUnitEx1.cs is not already open, then open it. We will show how to create some simple test cases within it and execute them using the NUnit executor. To write NUnit test cases within this class, you will need to add the using NUnit.Framework statement at the top of this file. NUnit is driven by reflection and attributes; if it is given a set of assemblies, it will examine those assemblies looking for classes that contain NUnit tests. When those classes are found, it will in turn look for and execute individual test cases contained in those classes. To signal that a class contains test cases, you must place the TestFixture attribute on the class and, to show that a method is a test case, add the Test attribute to it. NUnit uses a few other attributes; we will discuss some of those in a bit.

In the NUnitEx1.cs file, add the TestFixture attribute to the class. NUnit test cases have a few requirements:

- They must have a Test attribute.

- They must be a public method.

- They must return void.

- They must be parameterless.

In the NUnitEx1.cs class, create a method called TestStringEqual that meets the previous requirements. NUnit, like most other unit testing frameworks, uses assertions to determine what the expected behavior is. The NUnit.Framework.Assert class is used for this purpose, and each assertion method will contain an expected and actual value, a condition to check, or a reference to an object. Depending on the method called, a check will be generated against them to ensure that the expected value was produced during the test. You have six ways to invoke an assertion, as listed in Table 4-7.

Table 4-7. *NUnit Assertions*

Name	Description
AreEqual	Determines whether the expected value and actual value is the equal. This uses the System.Object.Equals method as opposed to the == operator.
AreSame	Compares the expected value to the actual value by the reference. This uses the System.Object.ReferenceEquals method to determine whether these two objects are the same instance.
IsFalse	Checks to ensure the condition evaluates to false.
IsTrue	Checks to ensure the condition passed in evaluates to true.
IsNotNull	Checks to make sure the object passed in is null.
IsNull	Checks to ensure the object passed in is null.

From the test case you created earlier, you can include a simple assertion. Refer to the following method:

```
[Test]
public void TestStringEqual()
{
    string testString = "Hello NUnit";
    Assert.AreEqual(testString, testString);
}
```

In this method, you have created a string, testString, and passed it into the Assert.AreEqual method for both the expected value and the actual value. When the NUnit engine passes over this class, it will notice that it contains test cases, and it will execute the TestStringEqual method inside it. Since the assertion passes, so should the test case. You'll now add a few more simple test cases, and then you'll run the test cases using NUnit's GUI runner. This is the class with a few more passing tests:

```
[TestFixture]
public class NUnitEx1
{
    [Test]
    public void TestStringEqual()
    {
        string testString = "Hello NUnit";
        Assert.AreEqual(testString, testString);
        Assert.AreSame(testString, testString);
    }
    [Test]
    public void TestIntEqual()
    {
        int intValue = 5;
        Assert.AreEqual(intValue, intValue);
    }
    [Test]
    public void IsTest ()
```

```
    {
        Assert.IsFalse(false);
        Assert.IsTrue(true);
    }
    public void NotATest()
    {   //will not be executed by NUnit..no Test attribute present
        Assert.IsTrue(false);
    }
}
```

This class contains four methods, but only three are test cases. The last method, NotATest, will not be recognized as a test case because it is missing the required Test attribute. At this point you can build this assembly and move on to executing it. Now, to execute these test cases to make sure they all pass, you have primarily two options; you can use the NUnit GUI runner or the command-line runner. For demonstration purposes, we will use the GUI runner.

When you installed NUnit, a shortcut to the GUI runner should have been installed in the NUnit directory. Start the GUI runner by using this shortcut. You should see the window shown in Figure 4-3.

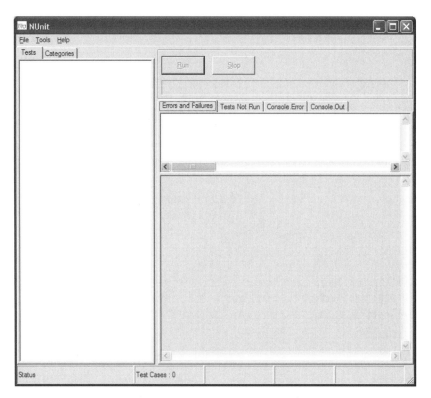

Figure 4-3. *NUnit GUI runner*

From this point you can run these tests by loading the assembly into the NUnit GUI runner. To do this, select File ➤ Open, and open the assembly that was just built. Following this, you will see the window shown in Figure 4-4.

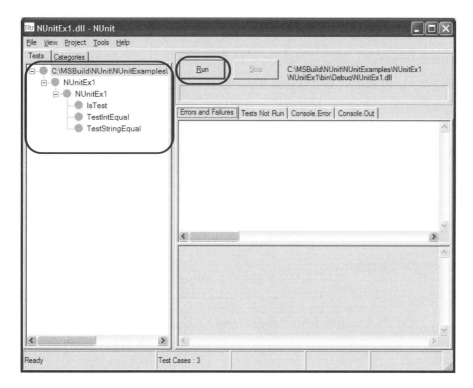

Figure 4-4. *NUnit GUI runner with* NUnitEx1 *assembly loaded*

In Figure 4-4, the Tests pane shows the loaded assembly and test cases that will be executed when the test is run. Notice that NotATest is not included in this list. To run this test, click the Run button. After running the tests, you'll notice all the test cases have a green circle to the right of their names. This signifies that the tests passed. A red circle represents a failing test, and a yellow circle indicates a skipped test.

In addition to creating test cases, NUnit has a much deeper capability; you have only scratched the surface. The emphasis of this section is not to teach you NUnit but to show you how you can integrate NUnit tests into your build process. With that said, we will now show how you can do exactly that.

NUnit MSBuild Task

The ideal case in integrating test cases into your code would be to simply write test cases and then have them executed when you are building your project or solution. Currently with NUnit, you build your application and then test it with two distinct tools. With MSBuild, you can integrate these tools and create a seamless build that will also run test cases over the latest version of code written. To do this, you need to write a NUnit MSBuild task. In this section, we will discuss how this was written and, more important, how you can use this in your projects.

In Chapter 3, we covered what was necessary to write your own tasks. We showed a few basic examples of tasks, but they were simple and just for demonstration purposes. In this section, we will introduce a task that you will find both useful and easy to integrate into your build process. This task is NUnitTask; it will examine the output assemblies of your project and execute any NUnit test cases contained within them. The three main components of NUnitTask are as follows:

- The C# file, NUnitTask.cs, that contains the task definition

- The event collector that will collect information about test execution

- The NUnit.targets file that wraps the task into a target for ease of use

We will cover the first two items and then move on to show the NUnit.targets file. The purpose of the NUnit.targets file is to help provide everything you need to easily integrate the task into your build process. Now let's look at the NUnitTask.cs file that defines the NUnitTask task.

NUnitTask is a generic task that will simply execute NUnit test cases that are contained in the assemblies passed to it. It will also generate some summary information made available as output properties, and it will write a log file to a location specified by the caller. In Table 4-8, you will find the names of all the inputs along with a description.

Table 4-8. *Inputs to the* NUnitTask

Input Name	Description
Assemblies	The list of assemblies that will be examined for NUnit test cases. If any are found, they will be executed.
LogFile	The location to which the log file will be written.
ContinueAfterError	If this is true, then test cases in all assemblies will be executed even if errors occur. Otherwise, after an error occurs, untested assemblies will not be tested.
CacheDirPath	NUnit requires a temporary directory while it is processing; this is the path to where you would like that temporary directory located.

All of these inputs are required inputs; the most important input is the Assemblies property. If there are any classes with NUnit test cases contained in these assemblies, then they will be executed when this task is executed. If you had an automated build process, you are most likely going to want to send the log file to your build engineers after this task has completed. This task generates outputs as well, as summarized in Table 4-9.

Table 4-9. *Outputs of* NUnitTask

Output Name	Description
NumExecutedTests	The number of test cases executed during this invocation of the task
NumIgnoredTests	The number of test cases ignored during this invocation of the task
NumFailedTests	The number of test cases that failed during the testing

These properties simply provide summary information about how the build concluded. This is information related to the testing process, if provided, via logging statements and via the log file that the task generates. Of these three properties, the most important is `NumFailedTests`. After the testing has completed, you can examine its value and determine how you should proceed with the build. Now you will examine how the `NUnitTask` task was written.

Previously, we gave examples of how to write MSBuild tasks; in this section we will briefly show how the `NUnitTask` task was written to give you a feel for the code base and to review. Some of the code for the `NUnitTask` task was based on code that you can find in the `NUnit` project, which is an open source project. All MSBuild tasks have to inherit from the `Microsoft.Build.Framework.ITask` interface. The `NUnit` task does this by having `Microsoft.Build.Utilities.Task` as its base class. You can observe this from the following class signature:

```
public class NUnitTask : Task
```

Inheriting from the `Microsoft.Build.Utilities.Task` class is the preferred method of implementing the `Microsoft.Build.Framework.ITask` interface, as opposed to directly implementing the interface itself.

An MSBuild task can have inputs and outputs; those are the ways your target file can pass data back and forth between the tasks. Inputs and outputs translate to public properties in the task definition class. These are called *parameters*. Two categories of parameters exist: scalars and vectors. A *scalar* parameter is a single value, and a *vector* is a list of values. An example of a scalar parameter is a string, and an example of a vector is an array of strings. Figure 4-5 summarizes the supported parameter types.

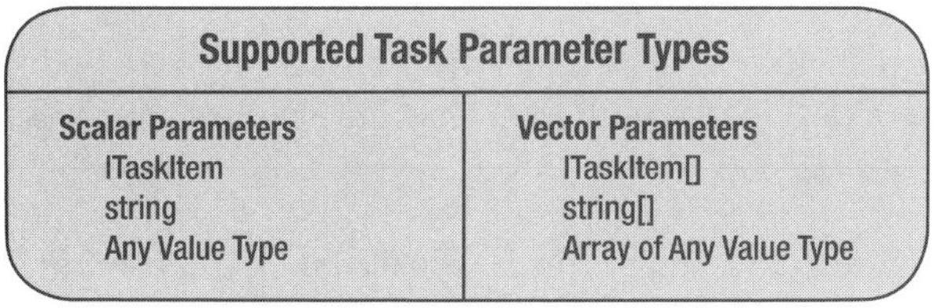

Supported Task Parameter Types	
Scalar Parameters ITaskItem string Any Value Type	**Vector Parameters** ITaskItem[] string[] Array of Any Value Type

Figure 4-5. *Supported task parameter types*

When using these types for inputs and outputs for tasks, you don't have to worry about building the objects. MSBuild will take care of this for you. Using an `ITaskItem` parameter is good for when you are referencing items because they have a rich feature set that can be used. You have access to the well-known metadata and any custom metadata that exists for the item. For example, see the following `Assemblies` input for `NUnitTask`:

```
[Required]
public ITaskItem[] Assemblies
{
    get
    {
        return this._assemblies;
    }
    set
    {
```

```
            this._assemblies = value;
        }
}
```

As you remember from Chapter 3, required task inputs have the Required attribute. This will guarantee that the property has been set before the task is invoked. The Assemblies property has both a get and a set, but only the set is required for MSBuild. Sample output, NumExecutedTests, is as follows:

```
[Output]
public int NumFailedTests
{
    get
    {
        return this._numTestsFailed;
    }
}
```

Since NumFailedTests is an output, it has the Output attribute attached to it. This signals to MSBuild that this property should be made available to the calling MSBuild target file. Another key element in an MSBuild task is the Execute method; this is the method that is called to run the task. The signature for the Execute method is public override bool Execute(). The Execute method in the NUnitTask will set up the NUnit environment and execute all the necessary tests. Also, it will generate a log file containing the results, as well as logging them. To get a better feel for how the task executes, you may have to look at the code that is available in the Source Code section of the Apress Web site (http://www.apress.com). Now that you have an idea how NUnitTask works, we'll cover how you can put it to use. We will show how to do this with the NUnit.targets file.

The purpose of the NUnit.targets file is to wrap up the NUnitTask file for ease of use and to increase portability across projects. The NUnit.targets file has two main sections—one related to executing the test cases and the other related to cleaning the project. We will first discuss the main section, which is the section related to executing the test cases. This section defines four items and one property, as follows:

```
<ItemGroup>
    <!--
        This is the location of the NUnit MSBuild task and
        all of its dependencies. This could come from an
        environment variable if desired
    -->
    <TaskBin Include="C:\MSBuild\TaskBin"/>

    <!-- NUnit requires a directory to temporarily
        store files; this is that directory -->
    <NUnitCache Include="$(OutputPath)\cache\"/>
    <!-- Name of the log file for successful builds -->
    <NUnitLog Include="$(OutputPath)\NUnit.log"/>
    <!-- Name of the log file for unsuccessful builds -->
    <NUnitFailLog Include="$(OutputPath)\NUnit.fail.log"/>
</ItemGroup>
```

```
<PropertyGroup>
  <!--
    This is the list of targets that will be executed, in order,
    if an error occurs during the course of the NUnit testing.
    You can extend this property in other project files in
    a similar fashion that the CleanDependsOn is overridden below.
  -->
  <NUnitErrorHandlers>
    HandleNUnitError
  </NUnitErrorHandlers>
</PropertyGroup>

<!-- This tells MSBuild where it can locate the task code -->
<UsingTask AssemblyFile="@(TaskBin->'%(FullPath)')\MSBuildTasks.dll" ➥
TaskName="NUnitTask"/>
```

At the bottom of the previous segment, you will find the `UsingTask` declaration. This state-ment tells MSBuild where to find the definition for the task to be used. For any custom tasks, this element is required to help locate the task definition. Table 4-10 describes the attributes of this element.

Table 4-10. `UsingTask` *Attributes*

Attribute Name	Description
AssemblyFile	The path to the assembly file that contains the class named `TaskName`. Either `AssemblyFile` or `AssemblyName` is required to be present. Only one can be used. This path can be either relative or absolute. If a relative path is used, then it is evaluated relative to the current directory. This causes the assembly to be loaded with the `System.Reflection.Assembly.LoadFrom` method.
AssemblyName	The name of the assembly that contains the class named in the `TaskName` attribute. This can be strongly named, but it is not required. Either this attribute or `AssemblyFile` is required, but only one can be present. This causes the assembly to be loaded by the `System.Reflection.Assembly.Load` method.
TaskName	The name of the class that is the MSBuild task to be loaded. If it is possible for name collisions with other tasks, then this attribute should be specified using the full namespace; however, this is not required.

You can use two attributes, `AssemblyFile` and `AssemblyName`, to specify how the assembly is loaded. Using the `AssemblyName` attribute will cause MSBuild to load the assembly by calling `System.Reflection.Assembly.Load`. This requires the long form of the assembly name to be provided. An example is `Microsoft.Build.Tasks, Version=2.0.0.0, Culture=neutral, PublicKeyToken=b03f5f7f11d50a3a`, which is found in the `Microsoft.CSharp.targets` file. If you use the `AssemblyFile` attribute, it will be loaded with the `System.Reflection.Assembly.LoadFrom` method. `TaskName` is the class name for the task; this class must implement the `Microsoft.Build.Framework.ITask` interface. Instead of directly implementing this interface, we recommend you extend the abstract `Microsoft.Build.Utilities.Task` class.

Now let's return to the other elements of the `NUnit.targets` file. The lone property in the previous snippet is the `NUnitErrorHandlers` property; this is a semicolon-separated list of tar-gets that will be executed when an error occurs. Table 4-11 describes the four items.

Table 4-11. NUnitTask *Items*

Name	Description
TaskBin	This is the directory that contains the NUnitTask assembly and all of its dependencies.
NUnitCache	This is the temporary directory that NUnit will use during the test execution.
NUnitLog	The location that a log file will be saved, if the tests are all successful.
NUnitFailLog	The location of the log file that will be generated if failed tests were detected. Only one of the two log files will be produced.

From these four items, two are directory locations, and the other two are locations to a log file that will be generated. The TaskBin is a location that will contain the NUnitTask assembly and all of its dependencies. This can be a central location that contains many different MSBuild tasks. This value can be driven from an environment variable or hard-coded as in this example. If the value is gathered from an environment variable, then you can reference it simply as if it were a defined property. The NUnitCache item is the location that NUnit will use during the course of executing the test cases. The other two items are log file locations.

During the course of execution of NUnitTask, there are three possible outcomes: all tests pass, one or more tests fail, or an error occurs to stop execution of the task. If an error occurs to stop the execution, most likely no log file will be created, depending on when the error occurs. If all tests pass, the log file will be written and the location will be pointed to by NUnitLog. If at least one test fails, then the log will be written to the NUnitFailLog path. It may seem kind of silly to write to two different locations depending on success/failure, but this technique has two advantages:

- It supports incremental building.

- Success/failure is easily detected by other tools.

Incremental building is when parts of a build are skipped because they are up-to-date. This is a critical component for building larger projects. By using incremental building, you may be able to skip some very costly build steps when they are not required. In the next section, we will discuss incremental building in detail. For the second aspect, any other tool can easily examine the log folder and determine whether the tests were a success.

Introducing Incremental Building

Incremental building is the process of building software completely without having to repeat unnecessary steps. An example of this would be building a solution that contains only a few modified source files. If you were to perform a complete rebuild, then you may be wasting resources and time. Most likely, you can skip building projects that do not depend on the modified files. This is incremental building. When creating tasks and targets, you have to remember to write them such that you can enable incremental building.

To enable incremental building, your targets must have inputs and outputs. When it is time to execute a target, MSBuild will examine the inputs and the outputs of the target to determine whether the target needs to be executed. If inputs were created after the outputs, then that target must be rebuilt; otherwise, it can be skipped. In this case, you want to execute the test cases if the assemblies you are testing have changed since you last tested them. Let's see how you facilitate this by looking at the beginning of the target definition, as shown here:

```
<Target Name="RunAllTests"
    DependsOnTargets="Build"
    Inputs="@(IntermediateAssembly)"
    Outputs="@(NUnitLog)">
```

The input is the IntermediateAssembly item; this is the list of assemblies that will contain the tested assemblies. The output is the NUnitLog file; this is the log file that will be written if there is a successful build. If the assemblies are older than the NUnitLog file, then the testing will be skipped. Since you are creating a different file for successful tests versus failed ones, MSBuild can properly determine whether the testing needs to occur. If you were to simply write the same file, then the target may be skipped when the tests need to be executed again.

Consider this scenario: you perform a build and a test, with some of these test cases failing. On this test execution, you will be notified that some test cases failed. Following this, you take the day off because you are frustrated fixing bugs. The next day you come back and perform the same build and test against unmodified assemblies, and you would not be notified that test cases failed. MSBuild will skip the RunAllTests target, because the outputs are up-to-date with respect to the inputs. Now let's examine the complete contents of the RunAllTests target, as shown here:

```
<Target Name="RunAllTests"
        DependsOnTargets="Build"
        Inputs="@(IntermediateAssembly)"
        Outputs="@(NUnitLog)">

    <MakeDir Directories="@(NUnitCache)" Condition="!Exists(@(NUnitCache))"/>

    <Delete Files="@(NUnitFailLog);@(NUnitLog)"/>

    <!--
      This works only for debug mode. To support release
      mode, then you need two CreateItems calls, one for debug
      and one for release mode. You should use a condition
      to determine which assemblies will be included in the testing.
    -->

    <!-- Can't use the IntermediateAssembly directly
         because it will cause the tests to fail. -->
    <CreateItem Include="bin\debug\**\*.dll; ➡
bin\debug\**\*.exe;">
        <Output TaskParameter="Include" ItemName="TestAssemblies"/>
    </CreateItem>

    <Message Text="Running unit tests in: @(TestAssemblies)"/>
    <NUnitTask  Assemblies="@(TestAssemblies)"
                CacheDirPath="@(NUnitCache->'%(FullPath)')"
                LogFile="@(NUnitFailLog)"
                ContinueAfterError="false"
        >
```

```xml
      <Output TaskParameter="NumFailedTests" PropertyName= ➡
"NumNUnitFailures"/>
      <Output TaskParameter="NumExecutedTests" PropertyName= ➡
"NumExecutedTests"/>
   </NUnitTask>

   <!--
      If the tests passed, then move the file to the target output
      location; that way we don't have to run this target again against
      the same code base. If it fails, we purposefully don't move to the
      successful location because incremental building will skip
      this target after failed tests.
   -->
   <Copy
      SourceFiles="@(NUnitFailLog)"
      DestinationFiles="@(NUnitLog)"
      SkipUnchangedFiles="false"
      Condition="'$(NumNUnitFailures)' == '0'"
         />
   <Delete Files="@(NUnitFailLog)"/>

   <Message Text="NUnitLogFile: @(NUnitLog->'%(FullPath)')" ➡
Condition="'$(NumNUnitFailures)' == '0'"/>
   <Message Text="NUnitLogFile: @(NUnitFailLog->'%(FullPath)')" ➡
Condition="'$(NumNUnitFailures)' != '0'"/>
   <Message Text="Num executed tests: $(NumExecutedTests)"/>

   <!-- If an error occurs during the process, these
        targets will be called -->
   <OnError ExecuteTargets="$(NUnitErrorTargets)"/>
 </Target>
```

This target has three main sections; one sets up for the test execution, one performs the execution, and the last follows up on the executed tests. In the set-up section, you'll notice the CreateItem task is being called. This is used to determine which assemblies need to be tested. This task will consume an item definition and dynamically create that item. As was previously stated, items are all evaluated before any targets are executed. This is the reason why you have to dynamically create a new item with CreateItem, because the necessary assemblies would not be present to populate the item before the build started.

When you call NUnitTask, you provide all the required inputs and read only the outputs in which you are interested. You are not required to read all the outputs from a task. An output from a task can either be placed in an item or be placed in a property; this depends on the task implementation. In this sample, all of the outputs are simple values that can be contained in properties. If you were outputting files or a list, then an item would be appropriate. Now let's finish up our discussion of this file by going over the last section.

In the final step to the process, you need to perform some actions depending on whether the tests cases passed or failed. This is determined by the NumFailedTests output of the task. As you can see in the previous invocation, that output is placed into the NumNUnitFailures property. You know that no test cases failed if the NumNUnitFailures is zero. This is written as a condition as '$(NumNUnitFailures)' == '0'. You know that failures existed if the condition '$(NumNUnitFailures)' != '0' evaluated to true. If the test cases are successful, then the log file is moved to the location of the successful path. Now that you know how the main section of the target file works, we'll show you how you can clean up after this target easily.

As you create new targets and tasks, you most likely will be creating files, especially if you are thinking about incremental building. Remember, incremental building requires inputs and outputs. When you are creating these new files, it is important to clean the files when the user desires as well. The best way to do this is to perform this action as a part of the normal Clean target. You have many different options about how to implement this, but the best solution would extend the normal clean to also clean any generated files, would not affect any other clean enhancements, and would be portable across different projects. The clean process defined in the NUnit.targets file meets all of these requirements. Now you will examine this to see how you should clean up newly generated files.

Cleaning NUnitTask Files

As you extend the build process, you are likely to generate new files. As part of your agreement with MSBuild, you are responsible for cleaning these files as well. NUnitTask creates files that need to be cleaned. You will examine how NUnitTask integrates into the clean process; then in the "Extending the Clean Process" section we will discuss cleaning in general. You can clean a project either at the command prompt or from within Visual Studio. If your targets are creating files that should be cleaned during this process, then you must extend the Clean target. The Clean target is defined in the Microsoft.Common.targets file. The best way to enhance the clean is to first create a target to clean your files and then add this target to the CleanDependsOn item. The CleanDependsOn is a property defined in the Microsoft.Common.targets file. It is a semicolon-separated list of targets that will be executed before a Clean is performed. The relevant portion of the NUnit.targets file is as follows:

```
<PropertyGroup>
    <!-- Extends CleanDependsOn to include cleaning
         the NUnit-generated files -->
    <CleanDependsOn>
      $(CleanDependsOn);
      CleanNUnit
    </CleanDependsOn>
</PropertyGroup>
<!--
    Run this target to remove NUnit-generated files
-->
<Target Name="CleanNUnit">
    <Delete Files="@(NUnitLog)" Condition= ➡
"Exists(@(NUnitLog))"/>
    <Delete Files="@(NUnitFailLog)" Condition= ➡
"Exists(@(NUnitFailLog))"/>
    <RemoveDir Directories="@(NUnitCache)" Condition= ➡
"Exists(@(NUnitCache))"/>
    <OnError />
</Target>
```

In the property declaration, you are taking the existing definition of `CleanDependsOn` and appending to it. Using this mechanism is simple and friendly for other targets that would like to clean their files as well. Consider this scenario: you have two targets that will create files that need to be cleaned; if they both extended `CleanDependsOn`, then both targets will be executed when a `Clean` is performed. There is no risk in creating modifications that will overwrite previous modifications because you are always appending to the `CleanDependsOn` item list. Now you know how to execute the unit tests and how to clean up after that process as well.

Seeing NUnit in Action

Now we will demonstrate the execution of the NUnit test execution against a simple project. First we'll show the project you will be building. This is the `DataAccess` project. In this project there is an `IContact` interface, which defines the behavior of your contacts, and a class that implements this interface, which is the `Contact` class. The interface definition is as follows:

```
namespace DataAccess
{
    public interface IContact
    {
        string FirstName
        {
            get;
            set;
        }
        string MiddleName
        {
            get;
            set;
        }
        string LastName
        {
            get;
            set;
        }
        string Email
        {
            get;
            set;
        }
        string Website
        {
            get;
            set;
        }
        ///<summary>
        ///Social security number (identifier)
        ///</summary>
        string Ssn
```

```
        {
            get;
            set;
        }
    }
}
```

IContact is a simple interface that simply exposes some properties. The Contact class implements these properties. Each of the properties will get/set its value to a private data member. The Contact class also provides a useful static method, BuildContacts, to create a list of contacts from a DataSet. The following shows one of the property implementations and the BuildContacts method:

```
public string Ssn
{
    get
    {
        return this._ssn;
    }
    set
    {
        this._ssn = value;
    }
}
public static IList<IContact> BuildContacts(DataSet ds)
{
    IList<IContact> contacts = new List<IContact>();

    if (ds == null || ds.Tables.Count == 0)
        return contacts;


    DataTable dt = ds.Tables[0];

    foreach (DataRow row in dt.Rows)
    {
        IContact current = new Contact();
        current.FirstName = row["FirstName"].ToString();
        current.MiddleName = row["MiddleName"].ToString();
        current.LastName = row["LastName"].ToString();
        current.Ssn = row["Ssn"].ToString();
        current.Website = row["Website"].ToString();
        current.Email = row["Email"].ToString();
        contacts.Add(current);
    }

    return contacts;
}
```

The `BuildContacts` method will simply convert the data contained in the passed-in DataSet, ds, to a list of IContacts. Now that you have seen the classes you will be testing, you'll examine how to create the tests for them.

There are many discussions about where unit testing should go with respect to the code that it is testing. Some prefer to have the testing code in a different solution from the project source code, and others like to have the testing code within the same project to allow white-box testing. In this sample, we will provide the test code in a separate project called `DataAccessTest`. Where you place your test code will be a decision based on the requirements of the test code and your organization's rules.

The `DataAccessTest` project contains a single class; this is the `DataAccessTest` class. One of the ideas behind Test-Driven Development (TDD) is to provide a test for each publicly available method or property. The `DataAccessTest` class provides this for the `Contact` class. You have six public methods to perform the testing and one method to set up the environment for the test case. With NUnit, if you apply the `SetUp` attribute to a method, then this method will be executed before every NUnit test gets executed within that test fixture. In this case, you will use this method to create a list of IContacts before you test each property. The set-up method, `SetUpContacts`, is as follows:

```
[SetUp]
public void SetUpContacts()
{
    FileInfo _tempFile = this.WriteFile();
    if (_tempFile == null)
        throw new Exception("Unable to write the Contacts test file");

    DataSet ds = new DataSet();
    ds.ReadXml(_tempFile.FullName);
    this._contacts = Contact.BuildContacts(ds);
    //now we can delete the file
    _tempFile.Delete();
}
private FileInfo WriteFile()
{
    string fileName = "tempContacts.xml";
    string fileText = @"
<Contacts>
    <Contact Ssn=""111-11-1111"">
        <FirstName>Sayed</FirstName>
        <MiddleName>Ibrahim</MiddleName>
        <LastName>Hashimi</LastName>
        <Email>sayed.hashimi@gmail.com</Email>
        <Website>www.sedodream.com</Website>
    </Contact>
    <Contact Ssn=""222-22-2222"">
        <FirstName>Sayed</FirstName>
        <MiddleName>Yahya</MiddleName>
        <LastName>Hashimi</LastName>
```

```
            <Email>sayed@sayedhashimi.com</Email>
            <Website>www.sayedhashimi.com</Website>
        </Contact>
        <Contact Ssn=""333-33-3333"">
            <FirstName>Mike</FirstName>
            <MiddleName>Ray</MiddleName>
            <LastName>Murphy</LastName>
            <Email>magickmike@gmail.com</Email>
        </Contact>
</Contacts>
";
        FileInfo theFile = new FileInfo(fileName);
        File.WriteAllText(theFile.FullName, fileText);
        return theFile;
}
```

The SetupContacts method sets up a new list of contacts before each test is performed. It is important to create NUnit tests that do not depend on any other tests cases and also to create NUnit test cases that are not disturbed by other test cases. This is why you are re-creating the list of contacts before each test method. Since all the test cases are similar, we will show only one. The following is the TestFirstName method:

```
[Test]
public void TestFirstName()
{
    IList<string> expectedNames = new List<string>();
    expectedNames.Add("Sayed");
    expectedNames.Add("Sayed");
    expectedNames.Add("Mike");

    Assert.AreEqual(this._contacts.Count, expectedNames.Count);

    for (int i = 0; i < expectedNames.Count; i++)
    {
        Assert.AreEqual(expectedNames[i], _contacts[i].FirstName);
    }
}
```

In this method, you are simply ensuring that the FirstName property for the Contact class is being properly set and retrieved. The other test methods are against the remaining public properties of the Contact class. Now you will see how to put everything together.

From this point, the only thing left is to integrate the NUnit execution task into this project. To do this, all you have to do is add the following to the project file:

```
<PropertyGroup>
    <SharedTargetsPath>..</SharedTargetsPath>
</PropertyGroup>

<Import Project="$(SharedTargetsPath)\NUnit.targets" />
```

Here you are declaring a property, SharedTargetsPath, that will contain all the target files that are shared across targets. In this example, this path is actually the location above the directory containing the project file. In your organization, you may have a location set aside for these types of tasks, and you can inject that path into the SharedTargetsPath declaration. The reason that this is declared as a property instead of an item is because you may choose to get this value from an environment variable instead of placing it into the file itself. If this is the case, you can simply remove the property declaration, and everything should work.

Now that you have successfully integrated the NUnit.targets file, you have two new targets that you are able to execute against your projects. Those targets are RunAllTests and CleanNUnit. Actually, another target exists, but it is related to error processing and shouldn't be called directly. We previously spoke about RunAllTests, so now we'll show how to execute it and show you the results against the DataAccessTest project. To invoke the tests at the Visual Studio command prompt, you can run >msbuild DataAccessTest.csproj /t:RunAllTests. Figure 4-6 shows the output.

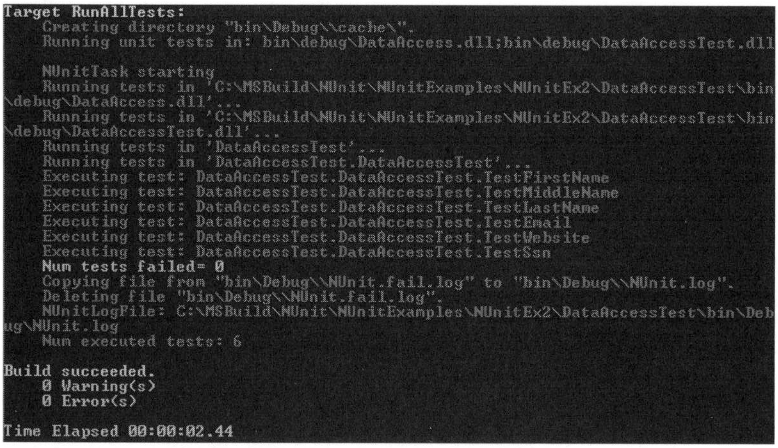

Figure 4-6. RunAllTests *target*

The RunAllTests target will be executed after a complete build is performed; as you can see, six test cases were executed, and all tests passed. Now to see incremental building at work, execute the RunAllTests target again. Figure 4-7 shows the result.

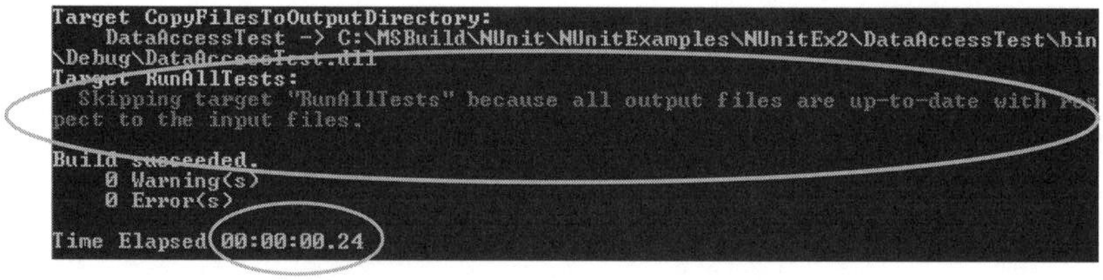

Figure 4-7. RunAllTests *target being skipped*

As you can see in Figure 4-7, the `RunAllTests` target was skipped. Also notice the time spent during the build. This last execution took 24 milliseconds whereas the previous execution took 2.4 seconds. This is because the `RunAllTests` targets, and possibly others, were skipped. If you are writing custom target, providing inputs and outputs to support incremental building is essential for builds that execute efficiently and quickly. Now we will move on to discuss how to clean your projects.

Extending the Clean Process

As you extend the build process, you are likely to create new files and place them in different places. If you extend the build process, you are also given the work of cleaning up after your extensions. Even if you place files in the `OutputPath` folder, they will not automatically be cleaned. They will simply be ignored. In this section, we will discuss how MSBuild cleans the files it generates and how you should clean the files you generate.

How does MSBuild clean its files? As your project is built, MSBuild keeps track of what files are generated so it knows to remove them on a clean. This file, `CleanFile`, is stored in `BaseIntermediateOutputPath`, which is usually the `obj\` directory. The `CleanFile` simply contains the path to files that were generated that need to be cleaned. Files that are eligible for cleaning with this process must be under either `OutDir` (usually a folder under the `bin` directory for the current configuration) or `IntermediateOutputPath` (usually a folder under the `obj` directory for the current configuration). When the `Clean` target is invoked, it will examine `CleanFile` and remove all the corresponding files that are placed under either of those locations. Any files that are generated as an extension to the build process will not be listed in this file and therefore will not be cleaned. To properly clean your files, you have two options:

- You can add entries to the clean file.

- You can extend the clean process.

The easier of these two tasks to complete is the first one, but the more flexible and robust option is to extend the clean process in a similar fashion as you did the build process. We will first discuss how to achieve the first approach because you may see others do this and because it is suitable for most cases. Following this, we will discuss how to extend the clean process by injecting your target to be executed with a call to `Clean`.

To have your files "automagically" removed upon a clean, all you have to do is list the generated files in the MSBuild clean file. To do this, you can simply call the predefined `WriteLinesToFile` task. Table 4-12 describes the input parameters to this task.

Table 4-12. `WriteLinesToFile` *Task Parameters*

Parameter	Type	Description
File	ITaskItem	The file to which the content will be written
Lines	ITaskItem[]	The items that will be written to the file
Overwrite	Boolean	If `true`, existing content will be overwritten; otherwise the file will be appended to

To demonstrate this in use, examine the following project file segment. This segment is taken from the `CleanEx1` project. This is a simple C# project that was created to simply demonstrate this cleaning integration.

```
<!-- Inject the custom target into the build process-->
<PropertyGroup>
  <BuildDependsOn>
    $(BuildDependsOn);
    WriteCompileFile;
  </BuildDependsOn>
</PropertyGroup>
<PropertyGroup>
  <OutputPathCopy>$(MSBuildProjectDirectory)\BinCopy</OutputPathCopy>
</PropertyGroup>

<!-- Item for the new file -->
<ItemGroup>
  <MyOutputFile Include="$(OutputPath)Myoutput.txt"/>
</ItemGroup>

<Target Name="WriteCompileFile">
  <Message Text="Writing the compile file"/>
  <WriteLinesToFile
    File="@(MyOutputFile)"
    Lines="@(Compile)"
    Overwrite="false"/>
  <!-- Append this file to the list of files to be removed upon a clean -->
  <WriteLinesToFile
    File="$(BaseIntermediateOutputPath)$(CleanFile)"
    Lines="@(MyOutputFile)"
    Overwrite="false"/>
</Target>
```

In this segment you have a property, an item, and a target defined. The property, BuildDependsOn, is used to inject the WriteCompileFile target into the build process, and the item represents the file that will be written to. When the WriteCompileFile is executed, the files that are contained in the Compile item will be written to the MyOutputFile file, and the CleanFile will have a new entry. You can verify that CleanFile has your new entry by viewing its contents. For this project, the CleanFile is located at obj\CleanEx1.csproj.FileList.txt. The contents of this file are as follows:

```
bin\Debug\CleanEx1.exe
bin\Debug\CleanEx1.pdb
obj\Debug\ResolveAssemblyReference.cache
obj\Debug\CleanEx1.exe
obj\Debug\CleanEx1.pdb
bin\Debug\Myoutput.txt
```

As you can see from the boldfaced line, the entry was successfully placed in CleanFile. Now when the Clean target is invoked, this file will be deleted. Another approach is to append to the FileWrites property. This property is defined in the Microsoft.Common.targets file, but this approach is also difficult to get working 100 percent correctly.

Despite this approach working, it is not recommended and wasn't meant for this purpose. Using this technique will make creating incrementally building targets difficult, because in most cases your output file will be deleted by MSBuild before the build takes place and therefore will be rebuilt. Also, this is not recommended because you can place only items in certain folders. Another reason to not use this technique is because when the clean is invoked, you have no control over what happens, and you cannot make other things happen. We will now describe a better technique that will enable all of these features.

You just saw how you can hook into the MSBuild clean process and include new files for deletion upon a clean. But you didn't extend the clean process; you just snuck your files into the list to be deleted. As was previously mentioned, it is much better to extend the clean process. We will discuss what this takes now. Similarly to how you extended the build process, you will extend the clean process.

When a clean is requested on a project, the Clean target gets invoked. What you want to do is to create a target that will clean the newly created files and to extend the Clean target to include the new target. To demonstrate this, you will examine the NUnit.targets file once again. This file contains the necessary elements to clean the files that the custom targets generate. The following is the relevant section from that file:

```
<!-- Extends the CleanDependsOn to include cleaning the NUnit-generated files -->
<CleanDependsOn>
  $(CleanDependsOn);
  CleanNUnit
</CleanDependsOn>
</PropertyGroup>
<!--
     Run this target to remove NUnit-generated files
-->
<Target Name="CleanNUnit">
  <Message Text="Clean File: $(BaseIntermediateOutputPath) ➥
$(CleanFile)"/>
  <Delete Files="@(NUnitLog)" Condition="Exists ➥
(@(NUnitLog))"/>
  <Delete Files="@(NUnitFailLog)" Condition="Exists ➥
(@(NUnitFailLog))"/>
  <RemoveDir Directories="@(NUnitCache)" Condition="Exists ➥
(@(NUnitCache))"/>
  <OnError ExecuteTargets="HandleNUnitError"/>
</Target>
```

First in this segment you redefine the CleanDependsOn item. This is the list of targets to be executed when a Clean is invoked. From this declaration, notice that you are first getting the current value for $(CleanDependsOn) and then adding CleanNUnit to it. You do this in the same manner as you extended the Build target in previous examples. Following this, you define the CleanNUnit target. This is a simple target that deletes all of the files that the RunAllTests target could have created. Also, an error handler is defined, in case an error occurs during the course of execution.

If you execute the RunAllTests target on the DataAccessTest example as shown previously (with >msbuild DataAccessTest.csproj /t:RunAllTests), this will create a file, NUnit.log, and the directory cache, both in the output folder. Now perform a clean to verify that these do get deleted. You can perform a clean with >msbuild /t:Clean. Figure 4-8 shows the results of this.

```
Project "C:\MSBuild\NUnit\NUnitExamples\NUnitEx2\DataAccessTest\DataAccessTest.c
sproj" (Clean target(s)):

Target CoreClean:
    Deleting file "bin\Debug\DataAccessTest.dll".
    Deleting file "bin\Debug\DataAccessTest.pdb".
    Deleting file "bin\Debug\DataAccess.dll".
    Deleting file "bin\Debug\MSBuildTasks.dll".
    Deleting file "bin\Debug\nunit.framework.dll".
    Deleting file "bin\Debug\nunit.util.dll".
    Deleting file "bin\Debug\DataAccess.pdb".
    Deleting file "bin\Debug\nunit.framework.xml".
    Deleting file "obj\Debug\ResolveAssemblyReference.cache".
    Deleting file "obj\Debug\DataAccessTest.dll".
    Deleting file "obj\Debug\DataAccessTest.pdb".
Target CleanNUnit:
    Deleting file "bin\Debug\\NUnit.log".
    Removing directory "bin\Debug\\cache\".

Build succeeded.
    0 Warning(s)
    0 Error(s)

Time Elapsed 00:00:00.05
```

Figure 4-8. Clean *"automagically" removing NUnit-generated files*

You can see from Figure 4-8 that the CleanNUnit target was executed automatically and that your files were successfully deleted as expected. Using this method, since a custom target is being executed, you can perform any necessary steps, even break into custom tasks for more complicated steps if necessary. We have now covered all the necessary bases to extend MSBuild to perform all the steps your application requires—and to do it nicely.

Summary

In this chapter, we presented the two most extensible aspects of MSBuild: custom loggers and custom tasks. We discussed how you can hook into the MSBuild logging process to create your own logger that meets the specific needs of your application if necessary. We covered how to create custom tasks to perform steps unattainable from existing MSBuild tasks. During this, we also discussed incremental building and how you can create targets and tasks that support it. We showed how to cleanly extend the build and clean process that MSBuild currently has in place. With these tools, you should be able to customize the build to meet the needs of your applications. All of the source code for this chapter is available in the Source Code section of the Apress Web site (http://www.apress.com). For brevity reasons, some details of that code could not be covered; for more information, see the source files.

■■■

CHAPTER 5

Introducing Team Foundation Server and Team Build

In this chapter, we will introduce some new solutions that Microsoft has created for enterprise organizations. These include Visual Studio 2005 Team Foundation Server (TFS) and Team Build, which are two products in the new Visual Studio Team System (VSTS) product line. Team Build is a powerful component that is built on top of MSBuild. Team Build is a build automation tool included in TFS. The primary goal of Team Build is to provide organizations with a "build lab out of the box." You need many prerequisites to be able to use Team Build, and we'll briefly discuss them in this chapter. Beyond this, we will introduce some of the other new components of VSTS, and we will cover how Team Build works and how you can use it to execute custom builds on a dedicated build machine. We will also discuss how you can extend the Team Build build process. Finally, we will discuss how to create an automated public build by using Team Build.

Introducing Visual Studio Team System (VSTS)

In this chapter, we will mainly discuss Team Build, which is a component in the new VSTS product line. VSTS is aimed at integrating all parties involved in the development life cycle, from the architect to the developer to the project manager. The team in *Team System* is the entire team involved in the development effort, not just the development team. VSTS is an effort by Microsoft to raise the bar for its software development tools and to capture more of the enterprise development marketplace. Discussing the details of what VSTS is and how you can use it in your organization is beyond the scope of this text, but we will discuss the components that are relevant to you in this chapter, namely, Team Build and TFS. For more detailed information about VSTS, you can refer to `http://msdn.microsoft.com/vstudio/teamsystem`.

One of the major additions in VSTS is TFS, which is an all-new source control management (SCM) utility. You may be wondering why Microsoft is releasing a new SCM tool when it already has Visual SourceSafe. TFS is targeted to enterprise software companies; Visual SourceSafe is more geared toward smaller corporations. TFS is not just an SCM tool; it introduces some new enterprise features that we will explain throughout the course of this chapter. Note that TFS is required in order to use Team Build and most of what is covered in this chapter.

Introducing Team Build

If you are using TFS as your SCM tool, you have the ability to add another component to it. This component is called Team Build, and you may have to install this component from your TFS install disc. Team Build is part of a larger product called Team Foundation Build, which is responsible for managing every aspect of team builds. As previously stated, the goal of Team Build is to provide organizations with a "build lab out of the box."

A *team build*, or public build, is a build created on a dedicated machine that the entire organization can reference later. Team builds are good because the configurations of the build machines are not in question like a developer's machine typically is, and you typically have a way to re-create these public builds. Team Build is the product you will use to create new public builds and execute them. Team Build is built on top of MSBuild and is extensible just like your typical build is. We will cover how to customize the team build later in the "Extending the Team Build" section.

So how do you create a team build? The idea is fairly simple; you have a machine that runs the Team Build service and waits for build requests. Once this happens, then it will get the latest code from the repository and proceed to build the specified product. When this is complete, Team Build will place the results at a specified location, which can be on the build machine or any other accessible network share. Along with building your product, you can also choose to have code analysis and unit tests executed along with your code. Team Build provides this out of the box. If you need to further control the execution, you can customize the team build similarly to how you customize other builds.

Introducing the Team Foundation Build Architecture

Before we start discussing in detail how to use Team Build, we will first describe how Team Build fits into the big picture of VSTS, and we will provide you with a look at the architecture behind Team Foundation Build. As mentioned earlier, Team Build is part of Team Foundation Build (see Figure 5-1).

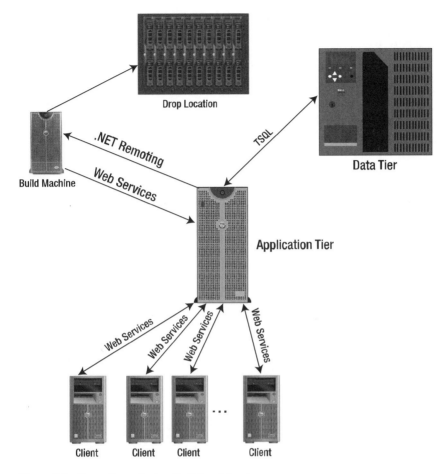

Figure 5-1. *Team Foundation Build architecture*

As shown, five primary responsibilities need to be fulfilled. Let's examine these roles a little more closely.

Team Foundation Build Client

Just as you would expect, this is the part of the application that the user interacts with. This is hosted inside Visual Studio. You can perform such tasks as start team builds, view reports for previous builds, or create new build types. A *build type* is simply a definition for what will be built and how it will be built. For example, you could create a new build type called `Release build` or `Nightly build`. You can also specify which users can perform which actions. For instance, you could have a group that is responsible for creating new build types. Other users would not be allowed to create new build types.

The security configuration of TFS is an important topic; unfortunately, this is outside the scope of this text. Each client must have the Team Foundation Build client installed; you can find this on the TFS install disc.

Application Tier

The application tier is the machine responsible for hosting most of the applications. For instance, the source control application will run from this machine, and the Web-based project portals will be driven from this machine. TFS uses a Windows Server 2003–based product for the project portals, which is Windows SharePoint Services 2003. SharePoint Services is a free Web-based tool designed to help share information and increase collaboration amongst team members and with customers. For more information about Windows SharePoint Services, you can visit the Windows Server 2003 home page at `http://www.microsoft.com/windowsserver2003/`.

Data Tier

The data tier is responsible for containing and managing all the data of the projects. For instance, the source control database is located on this machine, along with several other databases. This machine must have SQL Server 2005 installed and running. SQL Server 2005 has many new features that TFS utilizes. For instance, Reporting Services generates the build reports, and you can create your own new reports if you are familiar with this technology.

Build Machine

The build machine is a clean machine dedicated to conducting public builds. Typically you will not use this machine for any other purpose besides conducting the builds. This machine must have the Team Build service installed and running prior to any builds being produced on this machine. You can find the setup for this on the TFS setup disc.

Drop Location

This is any accessible network share; it will contain the binaries for all the builds. This will include every version that was built for each product. Source code will not be placed on this machine; it will contain only binary files and log files for each build. Typically you will want all the developers in the organization to be able to read from this share.

Using Team Foundation Build

In this section, we will discuss how you can use Team Foundation Build to create an automated public build for your projects. It is assumed that you have TFS installed and in use as your SCM tool. For demonstration purposes, we will be using an open source project named Codus. Codus is an object-relational mapping (ORM) tool. You can find more information about Codus at `http://adapdev.com/codus/index.aspx`. The complete source code for this project is available along with the other source for the exercises.

We had to slightly modify the Codus project to fit the needs of a public build. In particular, we placed all third-party assemblies in a common directory that is accessible to all projects and that was checked into source control. To use Team Foundation Build, your project must be part of a team project. A *team project* is not like the Visual Studio project that you are used to. A team project is part of VSTS and is designed to span multiple solutions. From the team project, you will reference the source control repository, manage work items and project documents, and do much more.

Now let's see how you can get started using Team Foundation Build. If you don't already have a team project defined, then you will need to create one. Follow the steps in the next section to create a new team project.

Creating a New Team Project

Open Visual Studio, and select File ➤ New ➤ Team Project. This opens the New Team Project Wizard shown in Figure 5-2. Simply specify the name of the team project, and click Next.

Figure 5-2. *New Team Project Wizard*

On the next page of the Team Project Wizard, you are asked to select a process template. This defines the development style that this project will use. By default you have two options: MSF for Agile Software Development or MSF for CMMI Software Development. The MSF for Agile template is the template you should use if your organization is using agile development methodologies. Select the MSF for CMMI template if your project requires longer software development life cycles and a more rigorous approach to software development. You can also create new process templates if needed. For this project, select the MSF for Agile template, and then click Next to move to the next page.

On the next page, you are asked to give your project portal a title and description. You can fill these in with appropriate values and then click Next to configure the source control settings. On the settings page, you have three options for your source control:

- You can create an empty source control folder.

- You can create a new source control branch.

- You *cannot* create a source control folder at this time.

For this project, you will go with the default, Create an Empty Source Control Folder. After you click Next, you will see a summary of the team project settings. At this time, you can click Finish to begin creating the team project. After the team project is built, the project portal appears in Visual Studio, as shown in Figure 5-3.

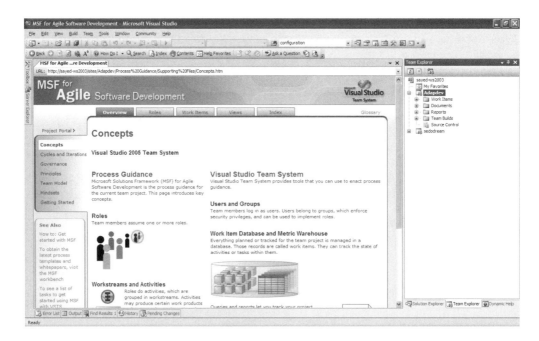

Figure 5-3. *Project portal view in Visual Studio*

The project portal opens in Visual Studio with the process guidance section. This section describes how you can manage your team project. It covers topics from member roles to team builds. Before you dive deep into team projects, we strongly suggest you examine the process guidance pages for a good description about how to proceed.

Understanding the Team Project Fundamentals

Now that you have set up your team project, we'll cover some of the contents of your team project. If the Team Explorer pane is not visible, you can open it by selecting View ➤ Team Explorer. Figure 5-4 shows the Team Explorer pane.

Figure 5-4. *Team Explorer pane*

As you can see from Figure 5-4, the team project has five main elements: Work Items, Documents, Reports, Team Builds, and Source Control. The following sections explain each of these elements.

Work Items

A work item summarizes work that needs to be completed on the project. This can be fixing a bug, creating new functionality, writing documentation, and so on. Don't limit yourself to thinking that work items are just for developers; this is the team project, and every team member can, and should, have work items. From the Work Items element, you can query the work items database for specific conditions.

Documents

When developing with previous versions of Visual Studio, you didn't have a good means to integrate project documents with the projects themselves. Sure, you could place them into a folder with the project, but this was certainly not an ideal solution. With TFS, this issue has been solved. You can place all files that relate to your project in the Documents node under your project. This can include, but is certainly not limited to, documents describing coding standards and documents addressing security vulnerabilities. When you create a new team project, you might be surprised to find many preexisting documents in this node.

Reports

Reports keep track of your project over a period of time. Many reports are available out of the box, including a report for all team project builds, a report for bug rates, and several others. You can also create new reports; these reports are built on top of Reporting Services. All reports are stored on the server and are available to other team members.

Team Builds

This is the section that the remainder of this chapter will focus on. This node displays all your defined team builds, and it allows you to create new team builds. Since you may have different products in this team project, you may have many different team builds available to build against all those products.

Source Control

Last but certainly not least is the Source Control section; from this node you can access the source control repository. If you double-click the Source Control item, the Source Control Explorer pane opens in Visual Studio. Currently the Adapdev team project, shown in Figure 5-4, does not have any files in the Source Control section.

We will now explain how you can add this project to source control.

Placing Code in Source Control

Now that you have an idea of what Team Foundation Build is, we'll show how to add the Codus project to source control. Before you do this, though, let's create a work item for this. To create a new work item, right-click the Work Items node in Team Explorer, and select Add Work Item. You also have to specify its type. Name the task Initial Checkin, fill in the other appropriate text boxes, and click Save. Now you can proceed to check the solution into the source control system. Follow these steps:

1. Open the solution in Visual Studio.

2. Right-click the solution in Solution Explorer, and select Add Solution to Source Control.

3. Following this, a dialog box will ask you which team project this belongs to; select Adapdev, and click OK, as shown in Figure 5-5.

Figure 5-5. *Selecting the team project for source control*

4. Now you have to commit your changes. Do this by right-clicking the Codus solution in Solution Explorer and selecting Check In. This presents you with the dialog box shown in Figure 5-6. Select Adapdev.

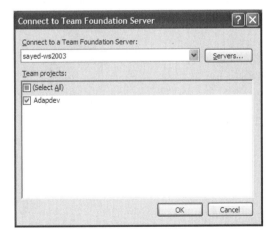

Figure 5-6. *Connect to Team Foundation Server dialog box*

5. After you click OK, you will see a page that displays the current change set being checked in. From this page you can add check-in notes and associate work items with this check-in change set, as shown in Figure 5-7.

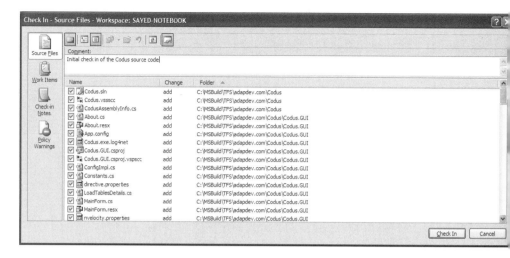

Figure 5-7. *Source Files view of the Check In dialog box*

6. In Figure 5-7, you can see four different views of your change set. These views are Source Files, Work Items, Check-in Notes, and Policy Warnings. You are especially interested in the Source Files view and the Work Items view. The Source Files view shows you the files that have been modified in the current change set and gives you a place to provide a comment about your check-in. The Work Items view allows you to associate this change set with any work items defined. To access any of these views, simply click the appropriate view icon. For this example, you want to associate this check-in with the Initial Check In work item created earlier. Do this by clicking Work Items and selecting the Initial Check In task, as shown in Figure 5-8.

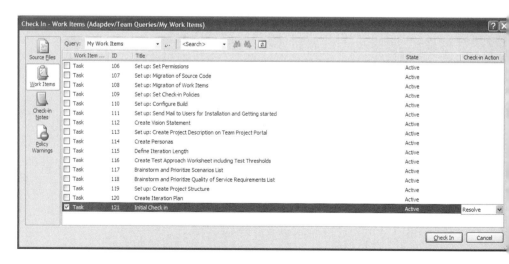

Figure 5-8. *Work Items view of Check In dialog box*

7. At this point, you are ready to check in your project, so simply click the Check In button.

Now that you have your project under source control and know a few more things about TFS, let's move on to Team Build and get started creating a new public build.

Using Team Build

Your first goal with Team Build is to get a public build running on a public machine that you can trust to build your products. In this scenario, you will actually be using the machine that TFS is installed on, but this is not recommended. When using Team Build in your organization, you will want a dedicated machine to perform builds. You must install Team Build on this machine; you can find it on the TFS disc.

Now you need to create a new team build from Visual Studio. First right-click the Team Builds node, and then select New Team Build Type. You will see the New Team Build Type Creation Wizard, as shown in Figure 5-9.

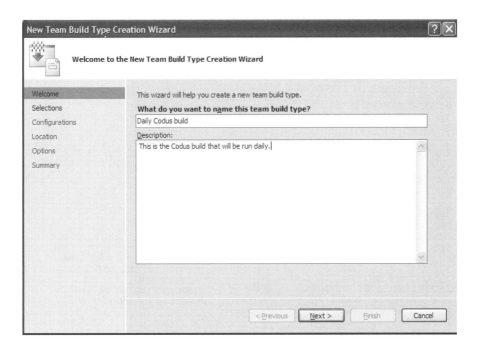

Figure 5-9. *New Team Build Type Creation Wizard*

On this page, you should specify the name and description of your team build. For this build, name it Daily Codus build. Later in this chapter we will discuss how you can automate this process. Click Next to proceed to the next page of this wizard, where you'll select which solutions you want to include in the build. On this page, you pick the only available solution, the Codus solution. Clicking Next brings you to the configuration selection page; for this build, select the Release configuration. On the next page, you will provide information about the build machine, as shown in Figure 5-10.

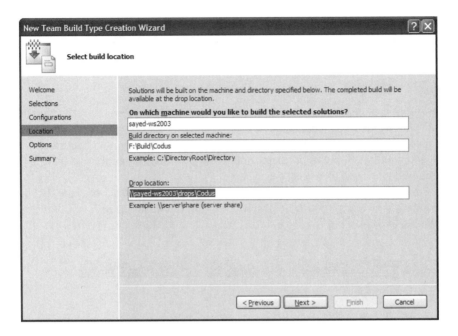

Figure 5-10. *Build location information*

In this example, since you are actually using the machine that is running TFS, you provide that information in the text boxes. For your team builds, you would provide the information about the dedicated build machine here. You must fill in three fields, as summarized in Table 5-1.

Table 5-1. *Build Location Parameters*

Field Name	Description
Build machine name	This should be the computer name on which you want the build to occur. You could alternatively use the Internet Protocol (IP) address.
Build directory	This is the directory on the build machine where you want the build to take place. Each time you build, you will find the sources used for the most recent build in this directory along with the binaries. Think of this as a temporary directory where the build will occur.
Drop location	This is the network share where the binaries will be saved after each build. Each build will have a unique identifier, so for each build you will be able to retrieve the binaries from this location. This location should be on a machine other than the build machine.

After you fill in this information, click Next to access the build options. On this page, you can specify to run test cases and to perform code analysis. Click Next to go to the summary page. The final page summarizes the team build type you are about to create, as shown in Figure 5-11.

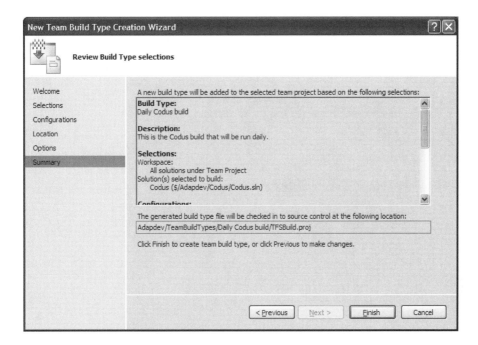

Figure 5-11. *Build type summary page*

On this page you can review everything to ensure you did not make any mistakes when defining the build type. Notice that it states the build type will be placed under source control. This means any changes to the build type will be tracked just like your source code. Also, this tells you where the build type file resides.

The New Team Build Type Creation Wizard is simply a GUI helper that creates the TFSBuild.proj file. This is the MSBuild file that will drive the team build. Before we discuss this file in great detail, we will discuss how you can kick off a build, and then we will show the results.

After completing the New Team Build Type Creation Wizard, you should see a new element under the Team Builds node in the Team Explorer. In this case, this is the Daily Codus build, as shown in Figure 5-12.

Figure 5-12. *Team Explorer with new team build*

To start the execution of this build, right-click the `Daily Codus build` element, and select Build Team Project Adapdev. This presents a dialog box that gives you a chance to override some of the configuration settings that you set previously, as shown in Figure 5-13.

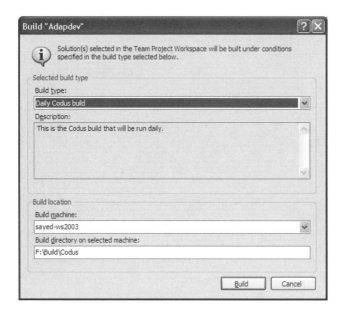

Figure 5-13. *Team build settings*

From here you can select the build type you want to execute, the build machine you want to execute it on, and the build directory of that machine. All other options are not configurable from this dialog box. For now, leave the defaults, and click Build. At this point, you should see a progress dialog box as your build information is sent to the build machine. Once the build progress dialog box disappears, you will see a view of the build in progress. This view will be updated as the build continues on the build machine. Figure 5-14 shows a view of the build starting on the build machine, and Figure 5-15 shows a view of the build progressing on the build machine.

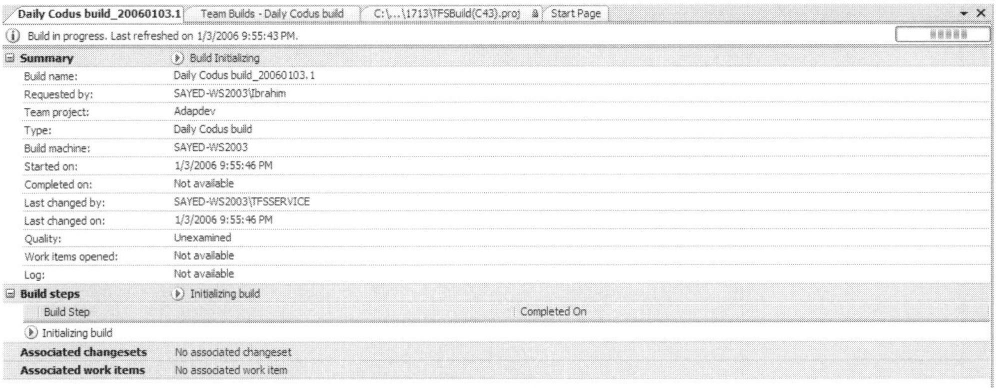

Figure 5-14. *View of build starting on build machine*

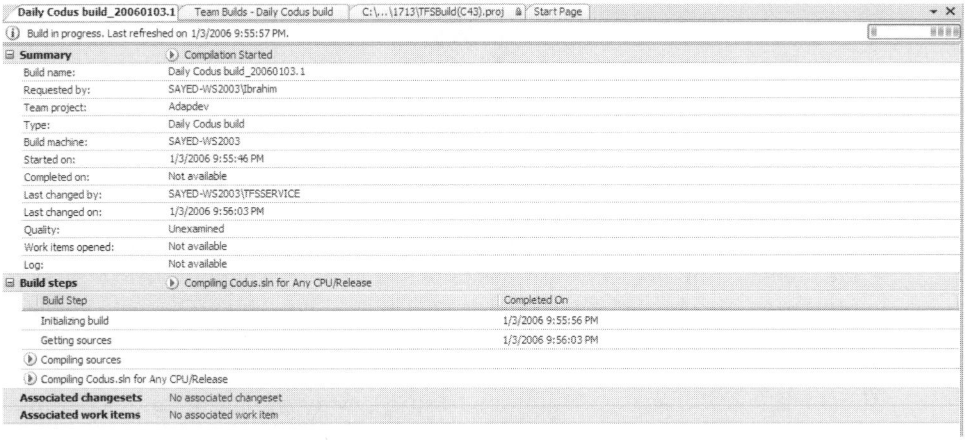

Figure 5-15. *View of build progressing on build machine*

The view of the build will continue to expand until the build has completed. The progress bar will continue to move until the build completes. Once the build has completed, the progress bar will disappear, and a few links will appear on the page. When you first create a public build from a solution, don't be surprised if your build doesn't pass initially. Typically, developer machines have items that may be forgotten. For instance, you may have installed some third-party libraries in the GAC that are missing from the build machine. This is just one good reason for a public build: you become aware of what it takes to build your project on a clean machine. Figure 5-16 shows the completed build report.

Release.txt	Daily Codus build_20060103.1	Team Builds - Daily Codus build	C:\...\1713\TFSBuild(C43).proj	Start Page		▼ ✕

ⓘ Last refreshed on 1/3/2006 9:57:30 PM.

⊟ Summary		⊗ Failed
Build name:		Daily Codus build 20060103.1
Requested by:		SAYED-WS2003\Ibrahim
Team project:		Adapdev
Type:		Daily Codus build
Build machine:		SAYED-WS2003
Started on:		1/3/2006 9:55:46 PM
Completed on:		1/3/2006 9:56:44 PM
Last changed by:		SAYED-WS2003\TFSSERVICE
Last changed on:		1/3/2006 9:56:44 PM
Quality:		Unexamined
Work items opened:		122 (Active/TFSSERVICE)
Log:		\\sayed-ws2003\drops\Codus\Daily Codus build 20060103.1\BuildLog.txt

⊟ Build steps	⊗ Failed	
Build Step		Completed On
Initializing build		1/3/2006 9:55:56 PM
Getting sources		1/3/2006 9:56:03 PM
⊗ Compiling sources		1/3/2006 9:56:11 PM
⊗ Compiling Codus.sln for Any CPU/Release		1/3/2006 9:56:11 PM
⊗ Compiling Codus.GUI.Extensions.csproj		1/3/2006 9:56:11 PM
Generating list of changesets		1/3/2006 9:56:35 PM
Copying binaries to drop location		1/3/2006 9:56:35 PM
Copying log files to drop location		1/3/2006 9:56:35 PM
Creating work item		1/3/2006 9:56:43 PM
⊗ Failed		1/3/2006 9:56:43 PM

⊞ Result details for Any CPU/Release	⊗ 6 error(s), 4 warning(s), no test result
⊞ Associated changesets	3 associated changesets
⊞ Associated work items	1 associated work item

Figure 5-16. *Completed build report*

It seems as though this build failed! As stated previously, when you try to create a public build for a product, you may have to make some modifications to be successful. You should note a few things on this page. You can access the drop site by clicking the build name link. Since the build failed, Team Build automatically opened a new ticket to resolve this issue. You can view this work item by clicking the work item's link. A summary of the build appears and tells you there were errors and warnings. You can also access the build log by clicking the log link.

Since your build failed, you are certainly interested in viewing the log for this build so you can resolve the issues. Here is a section of the build log file:

```
warning MSB3245: Could not resolve this reference. Could not locate the ➥
    assembly "log4net". ...
GUIConfigurator.cs(7,8): error CS0246: The type or namespace name 'Adapdev' ...
```

After viewing the log, it is obvious that the build machine didn't have access to the third-party assemblies that are required to build this solution. This is because they were never checked into source control. To add these files to source control, you first need to add the folder directly under the Codus solution folder and then add the files. To do this, you will use a few buttons on the Source Control Explorer toolbar, as shown in Figure 5-17.

Figure 5-17. *Source Control Explorer toolbar*

From this toolbar, click the New Folder button to create the Codus\Shared folder, and then click the Add Files button to add the files to that folder. After you add the files contained in the local directory, your source control directory should look similar to the one in Figure 5-18.

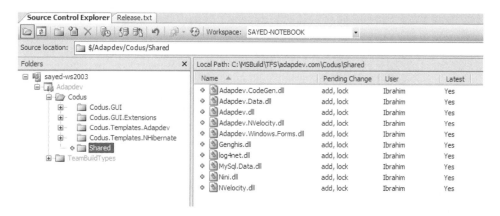

Figure 5-18. *Source Control Explorer*

You should notice a few things about the Source Control Explorer. The items you added are ready to be checked in, and now a new node appears under your Adapdev team project, the TeamBuildTypes node. This was created when you defined the Codus Daily build. At this point, you can check in the pending changes and rerun the build. When you check this in, you should associate this change set with the bug that was created by the failed build. Then you rerun the Codus Daily build. At this point, if all goes well, the build will succeed, and you can examine the build through the summary page. Now we will discuss how all this happens.

Understanding How Team Build Works

By now you are probably wondering how this whole process works. In a nutshell, at the client machine, the team build is initiated. This machine communicates with the app server using Web services. The application server then communicates with the build machine to initialize and run the build. From this point, the build machine conducts all the necessary steps to execute the build, including getting the latest sources from the repository. The build machine reports the status of the build to the application server, which is forwarded by the application tier to the client machine. After the build is complete, the binaries are placed on the drop machine.

Now you will look at how Team Build actually builds your project on the build machine. When you create a new team build type with the wizard in Visual Studio, you are actually creating a few files that will be placed into source control. The files that are created and their contents depend on what type of project you have and how you configure the team build type. Three files will be generated each time, and if you are building a C++ project, then another file will be created to assist with those projects. Table 5-2 summarizes these files.

Table 5-2. *Team Build–Generated Files*

Name	Description
TFSBuild.proj	This is the project file that will be built; it contains all the configuration options specified in the New Team Build Type Creation Wizard. This file will define values for your projects. The actual build process is imported through another file, similarly to how desktop builds are imported for managed projects.
TFSBuild.rsp	This is a response file you can use during the team build. In this file you can configure any command-line options that should be sent to msbuild.exe when building your project. By default this is empty.
WorkspaceMapping.xml	This is an XML file that describes which project is being built. This will drive which projects are pulled from source control. You can modify this file, but it is not recommended.
VCOverrides.vsprops	This file is processed by vcbuild.exe to build your C++ projects. If you are not building C++ projects, then this file will not be present.

Of these files, you are most interested in the TFSBuild.proj file; if you need to perform any customizations to the team build, then you will perform them within this file. We will discuss how to customize the team build in a bit. For now we will continue discussing how the team build actually takes place. The TFSBuild.proj file defines your team build, and it defines the build process by importing the details with the following statement:

```
<Import Project="$(MSBuildExtensionsPath)\Microsoft\VisualStudio\ ➥
v8.0\TeamBuild\Microsoft.TeamFoundation.Build.targets" />
```

The Microsoft.TeamFoundation.Build.targets file describes all the steps for a public build. You can compare this file to the Microsoft.Commons.targets and Microsoft.CSharp.targets files.

When you perform a team build, you have to follow several steps, as shown in Figure 5-19.

Note that after the sources are retrieved from source control, they are labeled. This ensures that the same build can be reproduced at any time in the future. When you are working on enterprise applications, this is essential. After the projects are built, the associated work items are updated. The work items are work items that have been resolved since the last good build, which is a build that completes without errors and has all its test cases pass. These work items will have their FixedIn field populated with this build, if it is a good build. If the build fails, then a new work item is generated to resolve the build failure. This is one of the powerful features of VSTS and TFS; all the major tools are very tightly integrated and work well together.

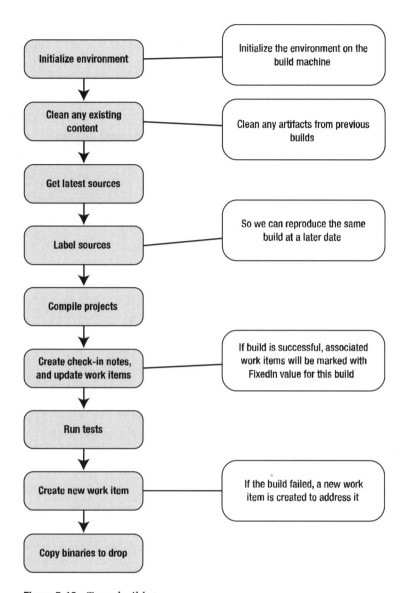

Figure 5-19. *Team build steps*

Now that you know what the build steps are, you'll look at the file that drives this entire process. This file is the TFSBuild.proj file that is created with the New Team Build Type Creation Wizard. To view or edit this file, you will have to get it from source control. To do this, open the Source Control Explorer by double-clicking the Source Control node in the Team Explorer pane, and navigate to the TeamBuildTypes folder, as shown in Figure 5-20.

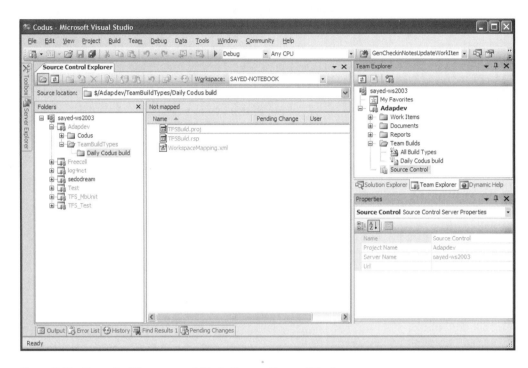

Figure 5-20. *Team Build–generated file in Source Control Explorer*

From the Source Control Explorer, you can either view the file or check it out for editing. For now you simply view the TFSBuild.proj file by double-clicking it. If you look in this file, you will notice that all the configuration options from the New Team Build Type Creation Wizard are placed in this file. If you would like to change a value from that configuration, you'll have to change this file manually. You have no way to launch the Team Build Type Wizard for an existing team build type. Here is part of this file, minus all the comments:

```
<Import Project="$(MSBuildExtensionsPath)\Microsoft ➥
\VisualStudio\v8.0\TeamBuild\Microsoft.TeamFoundation ➥
.Build.targets" />

<Import Project="$(MSBuildExtensionsPath)\Microsoft\ ➥
VisualStudio\v8.0\TeamBuild\Microsoft.TeamFoundation.Build.targets" />

<ProjectExtensions>
  <Description>This is the Codus build that ➥
will be run daily.</Description>
```

```
  <BuildMachine>sayed-ws2003</BuildMachine>
</ProjectExtensions>

<PropertyGroup>
  <TeamProject>Adapdev</TeamProject>
  <BuildDirectoryPath>F:\Build\Codus</BuildDirectoryPath>
  <DropLocation>\\sayed-ws2003\drops\Codus</DropLocation>
  <RunTest>false</RunTest>
  <WorkItemFieldValues>Symptom=build break;Steps To Reproduce ➥
=Start the build using Team Build</WorkItemFieldValues>
  <RunCodeAnalysis>Never</RunCodeAnalysis>
  <UpdateAssociatedWorkItems>true</UpdateAssociatedWorkItems>
  <WorkItemTitle>Build failure in build:</WorkItemTitle>
  <DescriptionText>This work item was created by Team ➥
Build on a build failure.</DescriptionText>
  <BuildlogText>The build log file is at:</BuildlogText>
  <ErrorWarningLogText>The errors/warnings log ➥
file is at:</ErrorWarningLogText>
</PropertyGroup>
```

From here it is obvious that many of these values came directly from the configuration that you created in the wizard earlier in this chapter. Also note that the first element in this file imports the file that will define the build process, `Microsoft.TeamFoundation.Build.targets`. When you perform a team build, you are actually executing the `EndToEndIteration` target. How can you customize this process? You can customize this in the same way you extended the normal build process in previous chapters. This is because Team Build uses MSBuild to perform the builds. In the next section, you will learn about some of the steps you can perform with this process.

Extending the Team Build

You previously learned how to extend the build process when you build a project or solution locally. To do this, you used MSBuild to inject steps into the build process. A team build is no different; it has a default way of building team projects, and you are free to extend or modify this process as much as you want. In fact, you can completely replace it if you want. Since you know how to use MSBuild, we don't need to cover the details of how to write an MSBuild target for Team Build. You simply need to know how and where to inject the appropriate steps into the Team Build process. You will want to place all modifications in `TFSBuild.proj`. You will have to check this file out to edit it and check it in to make the change take effect. You can also place the modifications in files that get imported into `TFSBuild.proj`. Remember to check in `TFSBuild.proj` and all other files that you would like imported into it.

You have a few ways to inject your steps into the process that will build your team projects. (We will cover the different methods and discuss the pros and cons of each. This is similar to some material that was discussed in previous chapters.) Many targets are already wired into the build process but have no steps contained within them. For example, before the project is compiled, the `BeforeCompile` target is invoked. In the `Microsoft.TeamFoundation.Build.targets` file, this is an empty target. The simplest way to extend the Team Build process is to define those targets. In Table 5-3, you'll find a list of these "empty" targets. These appear in the order they are defined in the `Microsoft.TeamFoundation.Build.targets` file.

Table 5-3. *Team Build Targets Designed to Be Overridden*

Name	Description
BeforeEndToEndIteration	EndToEndIteration is the target that drives the whole build process. Override this to perform some action before the entire process.
BuildNumberOverrideTarget	If you do not like the default build numbering provided by Team Build, then you can override it in the target. You'll need to create a custom task that outputs a property named BuildNumber. This will be used for your build number.
AfterEndToEndIteration	If you need something to occur after everything is completed, you can override this target.
BeforeClean	Called before the workspace is cleaned up. In this target you may want to perform some custom clean steps.
AfterClean	Called after the workspace has been cleaned; you can also perform some custom cleaning steps here as well.
BeforeGet	Called before the sources are gathered from source control. In this step you could get some other files from source control if necessary.
AfterGet	Called after the sources have been copied from source control. If you wanted to change the assembly version before the build process, you could do that here.
BeforeLabel	During a team build, the sources are labeled; this is the target before that process. If you modified any file previously in the build process, you could check them all in at this point.
AfterLabel	Called after the source tree has been labeled.
BeforeCompile	Called before the projects are compiled.
AfterCompile	Invoked after the projects have been compiled.
BeforeTest	This is called before the test cases in the projects are executed. If there were extra steps to set up your test cases, you could implement those steps in this target.
AfterTest	If you would like for some actions to take place after the tests are completed, such as creating summaries of the tests, then you could implement those here.
PackageBinaries	This target is to assist you in deployment; if you wanted to create a zip file of the binaries (or CAB files), you could do that here. If you'd like for these binaries to be located on the drop site, make sure you place them under the BinariesRoot folder.
BeforeDropBuild	The target called immediately before the build is placed in the drop site. If you'd like for other files to be copied to the drop site, this is your last chance to place them under BinariesRoot for copying.
AfterDropBuild	This is called immediately after the files are copied to the drop site. If you wanted to verify that the files made it there, you could implement that in this target.
BeforeOnBuildBreak	When an error occurs, this is the first target that gets called. You could perform any necessary error correction steps here, such as e-mailing admins or creating additional work items.
AfterOnBuildBreak	Last target that gets called after an error occurs.

By overriding one of these targets, you can easily extend the build process for your team build. We personally do not like overriding these targets, even though they're there for that sole purpose. As discussed in an earlier chapter, by overriding these targets you expose the potential for a difficult-to-locate hole in your build process. This hole would pop up when the same target is defined in more than one place for the same build. For instance, if the BeforeCompile target is overridden twice, only one implementation can exist; therefore, one is thrown away. This may not seem like a real possibility, but for projects with sophisticated builds, this can happen. Whenever possible, you should write MSBuild extensions that are generic and safely reusable. Implementations that override targets such as these are *not* safely reusable. To avoid this, you will use another technique.

Instead of implementing the predefined targets from Table 5-3 to extend the build process, you should inject your own targets into the build process. Many TFS targets specify the DependsOnTargets value with a list of targets; these targets will be executed before the target that is attached to it. Most of these targets extract this definition from a property, which you can extend to include your own targets. For instance, the following fragment is from the Microsoft.TeamFoundation.Build.targets file:

```
<PropertyGroup>
  <TeamBuildDependsOn>
    InitializeBuild;
    PreBuild;
    Compile;
    PostBuild;
    Test;
    PackageBinaries;
  </TeamBuildDependsOn>
</PropertyGroup>
<Target Name="TeamBuild"
        Condition=" '$(IsDesktopBuild)'!='true' "
        DependsOnTargets="$(TeamBuildDependsOn)" />
```

TeamBuild is a target that will be invoked during your public build process. This target actually does nothing! It just defines the target that must be executed before it. If you want to add your own steps to this list, you can do something like the following:

```
<PropertyGroup>
  <TeamBuildDependsOn>
    CustomBeforeTeamBuild;
    $(TeamBuildDependsOn);
    CustomAfterTeamBuild;
  </TeamBuildDependsOn>
</PropertyGroup>

<Target Name="CustomBeforeTeamBuild">
  <Message Importance="normal" Text="This is BEFORE the ➥
TeamBuild target gets invoked"/>
</Target>
```

```
<Target Name="CustomAfterTeamBuild"     >
  <Message Importance="normal" Text="This is AFTER ➥
the TeamBuild target finishes executing"/>
</Target>
```

This fragment is placed in the TFSBuild.proj file, after the import statement for Microsoft.
TeamFoundation.Build.targets. In the property group at the top of this fragment, you are
defining the TeamBuildDependsOn property. You are getting the current definition for the property
itself with $(TeamBuildDependsOn) and adding to it. Since this is after the import statement, you
know that this property has already been defined. Following this property declaration, the two
targets are defined. These targets simply print messages to the log. To verify that these customizations worked, you must check in the TFSBuild.proj file and begin another team build. The following
is a portion of the log that demonstrates its effectiveness:

```
Target CustomBeforeTeamBuild:
    This is BEFORE the TeamBuild target gets invoked
Target InitializeBuild:
    Creating directory "F:\Build\Codus\Adapdev\Daily Codus ➥
 build\BuildType\..\Sources".
    ...
    ...
Target GetChangeSetsAndUpdateWorkItems:
    GenCheckinNotesUpdateWorkItems TeamFoundationServerUrl= ➥
"http://sayed-ws2003:8080/" CurrentLabel="LDaily Codus build_20060109.3 ➥
@$/Adapdev" LastLabel="LDaily Codus build_20060105.3@$/Adapdev" ➥
UpdateWorkItems=True BuildId="Daily Codus build_20060109.3"
    Querying the contents of label 'LDaily Codus build_20060105.3@$/Adapdev'.
    Querying the contents of label 'LDaily Codus build_20060109.3@$/Adapdev'.
    Analyzing labels LDaily Codus build_20060105.3@$/Adapdev and LDaily ➥
Codus build_20060109.3@$/Adapdev.
    Querying item history.
    Changeset '56' was included in this build.
    Changeset '57' was included in this build.
    Changeset '58' was included in this build.
Target CustomAfterTeamBuild:
    This is AFTER the TeamBuild target finishes executing
```

As you can see from the previous snippet of the build log, your custom targets were executed successfully from the team build. You can extend a series of these DependsOn properties,
as listed in Table 5-4.

Table 5-4. *Available* DependsOn *Properties*

Target Name	DependsOn **Property Name**
EndToEndIteration	EndToEndIterationDependsOn
InitializeWorkspace	InitializeWorkspaceDependsOn
Clean	CleanDependsOn
TeamBuild	TeamBuildDependsOn
Test	TestDependsOn
PostBuild	PostBuildDependsOn
PackageBinaries	PackageBinariesDependsOn
DropBuild	DropBuildDependsOn
OnBuildBreak	OnBuildBreakDependsOn
CopyLogFiles	CopyLogFilesDependsOn

Using this method, you can confidently and safely extend the process that is executed when your public build takes place. When doing this, you must ensure that these declarations are *after* the import statement for the Microsoft.TeamFoundation.Build.targets file; otherwise, your changes will be overwritten.

Now you will look at how you can customize what happens after an error occurs during the build.

Handling Errors During a Team Build

Just like performing a normal build, you always have the possibility that errors will occur; arguably this possibility is actually higher when using Team Build. Handling an error during a team build is different from handling an error during a normal build, however. During the course of a normal desktop build, your main goal is to ensure that the person performing the build is notified that the error has occurred so that it can be resolved. If an error occurs during a team build, this affects the entire team, so you must ensure that the appropriate people get notified to correct the problem and that it is corrected as soon as possible.

When your team project is being built, a special target will be called if the build breaks. That target is OnBuildBreak. Typically, this target will create a new work item to have the build error resolved and drop the files at the drop location. But you may want to extend this process to increase awareness of the build failure. For instance, you may want to send an e-mail to the project manager or log the build error somewhere else.

Sometimes you would like to extend or replace how a build error is handled. To facilitate this, you first must know the default error-handling mechanism. When you invoke a team build, most of the work actually takes place in the CoreCompile target. This target will set up each project for building. This includes creating output directories, initializing properties, and generating items. It also includes executing the Build target on each project in the team project. Each of these projects will be built in their own instance of MSBuild. If a true build error occurs, then it will occur in this target. As discussed in a previous build, you can specify targets to execute if an error occurs during the execution of a target. You do this using the OnError element. This has to be the last statement of the target. If you look at the bottom of the CoreCompile target, located in the Microsoft.TeamFoundation.Build.targets file, you'll notice the statement

`<OnError ExecuteTargets="OnBuildBreak;" />`. This states the `OnBuildBreak` target will be invoked if an error occurs during the `CoreCompile` target. Now you will look at the `OnBuildBreak` target.

As mentioned previously, the `OnBuildBreak` target is invoked by MSBuild if an error occurs during the `CoreCompile` target. This target, like many other useful targets, actually does nothing! The purpose of this target is to simply invoke other targets to be executed in the correct order. Refer to the following fragment from the `Microsoft.TeamFoundation.Build.targets` file:

```
<PropertyGroup>
  <OnBuildBreakDependsOn>
    BeforeOnBuildBreak;
    GetChangeSetsOnBuildBreak;
    DropBuild;
    CreateWorkItem;
    AfterOnBuildBreak;
  </OnBuildBreakDependsOn>
</PropertyGroup>

<Target Name="OnBuildBreak"
        Condition=" '$(IsDesktopBuild)'!='true' "
        DependsOnTargets="$(OnBuildBreakDependsOn)" />
```

As you can see, the `OnBuildBreak` target simply dictates which other targets get executed, and in what order, by its `DependsOnTargets` list. Table 5-5 summarizes those targets.

Table 5-5. *Dependent Targets of the* `OnBuildBreak` *Target*

Target Name	Summary
BeforeOnBuildBreak	This is an empty target that is designed to be overridden; it's simply a placeholder.
GetChangeSetsOnBuildBreak	This gets the associated change sets, but obviously the `FixedIn` field will not be modified during a good build.
DropBuild	This places the build files that were generated on the drop location.
CreateWorkItem	This creates a work item for the build error.
AfterOnBuildBreak	This is an empty target designed for overriding.

From these targets, you can override two of them to add custom functionality; those are `BeforeOnBuildBreak` and `AfterOnBuildBreak`. As mentioned, even though this approach will work, a better method is to inject your target by extending the dependency list; in this case, that list is defined by the `OnBuildBreakDependsOn` property. An example of this is as follows:

```
<PropertyGroup>
  <OnBuildBreakDependsOn>
    CustomDoBeforeBuildBreak;
    $(OnBuildBreakDependsOn)
  </OnBuildBreakDependsOn>
</PropertyGroup>
```

```
<Target Name="CustomDoBeforeBuildBreak">
  <!-- Insert your custom error handling here -->
</Target>
```

For this to work, you have to place this declaration in the TFSBuild.proj file *after* the import statement for Microsoft.TeamFoundation.Build.targets. Once again, in the case that the OnBuildBreakDependsOn is overridden many times, this technique is safe because you are always adding to the list instead of overwriting it. For more specific information regarding error handling, refer to the previous chapters, which contained many examples.

Automating Team Build

Since we have already defined what a public build is and you have dedicated resources for this purpose, it only makes sense to automate this process. When you are developing large projects, this is a critical part of the development plan. It is critical that you detect when a public build error has occurred and resolve it before any further damage can be done.

You can use a simple command-line utility to build your team projects. This command-line utility is tfsbuild.exe and is installed on the TFS machine. You can use this command-line utility with the Windows Task Scheduler (or the schtasks command) to run this build on a regular basis. In this section, you will first learn how you can run a build using the command line, and then you will learn how to schedule it.

You can find the tfsbuild.exe file on the TFS machine in the %ProgramFiles%/Microsoft Visual Studio 8/Common7/IDE directory. This utility can perform three major operations: starting a build, deleting completed builds, and stopping a build that is in progress. Here we will discuss only how to start a build. To start a build, you will use the tfsbuild.exe start command. This command has five parameters, as summarized in Table 5-6.

Table 5-6. tfsbuild.exe start *Parameters*

Name	Summary	Required?
TeamFoundationServer	This is the name of the TFS server you want to use for this build.	Yes
TeamProject	Name of the team project to build.	Yes
BuildType	Build type for this build.	Yes
Machine	Machine to use for the build. Only necessary if different from the machine name specified in the build type.	No
Directory	Directory on the build machine where the build is to take place. Only necessary if different from directory specified in the build type.	No

The syntax for the command is as follows:

```
tfsbuild.exe <TeamFoundationServer> <TeamProject> <BuildType> ➥
[/m:<Machine> /d:<Directory>]
```

From this syntax to kick off your Daily Codus build for the Adapdev team project, you would use the following statement:

```
tfsbuild.exe start sayed-ws2003 Adapdev "Daily Codus Build"
```

After executing this, you get the following result:

```
>tfsbuild.exe start sayed-ws2003 Adapdev "Daily Codus Build"
Microsoft (R) TfsBuild Version 8.0.0.0
for Microsoft (R) Visual Studio 2005 Team System
Copyright (C) Microsoft Corporation 2004. All rights reserved.

Build number: Daily Codus Build_20060111.1
    Initializing build
    Getting sources
    Compiling sources
    Compiling Codus.sln for Any CPU/Release
    Compiling Codus.GUI.Extensions.csproj
    Compiling Codus.Templates.Adapdev.csproj
    Compiling Codus.Templates.NHibernate.csproj
    Compiling Codus.GUI.csproj
    Generating list of changesets and updating work items
    Copying binaries to drop location
    Copying log files to drop location
    Successfully Completed
```

From this output you can see the build was successfully completed, and you can see which projects were included in the build process. This output is purposefully brief. To verify that the build did indeed take place and was registered with your TFS, you can examine the Daily Codus build from the Team Explorer. Now we will discuss how to automate this using the Windows Task Scheduler, also known as Scheduled Tasks.

The Windows Task Scheduler allows you to schedule tasks that should execute on a regular basis. To access this utility, you can open it via Start ➤ Programs ➤ System Tools ➤ Scheduled Tasks. This opens the Scheduled Tasks dialog box. Select File ➤ New to create a new scheduled task. This adds a blank task to the scheduled tasks. To edit this task, simply double-click it. You can configure many different properties of how you want the task to be run.

To make this process easier, you can wrap up the command to start the build into a batch file. You simply place the previous statement in a BAT file and place it on the TFS. You can actually place this on other machines, but in this scenario you are actually placing it on the TFS machine. This file is named startCodusBuild.bat. By doing this it is easy to modify the build parameters or to even run other builds. Then you use the command to schedule the script to be run. From the configuration for the scheduled task, give the parameters shown in Figure 5-21.

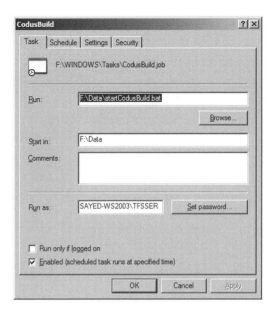

Figure 5-21. *Codus build scheduled task configuration*

Notice here that you specify the user who will run this scheduled task to be the TFS user; in this case, this user is named TFSSERVICE. If you don't know this value, consult with the person who installed TFS on that machine. On the Schedule tab, you specify the time you want to run (2 a.m.) and that you want it to execute each night. Following this, the build will run each night at 2 a.m., and the team will have a fresh build report waiting for them in the morning. For this to work, you must have the Windows Task Scheduler running on the machine that is scheduling this task. You can check the status of this service by running the services.msc MMC snap-in to open the Windows Services utility. From there you can configure the Windows Task Scheduler.

Summary

In this chapter, we introduced many new topics, the most important being Team Build. Team Build is flexible because it is built on top of MSBuild. Also, you can reuse your knowledge of MSBuild to fine-tune your team build process. Covering the new topics that were addressed here in great detail is outside the scope of this chapter, but it certainly has given you a starting point to creating a solid public build on which your team can rely.

If you are working on enterprise applications, then it is essential that scheduled, automated builds are part of your process. By using TFS and Team Build, you are able to do this simply and easily. Not only is it easy to create an automated public build process, but it also integrates with the other components available in Visual Studio. You no longer have to rely on hooking up many different third-party tools to achieve this.

CHAPTER 6

■ ■ ■

Deploying Smart Clients with ClickOnce

Over the course of the past 15 years, technology decision makers (CTOs, architects, and so on) have bypassed thick clients in favor of thin clients. When you look at the benefits of a thin client versus a thick client (Table 6-1), you can see that even though a thick client is more powerful, organizations still choose thin clients because of easy deployment and global reach. That is, because thick clients are more difficult to deploy, companies choose to give up the rich controls, dynamic user interface, local resource access, and so on, for easy deployment.

Table 6-1. *Benefits of a Thick Client vs. a Thin Client*

Feature	Thick Client?	Thin Client?
Rich functionality*	Yes	No
Dynamic user interface	Yes	No
Offline support	Yes	No
Uses desktop resources	Yes	No
Global reach	No	Yes
Easy to deploy	No	Yes

Thick client applications often have controls that offer more functionality than their Web-based counterparts. For example, it's not uncommon to see thick clients with grid controls that support shuffling columns; it is, however, uncommon to see the same functionality in thin clients.

This begs the question: if thick clients are so much better than thin clients, why didn't someone come up with a solution earlier? The truth is, Microsoft has been working toward this solution for, probably, more than ten years. The difficulty with thick clients is that they have to be installed on the user's machine, and this introduces several problems:

- How do you do updates?

- How do manage versions?

- How do you avoid DLL Hell?

To solve all of these issues, Microsoft had to come up with a solution that solved the DLL Hell problem first. The solution is called *side-by-side deployment* and was introduced with Windows XP[1] (we'll talk about side-by-side deployment in the next section). With this in place, Microsoft then introduced Web-based deployment with the initial release of .NET, called no-touch deployment (NTD). NTD unfortunately was well short of a satisfactory solution, as you'll see in the later "No-Touch Deployment" section, but it set the groundwork for a suitable solution—ClickOnce.

In the next sections, we will discuss side-by-side deployment and then touch on the previous deployment methods for Windows Forms applications.

Introducing Side-by-Side Deployment

The purpose of side-by-side deployment is to allow application authors to safely deploy and update applications/assemblies while allowing assemblies to be shared safely. Windows XP does this by supporting two key features: side-by-side assemblies and isolated application installation. Support for side-by-side assemblies allows multiple versions of an assembly to be installed and run at the same time. Support for isolated applications ensures that the installation of one application does not affect an application that is already installed.

The benefits of side-by-side deployment are as follows:

- Applications written, and tested, against a specific assembly are executed against the same assembly.

- You can deploy an application by simply using an xcopy mechanism.

- Installing an application no longer requires a reboot.

Side-by-side deployment relies on components, and applications use metadata to describe themselves rather than the registry (which is what previous versions of Windows recommended). Moreover, shared assemblies go into a well-known folder, %WinDir%\WinSxS, where they are managed by version. Side-by-side deployment exploits the idea of self-containment, as depicted in Figure 6-1.

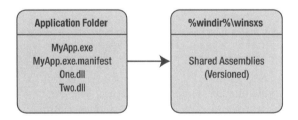

Figure 6-1. *Side-by-side deployment*

The side-by-side deployment concept introduced in Windows XP has also been implemented in the CLR in the .NET Framework. This means with .NET you also use side-by-side deployment and xcopy to deploy .NET applications. Thus, you get all the benefits of side-by-side deployment discussed earlier.

---

1. Side-by-side deployment was actually introduced in Windows 98 but had some shortfalls and was not accepted as a formal solution.

A typical .NET deployment will have an executable, an application configuration file (MyApp.exe.config), a few private assemblies, and zero or more references to shared assemblies.[2] With .NET, shared assemblies go into the GAC, not WinSxS.

Looking at the Previous Approaches of Deploying Windows Forms Applications

We will now cover how people have deployed Windows Forms applications in the past. We'll discuss only two relevant approaches here, even though others exist, simply because the others are either variations or combinations of these two. The two methods we will discuss are MSI deployment and NTD. We'll start with MSI.

MSI Deployment

In the early 90s, Microsoft saw that organizations were building custom solutions to deploy their thick client applications, so it surveyed a score of clients about what problems they faced with deployment and what they would like to see in an installer solution. With that information in hand, Microsoft built and then released MSI in 1999.[3] MSI is an operating system component that uses a well-defined standard to describe a deployment. Table 6-2 outlines the benefits and shortfalls of an MSI solution.

Table 6-2. *Advantages and Disadvantages of Using an MSI Solution*

Advantages	Disadvantages
Can install to the GAC.	Requires that you get the MSI to the client somehow.
Can install Windows services and Component Object Model (COM) components.	Requires administrator privileges.
Can write to the registry.	Users generally have to go through a wizard with many steps.*
Can deploy a database and create Open Database Connectivity (ODBC).	
The MSI can create databases, shortcuts, and so on.	
Allows custom actions to control every step of the deployment.	
Built upon a well-known standard.	
Can create Windows Installer Transforms (MST).	

* Note that you can automate the installation of MSI solutions using tools such as IntelliMirror in Active Directory.

---

2. An assembly has zero or more dependent assemblies, and references to these assemblies are stored as metadata within the assembly. The .NET Framework SDK comes with a tool, ILDASM.exe, that you can use to verify this.

3. Windows Installer became an operating system component starting with Windows 2000.

As you can see, an MSI solution has a lot of advantages and only a few disadvantages. The primary shortfalls with MSI, however, are that you have to get the MSI to your clients for them to install your application and you have to be an administrator to run the installer.

You'll see how ClickOnce does a much better job shortly.

No-Touch Deployment

NTD enables Windows Forms applications to be deployed in a manner similar to how thin clients are deployed; thin clients are deployed by copying the application to a Web server, and then users can access the application via a uniform resource locator (URL). Similarly, smart clients can be deployed by copying the application to a virtual directory on a Web server and then distributing a link that points to the executable. When the user clicks the link, Internet Explorer (IE) downloads the application to the user's machine and then tells a special executable (IEExec.exe) to run the application. The beauty behind NTD is that it does not require application authors to touch the client machine in order to deploy the application, which is where it gets its name, *no-touch* deployment. This is also true for updates; to do an update, you simply copy the new version of the application to the server, and the next time the application is launched, IE checks for a newer version—and *voila*! Figure 6-2 shows NTD.

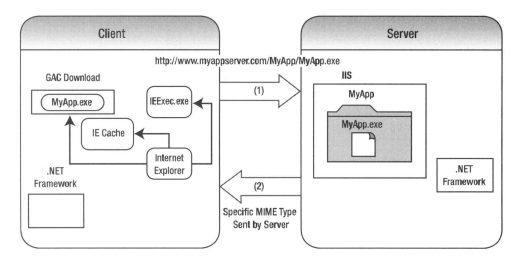

Figure 6-2. *NTD architecture*

Figure 6-2 shows that a client makes a request to a Web server for an executable, and the Web server sends the response with a particular Multipurpose Internet Mail Extensions (MIME) type that IE knows about (IE versions 5.01 and newer). This MIME type indicates to IE that the requested executable is a .NET assembly. When it sees this, IE downloads the application and kicks off IEExec.exe to launch it. Figure 6-2 also shows that the application is potentially downloaded to several places: the GAC[4] download[5] and the browser cache (Temporary Internet Files). Note

---

4. For more information about the GAC, see http://msdn.microsoft.com/library/default.asp?url=/library/en-us/cpguide/html/cpconglobalassemblycache.asp .

5. You can check the contents of the GAC download cache by running the GAC utility with a specific command-line switch (such as GACUTIL /LDL).

also that for NTD to work, the client has to have the .NET Framework installed. Table 6-3 covers the advantages and disadvantages of NTD.

Table 6-3. *Advantages and Disadvantages of No-Touch Deployment*

Advantages	Disadvantages
Easy to deploy.	Requires Internet Explorer greater than 5.0 and doesn't work with non-Microsoft-friendly browsers.
Easy to update.	Application runs in the code access security (CAS) sandbox, so you lose a lot of the advantages of having built a Windows application. For example, the application cannot use the disk, the printer, interoperate with Microsoft Office, and so on.
User does not have to be an administrator to install the application, which is generally the case with thick clients.	The entire application has to be downloaded prior to running the application.
	There is no support for install-time actions. For example, you can't create shortcuts at install time.
	It's virtually impossible to work offline.
	Resembles a Web application because users are clicking a link.
	The client has to have the .NET runtime on their machines prior to downloading the application.

Deploying smart clients with NTD has some drawbacks. Notably, because the application is downloaded from an unknown source, the application is treated as potentially malicious and has to run within the CAS sandbox. This prevents the application from using local resources (such as a printer), so the application is limited in its functionality. Conversely, the application is easy to deploy and update; when the user clicks the link, if a new version of the application is available, it is downloaded, and the new version is launched.

As you can see, NTD is restrictive and best suited for applications that do not require interaction with local resources. This removes a lot of the benefits of building smart clients; however, you do get the responsive user interface with ease of deployment.

Now we'll discuss the updater application block.

The Updater Application Block

The updater application block[6] (UAB) is a flexible and scalable application updater component. It is easy to use and provides the options needed when deploying large-scale distributed applications. For example, for a large application it may be necessary to download large binaries and be able to monitor their download progress. The UAB provides this flexibility while not intruding on smaller applications that need to be easy to use. Figure 6-3 shows a high-level architecture of the UAB.

---

6. You can get the latest version of the updater application block from `http://www.microsoft.com/downloads/details.aspx?FamilyID=C6C09314-E222-4AF2-9395-1E0BD7060786&displaylang=en`.

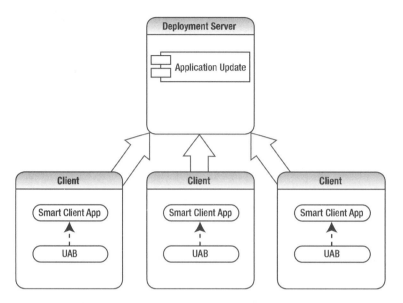

Figure 6-3. *High-level architecture of the UAB*

How the UAB Works

At a high level, the UAB sits on the client machine and is responsible for detecting, downloading, and installing application updates. Similar to ClickOnce, the UAB is driven by a manifest file that contains an application's dependencies (binaries, resources, and so on). When an application is installed on a client's machine, the UAB manifest is also installed along with the UAB. The UAB looks at the manifest file on the local machine and compares it to the manifest on the server to determine whether an update is available. When it detects an update, the UAB can perform one of two tasks:

- Notify the application that an update is available, via an event-based notification system, and subsequently download and install the update.[7]

- Download the update and install it silently; the client will see the new version the next time the application is launched.

Elements of the UAB

The UAB block consists of some key elements. We already mentioned that the UAB is driven by a manifest file. This manifest file defines everything making up the application. For example, most applications have an executable, some dependent assemblies, and likely some resource files (for example, some icons). The UAB has several other key elements. The UAB defines something called a *controller* and a *bootstrapper*. The controller manages the update process. This includes starting and stopping the updater and handling events that are raised during the update process. The UAB defines two types of controllers:

---

7. Note that this feature allows clients to plug into the update process and thus create customized update solutions.

Computerwide controller: The computerwide controller is an external application that is used to manage the update process for one or more smart client applications on a machine. This controller is implemented as a Windows service and driven by a configuration file that defines the applications that are going to be updated.

Application-launcher controller: The application launcher controller ensures that clients run only the latest version of an application and nothing else. This type of controller is useful when you want to force clients to run the latest version of an application.

The controllers mentioned here are external to the application being updated. The UAB also provides a programmatic interface to the UAB and can be used by self-updating applications. Self-updating applications are those applications that manage the updates process but use the UAB facilities to detect, download, and install updates. In this scenario, the UAB provides events when updates are available directly to the application, and the application reacts accordingly. For example, when an update becomes available, the application can notify the user of the update and allow the user to choose to install it.

We also mentioned that the UAB defines a bootstrapper. The bootstrapper is also an external application that is used to launch the application being updated. The bootstrapper serves two purposes:

• After an update, it ensures that the correct version of the application launches.

• It ensures that shortcuts to the application don't break after the installation of an update.

Figure 6-4 shows the relationship between the application, the bootstrapper, and the controller.

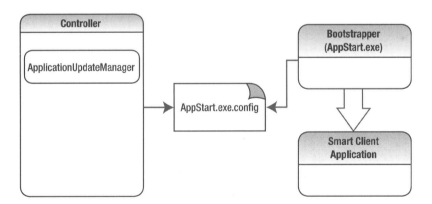

Figure 6-4. *The relationship between the application, the bootstrapper, and the controller*

As shown, the controller contains something called an ApplicationUpdateManager. This manager is the entity that knows how to detect, download, and install updates. When an update is installed, the controller updates the bootstrapper's config file to reflect the new installation. When the user launches the bootstrapper, the bootstrapper looks at the config file to determine which application to launch and then launches the application. For example, assume that version 1.0.0.0 of an application is installed on a client's machine. In this case, the client would have a shortcut that pointed to AppStart.exe, and the AppStart.exe.config file would have a reference to version 1.0.0.0 of the application (see Figure 6-5).

```xml
<?xml version="1.0" encoding="utf-8" ?>
<configuration>
        <configSections>
                <section name="appStart"
                    type="Microsoft.ApplicationBlocks.ApplicationUpdater.A|
        </configSections>

        <appStart>
                <ClientApplicationInfo>

                        <appFolderName>D:\ConsultingEngagements\PAG\Ap|

                        <appExeName>SampleAssembly.exe</appExeName>

                        <installedVersion>1.0.0.0</installedVersion>

                        <lastUpdated>2003-05-04T14:49:18.4483296-05:00·

                </ClientApplicationInfo>
        </appStart>
        |
</configuration>
```

Figure 6-5. *Contents of the* AppState.exe.config *file*

When the user clicks the shortcut, AppStart.exe launches version 1.0.0.0 of the application. After an update is installed, the controller modifies the AppStart.exe.config file to reflect the new version (that is, 2.0.0.0), and AppState.exe will launch the new version the next time the user clicks the shortcut.

The UAB is a great tool; however, it has a few problems that prevent its use at a global level. For example, the tool uses the Binary Intelligent Transfer Service (BITS) to manage updates. This poses a major problem because this service is not guaranteed to be installed on all operating systems that might have a smart client running.[8] As you'll see in the next section, ClickOnce solves this problem by using raw HTTP to distribute updates.

Introducing ClickOnce

ClickOnce is a technology that allows you to easily deploy and update smart client[9] applications. ClickOnce allows easy deployment of smart clients while removing the side effects of the previous methods of deployment. For example, traditionally people used MSI to deploy Windows Forms applications. With an MSI-based deployment, users need administrative privileges to install applications, and updates are difficult; updates usually require users to run another MSI, which then wipes out the older version because you can't have more than one version of the application on your machine. With ClickOnce, applications are usually installed using a Web-based model, updates are configurable, and users don't have to be administrators to install applications. If that's not enough, you can install multiple copies of an application on a machine per user.[10] This is in contrast to MSI, which forces you to uninstall an application before you can install another version.

The ClickOnce technology automates application installation, updates, and version management. It automates installation by supporting several deployment methods that allow users to

---

8. Note that BITS is used by Windows Update; therefore, most systems will have BITS already installed.

9. Technically speaking, you can deploy any Windows Forms or console application using ClickOnce.

10. This feature enables rolling back to a previous version of an application.

download an application to their local machine. It automates updates by allowing application authors to define the update policy for the application and then enforces that on the client. For example, an application author can dictate that an application should check for an update when the application starts and, if available, download and run the new version. Note that you can also roll back installations if necessary. ClickOnce also automates the installation of multiple versions of the same application by installing the application in an isolated "application cache" on the user's machine, which is relative to the user logged in to the machine. This prevents the installation of one application breaking another application, or another version of the same application.

ClickOnce is an end-to-end deployment solution. It not only does a great job of installing, updating, and versioning applications, but it also offers the little features that make an application deployment look professional. For example, after an application deployment with ClickOnce, the application has an icon in the user's Start menu and an entry in the Add/Remove Programs list. Note that nothing is added to the registry or `Program Files` folder since the application is installed on a user-by-user level.

The remainder of this chapter will discuss the fundamentals of ClickOnce. We'll start by discussing the various methods of deployment using ClickOnce.

Introducing the ClickOnce Deployment Methods

To deploy an application with ClickOnce, you first have to publish the application to a Web server, a file server, or some form of removable media (for example, a CD or DVD). Once published, users can download the application to a local machine by clicking a link. Web and file-share deployments are best suited for deployments where users have network connectivity because the application will have to be downloaded over the network to the local machine. The removable media option is best when you know your users will not have a network connection. The default and recommended choice is definitely Web/file server deployment because this makes updating the application a breeze (among other things).

ClickOnce applications are generally downloaded and run from the user's machine. This, however, doesn't have to be the case. ClickOnce offers a deployment option where the application can be downloaded to a temporary location on the user's machine and run from there, rather than being installed. With this option, there are no updates because users need connectivity in order to run the application. You can think of this deployment scenario as similar to how Web pages are downloaded by the browser and cached in temporary folders.

Introducing the ClickOnce Architecture

Figure 6-6 shows the ClickOnce architecture.

ClickOnce is driven by two XML-based manifest files called the *deployment manifest* and the *application manifest*. Ironically, the deployment manifest has an `.application` extension, and the application manifest has a `.manifest` extension. The deployment manifest contains information specific to the deployment of the system as a whole, and the application manifest captures the details specific to a version of the system. For example, if your company has deployed three versions of its system using ClickOnce, then this means you have one deployment manifest and three application manifests, one for each deployed version.

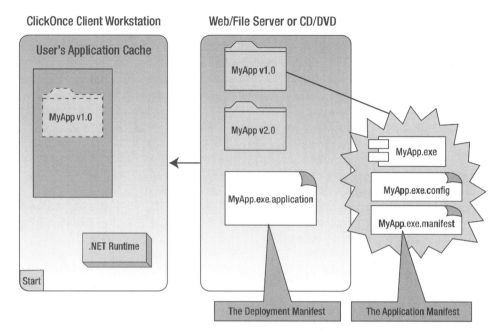

Figure 6-6. *ClickOnce architecture*

The deployment manifest captures information specific to the deployment of the system as a whole. In a deployment scenario, the deployment manifest tells ClickOnce how the application should be deployed and updated. Figure 6-7 shows an example deployment manifest.

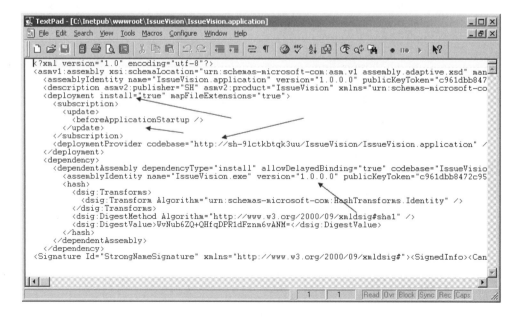

Figure 6-7. *An example of the ClickOnce deployment manifest*

Note that the deployment manifest tells ClickOnce whether to install the system onto the client machine, the current version of the system, and the update policy of the system. Also realize that the deployment manifest has some security settings, which we will talk about in the "Introducing ClickOnce Security" section.

Another important aspect of the ClickOnce architecture, shown in Figure 6-7, is that the .NET runtime is required on the client because ClickOnce is embedded within the runtime.[11] Note that you don't need the runtime on the server side. This goes without saying because you can deploy ClickOnce applications from a removable media source (such as a CD).

Figure 6-8 shows an application manifest.

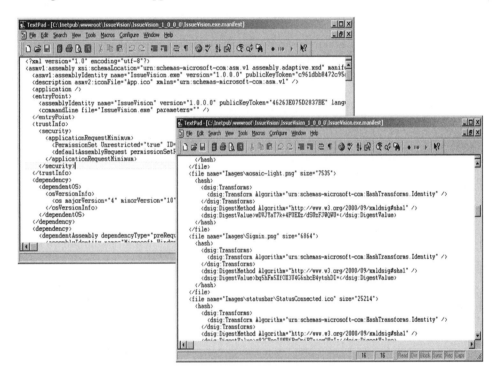

Figure 6-8. *The ClickOnce application manifest*

The application manifest tells ClickOnce everything about a particular version of the system. This information includes the files that make up the system (DLLs, icons, and so on) and the security requirements of that particular version.

We'll delve into all the details of each manifest file in Chapter 7. For now, know that ClickOnce is integrated within Visual Studio 2005, so you won't have to create the files yourself. Moreover, Visual Studio 2005 comes with a tool known as the Manifest Generation and Editing tool, mageui.exe,[12] which you can use to create the deployment and application manifest files, as shown in Figure 6-9. We'll talk about this tool in Chapter 9.

---

11. Note that you can deploy the .NET runtime via an application prerequisite. We'll talk about deploying prerequisites in the next few chapters.

12. This tool comes with the .NET Framework 2.0 SDK. There is also a command-line version of this, mage.exe.

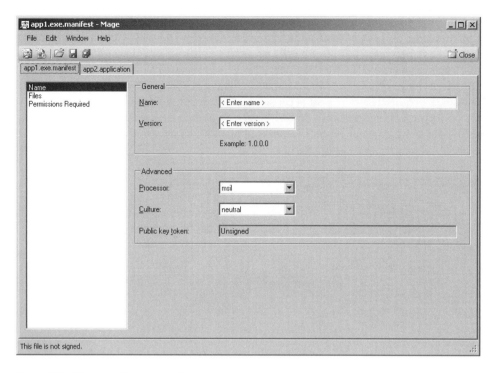

Figure 6-9. *The* mageui.exe *interface*

Seeing ClickOnce in Action

Now we'll walk you through creating and deploying an application with ClickOnce. To create and deploy the application, follow these steps:

1. Launch Visual Studio 2005.

2. Create a new Windows application, and call it **HelloFromClickOnce**.

3. Using the Form Designer, place a label on the form. Set the label's Name property to **label1**; you can do this by selecting the label and then changing the Name property using the Properties window.

4. Create a new class library project, and call it **DependentAssm**.

5. Create a new class in DependentAssm, and call it **SayHelloComp**.

6. Add a public instance method to this class called **SayHello()**, and return the **hello world!** string.

7. From Solution Explorer, right-click the project, and then choose Add Reference. Then, add DependentAssm as a referenced project to HelloFromClickOnce.

8. When you created the project, Visual Studio generated a form named Form1.cs. Open Form1.cs, and add a using statement to make SayHelloAssm visible.

9. In the default constructor of Form1.cs, set the label's Text property to the string returned by the method created in SayHelloComp:

```
label1.Text = new SayHelloComp().SayHello();
```

10. Open the AssemblyInfo.cs file under the Properties node, and set the AssemblyVersion for both projects to **1.0.0.0**, if not already set to this. You can also do this by selecting Project ➤ Properties and clicking the Assembly Information button. Note that this is not the deployment version.

11. Build the application.

At this point, you have a smart client application that has a dependent assembly. To deploy the application using ClickOnce, follow these steps:

1. In Visual Studio 2005, pull down the Project menu, then choose the Publish tab, and finally click the Publish Wizard button. You will see the Publish Wizard, as shown in Figure 6-10.

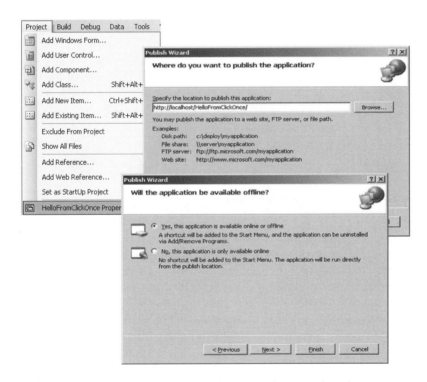

Figure 6-10. *Stepping through the Publish Wizard in Visual Studio 2005*

2. Accept the default location for the deployment. ClickOnce will create a virtual directory at the specified location and will copy the application to the directory. Click Next.

3. Choose the Yes, This Application Is Available Online or Offline option to set the install mode. Click Next.

4. You will now see a dialog box to sign the deployment. Leave the default, click Next, and then click Finish to complete the deployment.

At this point, ClickOnce will publish the application and present you with a Web page in Internet Explorer that looks similar to Figure 6-11.

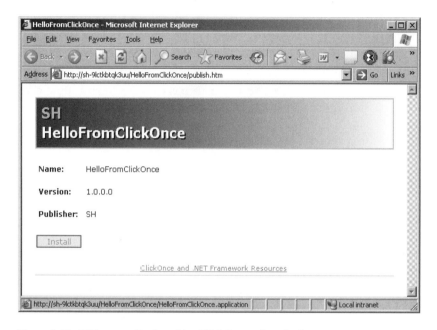

Figure 6-11. *Web page displayed by ClickOnce after deployment*

The Web page shown in Figure 6-11 allows you to install the application to your machine. Note that if you hold the mouse over the Install button, you'll see the target of the button in the status bar, which is the deployment manifest. Click the Install button, and note that you'll see a security warning from ClickOnce because ClickOnce doesn't know the publisher of the application (more about this in Chapter 7).

It is instructive to see what was installed when you published the application. Assuming you have IIS installed locally, browse to c:\Inetpub\wwwroot\. ClickOnce should have created a directory under wwwroot with the name HelloWorldClickOnce, and the contents of the folder should be similar to what is shown in Figure 6-12. Note that ClickOnce created the deployment manifest (HelloFromClickOnce.application) and the application manifest (HelloFromClickOnce.exe.manifest). You can also see that ClickOnce created a setup.exe file, which is a bootstrapper that can be used to ensure all of the prerequisites of your application are installed on a client's machine prior to installing your application. For example, if your application needs to install SQL Server 2005 Express Edition, the bootstrapper can ensure that this component is installed prior to running your installation.

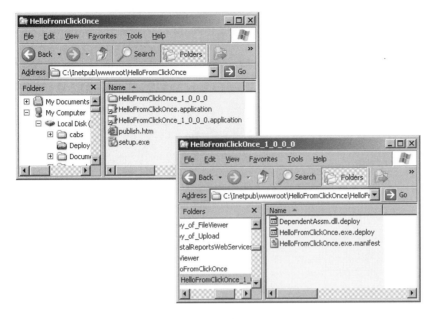

Figure 6-12. *Contents of the published folder*

Updating and Versioning with ClickOnce

Now we'll explain how updates work with ClickOnce. To do that, we'll show how to slightly modify the component assembly and deploy the application again with a new deployment version. Note that the deployment version is not the same as the assembly version; the deployment version is the version you set in the deployment manifest, and the assembly version is the version you set in the `assemblyInfo.cs` file. The deployment version is the version number that ClickOnce is concerned with, and the version number in the `assemblyInfo.cs` file is the assembly's version number. In this case, you will modify the application and create another deployment version. The previous version was set to 1.0.0.0, and you'll kick that up to version 2.0.0.0. Recall that when you deployed the `HelloFromClickOnce` application, you didn't specify any information specific to doing updates. If you take a peek at the deployment manifest, you'll see that Visual Studio 2005 set the update policy to check for updates before start-up (that is, to `beforeApplicationStartup`). Since you have deployed the application once already, we'll show how to modify the sample and publish the new version to the Web server; then you can run the application again to see whether ClickOnce realizes that a new version is available.

To test updating with ClickOnce, modify the `SayHelloComp` class so that the `SayHello()` method returns a different string, and build the solution. Next, modify the version number of the deployment. Recall that when you wrote the initial version of this sample, you didn't set a version number. This means Visual Studio 2005 (VS 2005) by default set the version number to 1.0.0.0. To modify the version number, you have to acquaint yourself with the Project Designer in VS 2005. The Project Designer has three tabs specific to ClickOnce: Signing, Security, and Publish; Figure 6-13 shows the contents of the Publish tab.

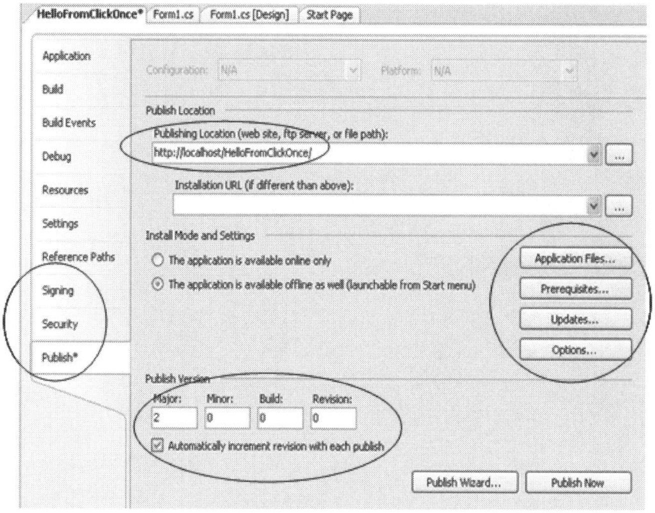

Figure 6-13. *The Publish tab in the Project Designer*

The Publish and Security tabs allow you to customize and manage the contents of the deployment manifest and application manifest. The Signing tab is used for code/manifest signing. We'll talk about this in Chapter 7. Notice that the Publish tab allows you to set the initial deployment location, the publish version, and the install mode of the application. From the Publish tab you can also launch dialog boxes to specify the update policy and the prerequisites to the deployment (for example, client must have Microsoft Data Access Components [MDAC] installed prior to installing your application). You can even customize the language presented to the user during the install and whether the publish.htm file should be shown (see Figure 6-14); recall that after ClickOnce installed the sample application, it launched IE with a Web page that allowed you to install the application.

With that out of the way, increment the publish version number to 2.0.0.0,[13] and then click the Publish Now button in the Publish pane. VS 2005 will build the solution and then publish the application to the Web server. Since you incremented the version number, VS 2005 will create another folder on the Web server with the newer version and will also update the deployment manifest to point to this new version (see Figure 6-15). To see whether the update is detected by ClickOnce, go to the Start menu, and launch the application from the Program Files menu shortcut.[14]

When you launch the application from the Program Files shortcut, ClickOnce detects that there is an update to the application and prompts you to install the latest version. If you click OK, the new version of the application is downloaded and installed to the machine, and then the new version is launched.

We'll get into the details of how ClickOnce does updates in Chapter 7.

---

13. You can have Visual Studio 2005 automatically increment the publish version number each time you publish; all you have to do is select the Automatically Increment Revision with Each Publish checkbox on the Publish tab.

14. The application icon will be placed within a menu group named after the publisher of the application.

Figure 6-14. *The Application Files, Prerequisites, Application Updates, and Publish Options dialog boxes*

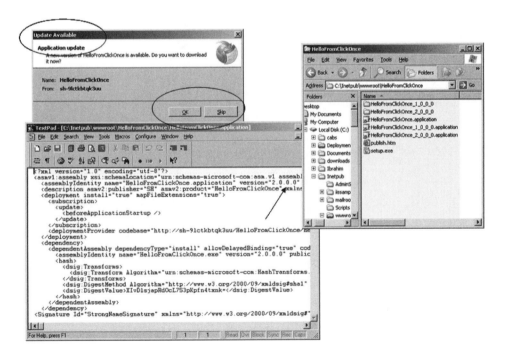

Figure 6-15. *ClickOnce updates*

Introducing ClickOnce Security

When you deployed the sample application, you probably noticed that ClickOnce prompted you with a security dialog box prior to installing the application. By default, ClickOnce-deployed applications run within a CAS sandbox. This prevents the application from performing privileged actions on the client if it's not allowed to. If an application needs additional permissions, you have two approaches for expanding the CAS sandbox or getting the permission your application needs to perform its tasks. The first is to declare the permissions your application needs in the application manifest. VS 2005 helps with this by providing a user interface to customize application security via the Project Designer. With this approach, you identify what permission you need, and when the users install the application, they are presented with a dialog box to allow the application to be installed or not. The second approach is to use a trust license. With this method, the application author obtains a trust license from a trust license issuer by submitting a public key. With the trust license in hand, the application publisher also signs the two manifests and deploys the application. When the client installs the application, ClickOnce compares the digital signatures in the manifest files against the key in the trust license (in the background); if they match, the permissions requested by the application are granted, and the application runs as expected, without prompting the user. We'll cover how you can use trust licenses in Chapter 7.

Figure 6-16 shows the Security tab in the Project Designer for HelloFromClickOnce.

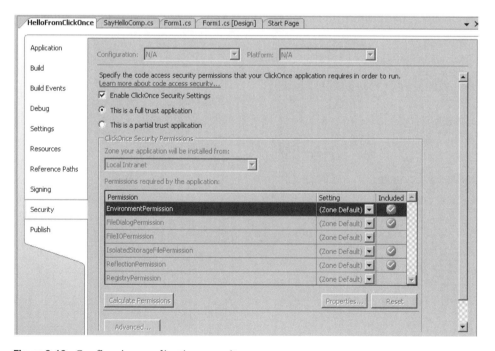

Figure 6-16. *Configuring application security*

By default, ClickOnce-deployed applications are set to have full trust on the client machine. With this in place, the application can do whatever it needs on the client;[15] however, the client is prompted with a dialog box to verify the installation of an untrusted application during the install.

Customizing Deployment with the ClickOnce API

The ClickOnce technology also has a programmatic interface that you can use to customize deployment and updates. For example, if you have a plug-in where the core of the application is deployed initially and then users are allowed to choose optional features (plug-ins) and have them installed on demand, the ClickOnce API can help.

To demonstrate the ClickOnce API, we'll show how to build an application that has an optional feature, called PluginOne, and the user can install this feature via a menu item, as depicted in Figure 6-17.

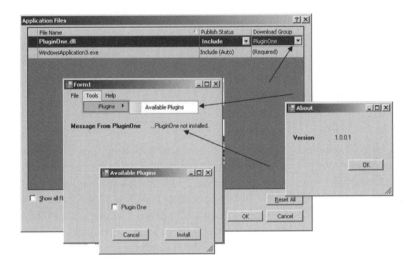

Figure 6-17. *Using the ClickOnce API*

As shown, the application has a simple user interface: a form with two labels, a menu bar, and a few dialog boxes. The menu bar has several menu items. The Tools ➤ Plugins ➤ Available Plugins menu item displays the application's optional plug-in and allows the user to install it on demand. The other interesting menu is the About menu. When this menu item is selected, it displays a dialog box that shows the application's current deployment version number. Note that the main user interface (MainForm) displays a message that says "Message From PluginOne." This label points to a message from PluginOne. When the application starts, it checks to see whether the plug-in has been installed, and if so, it loads a class and gets a message from the plug-in.

---

15. Strictly speaking, the application is limited to the permissions the user has on the machine.

Here's the code that shows how you can use the ClickOnce APIs:

```
public MainForm()
{
    InitializeComponent();
    CheckForPluginOne();
}
private void CheckForPluginOne()
{
    try
    {
    Assembly asm = Assembly.Load("PluginOne");
    if (asm == null)
    {
        throw new Exception("Failed to get reference to PluginOne");
    }
    msgLbl.Text = asm.GetType("PluginOne.Class1").ToString();
    }
    catch (Exception ee)
    {
    msgLbl.Text = "...PluginOne not installed.";
    }
}
```

This scenario has several interesting tidbits. First, the ClickOnce technology defines something known as a *download group* (found via the Publish Wizard ➤ Application Files button). The features of a deployment can be organized into groups, and these groups can be downloaded on demand or set to download initially with the application. Figure 6-17 shows that the application assembly, WindowsApplication3, is in a group by itself, called Required; its publish status is set to Include (Auto). This configuration tells the ClickOnce runtime that this assembly needs to be installed in order to run the application. Second, the application also has a dependent assembly called PluginOne. This assembly has been configured in a separate download group named PluginOne, and this assembly's publish status is set to Include, not to Include (Auto). This tells the ClickOnce runtime not to download the assembly at install time. In Figure 6-17, when the user chooses Tools ➤ Plugins ➤ Available Plugins, then selects PluginOne, and finally clicks Install, the application uses the ClickOnce APIs to download and install the named group PluginOne.

Here's the code that shows how you can download a file group using the ClickOnce APIs:

```
private void availablePluginsToolStripMenuItem_Click(object sender, EventArgs e)
{
    AvailablePluginFrm frm = new AvailablePluginFrm();
```

```
if (frm.ShowDialog() == DialogResult.OK)
{
        If(!ApplicationDeployment.
         CurrentDeployment.IsFileGroupDownloaded("PluginOne"))
        {

ApplicationDeployment.CurrentDeployment.DownloadFileGroup("PluginOne");
    CheckForPluginOne();
        }
    }
}
```

Note that the ClickOnce APIs are packaged in the System.Deployment assembly, and the deployment details of an application are in classes within the System.Deployment.Application namespace. This namespace holds the ApplicationDeployment class shown previously. This class is used to support programmatic updates of an application. This class defines methods to, for example, download groups synchronously and asynchronously. In this example, the ApplicationDeployment class downloads the PluginOne group synchronously. After the download is complete, the application calls the CheckForPluginOne() method to instantiate a class from the downloaded plug-in and to call a method on it to update the label shown on the main form.

Figure 6-17 also shows that the menu bar has a Help ➤ About menu item. When the user clicks the About menu item, the application displays a dialog box that shows the current version of the application. The following code uses the ClickOnce APIs to retrieve the current version of the deployment and sets a label's Text property:

```
ApplicationDeployment ad = ApplicationDeployment.CurrentDeployment;
versionLbl.Text=ad.CurrentVersion.ToString() ;
```

In this example, we show one of the tasks you can perform with the ClickOnce APIs is that you can customize the deployment of your application so that not all of the application's referenced assemblies are downloaded initially. That's just one scenario; with the ClickOnce APIs exposed, you can take over the entire deployment process—from the user interface options to what gets downloaded and what doesn't. Moreover, you can also control what and how updates are done.

Understanding the Bootstrapper

We mentioned earlier that when VS 2005 publishes an application, it can also generate a bootstrapper that can install any prerequisites required by the application. The bootstrapper is an executable (setup.exe) application that is published next to the deployment manifest. The job of the bootstrapper is to check for a list of prerequisites on the client's machine; if any of the prerequisites are missing, then it ensures they are installed prior to running the ClickOnce installation. VS 2005 provides a user interface, via the Project Designer, to configure the bootstrapper with the prerequisites (see Figure 6-18).

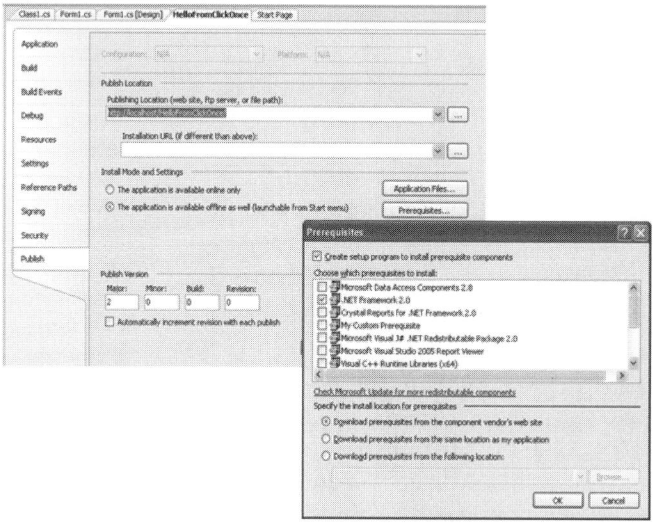

Figure 6-18. *Configuring the bootstrapper with deployment prerequisites*

As shown in Figure 6-18, you can configure the bootstrapper to install one or more of the components from the list or specify a custom component at a specific location. To configure the bootstrapper to install a custom component, select the Download Prerequisites from the Following Location radio button, and then click the Browse button. This opens a dialog box that allows you to choose a location from the local file system, a local Web server, an FTP site, or a remote Web site (see Figure 6-19).

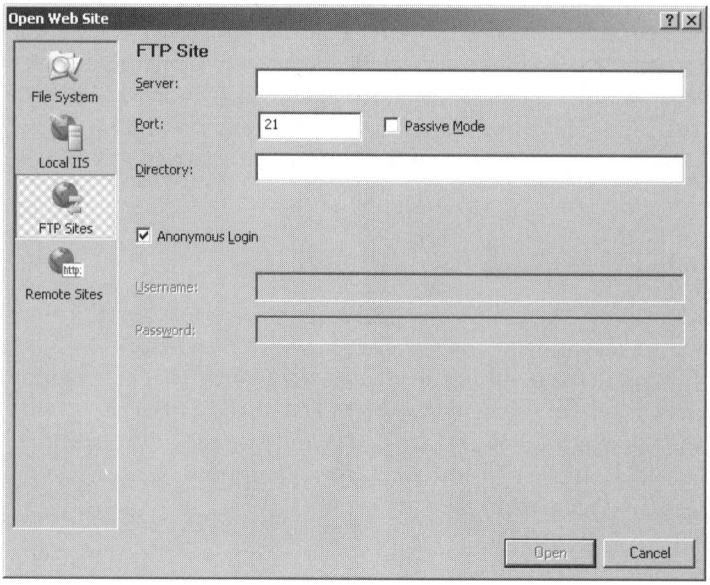

Figure 6-19. *Configuring the bootstrapper to download a custom component from a specific location*

As mentioned, the bootstrapper is an executable, and this executable has to run prior to running the deployment manifest. There is not a process that kicks off the bootstrapper first, so to run the bootstrapper, you distribute a link to the `publish.htm` page, which provides a link to run `setup.exe`. After installing the prerequisites, the bootstrapper will take care of launching the deployment manifest. The bootstrapper is not a managed executable that can be launched from Internet Explorer like with NTD applications. Instead, the bootstrapper has to be downloaded and launched manually. The good news is that the bootstrapper is a small application and will take only a few seconds to download (even over a dial-up connection). Once the bootstrapper is downloaded, the user can run the application to install the entire product.

Summary

The focus of this chapter was ClickOnce, which is a technology that ships with the .NET Framework 2.0 and is used to autodeploy and update Windows Forms and console applications. ClickOnce supports three sources for where a ClickOnce application can be deployed. They include a Web server, a file server, and some form of removable media (such as a CD).

ClickOnce is a major improvement over the previous approaches to deploying rich client applications. ClickOnce has a rich and configurable deploy, update, and security policy. Moreover, you can use the ClickOnce APIs to customize your deployment solutions.

This chapter was a tour of ClickOnce. In the next chapter, we will go into great detail about the concepts discussed here. Furthermore, we'll identify what ClickOnce can't do and how to work around that.

CHAPTER 7

■■■

ClickOnce Updates, Security, and the Bootstrapper

In Chapter 6, we gave you a tour of ClickOnce. We deployed a simple application and showed how to update it. We also discussed the ClickOnce APIs and touched on security. In this chapter, we will start to discuss the details of deploying with ClickOnce.

We will dive a bit deeper into ClickOnce by showing how you can configure an application for automatic updates. You can take several approaches for updating an application, and we'll cover each approach in this chapter.

We will also talk about security issues regarding ClickOnce applications. You saw with the sample application in the previous chapter that a user is prompted with a security dialog box during installation if the application author is unknown. We'll talk about how to overcome this security prompt by looking at trusted publishers. We'll also talk about partially trusted applications in this chapter.

In addition, we'll cover how you can deploy prerequisites with ClickOnce. For example, if your application depends on a Windows service, then you'll learn how you can ensure that the prerequisite is installed on the target machine and if not installed, how you can install it to ensure your application runs correctly.

You'll see all this in this chapter. We'll start the discussion, however, by looking at the ClickOnce deployment and application manifest files.

Understanding the ClickOnce Manifest Files

The ClickOnce deployment manifest describes everything about the overall deployment of a system (see Figure 7-1).

```
<?xml version="1.0" encoding="utf-8"?>
<asmv1:assembly xsi:schemaLocation="urn:schemas-microsoft-com:asm.v1 assembly.adaptive.xsd" manifestVersion
  <assemblyIdentity name="HelloFromClickOnce.application" version="2.0.0.0" publicKeyToken="2c1b3ed028dafcd
  <description asmv2:publisher="SH" asmv2:product="HelloFromClickOnce" xmlns="urn:schemas-microsoft-com:asm
  <deployment install="true" mapFileExtensions="true">
    <subscription>
      <update>
        <beforeApplicationStartup />
      </update>
    </subscription>
  </deployment>
    <deploymentProvider codebase="http://sh-91ctkbtqk3uu/HelloFromClickOnce/HelloFromClickOnce.application"
  </deployment>
  <dependency>
    <dependentAssembly dependencyType="install" allowDelayedBinding="true" codebase="HelloFromClickOnce_2_0_
      <assemblyIdentity name="HelloFromClickOnce.exe" version="2.0.0.0" publicKeyToken="2c1b3ed028dafcd4" la
      <hash>
        <dsig:Transforms>
          <dsig:Transform Algorithm="urn:schemas-microsoft-com:HashTransforms.Identity" />
        </dsig:Transforms>
        <dsig:DigestMethod Algorithm="http://www.w3.org/2000/09/xmldsig#sha1" />
        <dsig:DigestValue>XIvDlsjapRdOcL7S3pKpfn4txnk=</dsig:DigestValue>
      </hash>
    </dependentAssembly>
  </dependency>
<Signature Id="StrongNameSignature" xmlns="http://www.w3.org/2000/09/xmldsig#"><SignedInfo><Canonicalizatior
```

Figure 7-1. *A ClickOnce deployment manifest*

The deployment manifest shown in Figure 7-1 has five higher-level tags within the root `assembly` element. The `assembly` element is required and has the required attribute `manifestVersion`. Since `assembly` is the root element, you also see the deployment manifest schema[1] attached to this tag. Within the `assembly` element, you have `assemblyIdentity`, `description`, `deployment`, `dependency`, and `Signature`.

The `assemblyIdentity` element determines the application being deployed. This tag has five required attributes and no child elements. The `name` attribute is the name for the application being deployed. In this case, the deployment manifest was generated with Visual Studio 2005, and it generated a default value for this tag. The `version` attribute determines the current deployment version of the application. The `publicKeyToken` is used for signing the deployment manifest, and the `processorArchitecture` attribute determines the application's processor architecture (valid values for this tag include `msil`, `x86`, `IA64`, and `amd64`). Note also that this tag contains an optional `language` attribute that determines the language that ClickOnce presents to the user while doing the deployment. Note that this is not the application's preferred language. The value `neutral` tells ClickOnce to refer to the client's machine settings to determine what language to use. Finally, the `assemblyIdentity` element has a required `type` attribute. This attribute has to have the value `win32` and is used for compatibility with side-by-side deployment.

The `description` element describes the application. The information in this tag is used when the application is deployed in install mode (we'll talk about install mode in the "Offline vs. Online Applications" section).

The `deployment` element determines the mode of deployment and identifies the update policy for the application. ClickOnce applications can be deployed in one of two modes: offline or online. Offline mode–deployed applications can run without a network connection, while online deployments can't. Applications that are deployed in online mode require that their users always run the application by pointing to the deployment manifest; that is, users will always go to a Web page and click a link that points to the deployment manifest. Additionally, online mode requires that the client have a network connection when launching the application.

---

1. You can see the entire schema at `http://msdn2.microsoft.com/en-us/library/k26e96zf.aspx`.

Online applications are downloaded (to the ClickOnce cache) every time the application is launched. After the application is downloaded, however, there is no need for a network connection, unless the application requires it (for example, to get data). Offline applications are installed locally and executed via a shortcut from the Start menu. Moreover, this mode of deployment does not require a network connection because the application, along with the deployment manifest, is cached locally on the client machine. Offline-mode applications also get versioned on the client and are available through Add/Remove Programs, just like traditional thick clients. Finally, offline applications can have various update policies (for example, checking for updates at start-up) and are installed on a per-user basis (that is, do not require an administrator). Note that the `deployment` element also has an optional attribute named `minimumRequiredVersion` that can control the earliest version that can be run by clients. For example, you could use this tag to ensure that all clients run version 1.2.7.5 of the application and nothing older.

The `subscription` element within the `deployment` element is an optional element that determines when to check for updates for the application. If the tag is not defined in the deployment manifest, then ClickOnce does not check for updates for the application. Note also that if the application is deployed in online mode, then ClickOnce will ignore this tag because the application will always run the latest version of the application from its deployed location (for example, the Web server). When the `subscription` element is defined and the application is deployed in offline mode, then ClickOnce can be configured to check for updates, either on application start-up or on an interval after start-up, by using the required `update` element. The `update` element has two optional elements: `beforeApplicationStartup` and `expiration`. To check for updates at start-up, the `beforeApplicationStartup` element has to be defined within the `update` tag. Alternatively, you can use the `expiration` element to construct a finer-grained update-check policy. For example, you can configure update checks to happen on an hourly, daily, or weekly basis. Note that when using the `expiration` update policy, ClickOnce checks for updates in the background while the application runs. When an update becomes available, the user sees a dialog box to install the newest version the next time the application is launched, not immediately.

The `deploymentProvider` element defines where the deployment manifest lives and where updates come from. This may seem like overkill because the user first clicks a link to get to the application manifest, and now the manifest has a link to itself. This turns out to be useful in situations where the application is deployed outside ClickOnce but uses the update facility provided by ClickOnce. For example, large applications can be distributed with a DVD and can still be updated via ClickOnce by using `deploymentProvider`.

The `dependency` element determines the specifics of the application to install (for example, the version and actual assemblies). Note that this tag actually points to the application manifest (via the `codebase` attribute). An application manifest file is how ClickOnce enables application authors to deploy and manage versions of an application on the client and the server. Application manifest files are also XML files that end with the `.manifest` extension and contain everything required by the application for a particular version. Figure 7-2 shows a sample application manifest file.

```
<?xml version="1.0" encoding="utf-8"?>
<asmv1:assembly xsi:schemaLocation="urn:schemas-microsoft-com:asm.v1 assembly.adap
  <asmv1:assemblyIdentity name="ClickOnceSample.exe" version="1.0.0.0" publicKeyTo
  <entryPoint>
    <assemblyIdentity name="ClickOnceSample" version="1.0.1906.22742" language="ne
    <commandLine file="ClickOnceSample.exe" parameters="" />
  </entryPoint>
  <trustInfo>
    <security>
      <applicationRequestMinimum>
        <PermissionSet Unrestricted="true" ID="Custom" />
        <defaultAssemblyRequest permissionSetReference="Custom" />
      </applicationRequestMinimum>
    </security>
  </trustInfo>
  <dependency>
    <dependentAssembly codebase="ClickOnceSample.exe" size="16384">
      <assemblyIdentity name="ClickOnceSample" version="1.0.1906.22742" language="
      <hash>
        <dsig:Transforms>
          <dsig:Transform Algorithm="urn:schemas-microsoft-com:HashTransforms.Iden
        </dsig:Transforms>
        <dsig:DigestMethod Algorithm="http://www.w3.org/2000/09/xmldsig#sha1" />
        <dsig:DigestValue>GjRUUCXOLrCfva9nX5igSv9WGxw=</dsig:DigestValue>
      </hash>
    </dependentAssembly>
  </dependency>
  <dependency>
    <dependentAssembly codebase="ComponentsLib.dll" size="16384">
      <assemblyIdentity name="ComponentsLib" version="1.0.1906.22657" language="ne
      <hash>
        <dsig:Transforms>
          <dsig:Transform Algorithm="urn:schemas-microsoft-com:HashTransforms.Iden
        </dsig:Transforms>
        <dsig:DigestMethod Algorithm="http://www.w3.org/2000/09/xmldsig#sha1" />
        <dsig:DigestValue>M1xx7D5ZulxwZPFiw8L+2VfaLrE=</dsig:DigestValue>
      </hash>
    </dependentAssembly>
  </dependency>
```

Figure 7-2. *A sample application manifest file*

Every version of an application has an associated application manifest file. This manifest file defines the version number of the application, the security requirements of the application, the dependent assemblies of the application, and so on. In other words, it tells ClickOnce everything it needs to download and run the application on a client's machine. As shown in Figure 7-2, the entryPoint element defines the executable that holds the entry point method (that is, the Main() method), and an entry exists for every dependent assembly that needs to be downloaded to run the application. Moreover, the trustInfo tag defines all the permissions necessary to run the application, from a CAS standpoint.

The Signature element defines a public/private key signature for the deployment. Deployment manifests and application manifests both have to be signed with the same signature to tell the ClickOnce runtime that the same organization that published the application is the same publisher doing updates to the application. If the signatures in the two manifest files don't match, ClickOnce will not allow updates.

Offline vs. Online Applications

ClickOnce applications have to be deployed to a Web server, to a file server, and/or to removable media (such as a CD/DVD). Moreover, you can deploy these applications in one of two modes: offline or online. *Offline applications* are meant to function without a network connection. *Online applications* behave more like Web applications and require network connectivity.

When you deploy an application using Visual Studio 2005, you configure the deployment mode of the application when you run the Publish Wizard (see Figure 7-3).

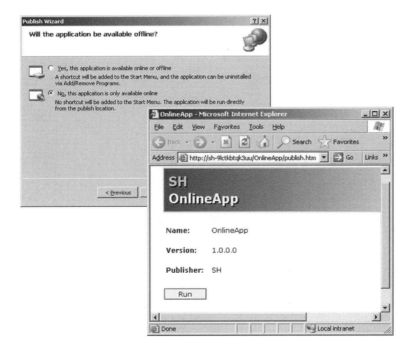

Figure 7-3. *Online deployment mode*

Note that after deployment, the publish.htm page shows a Run button rather than an Install button, which you saw when you deployed the sample offline application in Chapter 6.

Also note that online applications have the install attribute's value set to false to indicate that the application should not be installed locally on the client. That is, it should not have a shortcut under the Start menu or an entry in Add/Remove Programs. For example:

```
<deployment install="false" mapFileExtensions="true" />
```

Moreover, online applications don't have a deploymentProvider element. Recall that this tag is useful for cases when you install a very large application using a CD/DVD and then use the deploymentProvider element to dictate where updates should come from. Since online applications don't have versioned updates, you do not need this tag.

Online applications don't get installed like offline applications. However, to run the application, the current version of the application is downloaded when you click the Run button and is placed into the ClickOnce cache. ClickOnce creates an application cache on a user-by-user basis for each application version (see Figure 7-4) and thus does not require administrative permissions.

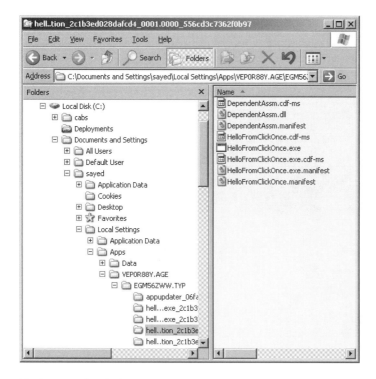

Figure 7-4. *The ClickOnce application cache*

Note that the ClickOnce application cache is located at %userprofile%\Local Settings\ Apps\.

In Figure 7-4, you can see that there are a host of applications for user sayed. Furthermore, note that the contents of the cache shown in the right pane are for the HelloFromClickOnce application discussed in Chapter 6. The contents of the cache has .exe, .dll, .manifest, and .cdf-ms files. It turns out that the .cdf-ms files are precompiled versions of the manifest files and are used for performance reasons.

We'll talk more about the ClickOnce cache throughout the discussion of ClickOnce in this book.

Performing ClickOnce Updates

ClickOnce offers automatic update support for online and offline applications. Online applications are updated when they are accessed, and users don't have a choice of running an older version; the latest version is downloaded and executed. With offline applications, however, you have a lot of choices.

Configuring Update Notification

For starters, when a newer version of an application becomes available, ClickOnce notifies users when the update check is executed (for example, beforeApplicationStartup). Users then have a choice whether to download and run the newer version or stay with the older version (see Figure 7-5).

Figure 7-5. *Update detection in ClickOnce*

   To get the latest version, users have to click OK in the Update Available dialog box. If they click Skip, the ClickOnce runtime will not show them the Update Available dialog box again for one week. Note that this value is not configurable.[2] Also, if the user doesn't click OK or Skip and instead closes the dialog box, ClickOnce runs the older version but then prompts the user of an update the next time the application icon is executed from the Start menu.

Configuring Application Update Policy

You can configure the update policy of an application by clicking the Update button on the Publish tab (accessed from the Project Designer, which is also referred to as the Project Properties page). To see this, create a new Windows application and then select the project in Solution Explorer. Then, pull down the Project menu and choose the Properties menu item. From the Project Designer, click the Publish tab, and then click the Updates button. You should see the dialog box shown in Figure 7-6.

---

2. ClickOnce does provide an API, however, that you can use to customize the installation and update of your applications. We'll talk about this later.

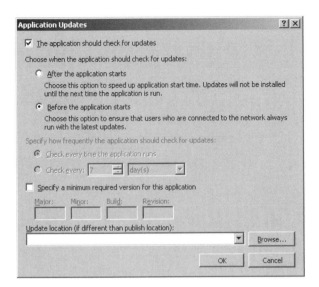

Figure 7-6. *Application Updates dialog box*

As shown, you can set an application to not be updated at all. If an update is configured, the default is to check for an update prior to application start-up. You can also opt to check for updates after the application starts. In this case, you can configure how often the update check should run. For example, you can configure the check to run every time the application runs or on an hourly, daily, or weekly basis. Note that with this option, users are notified that an update is available the next time they run the application.

Note also that you can specify a minimum required version for an application. For example, if you deploy version 1.0.0.0 and you discover a major security bug in your application, you can fix the bug, issue a new version (say 1.1.0.0), and via this option ensure that your users are not running the older version. Note that when ClickOnce detects a required update, ClickOnce disables the older version and automatically downloads, and then runs, the new version (see Figure 7-7).

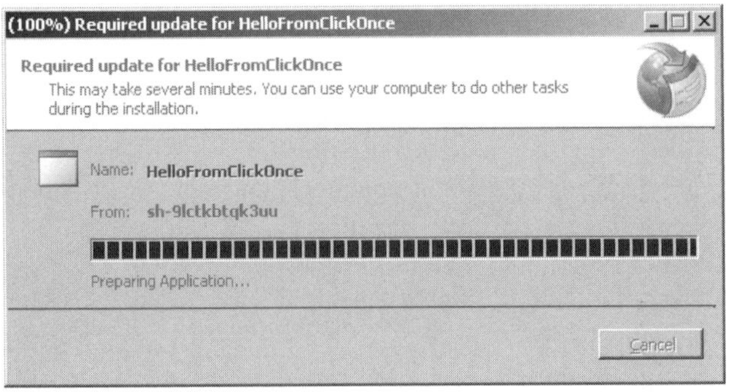

Figure 7-7. *Automatic detection and download of a minimum required version*

Application authors can also either modify the deployment manifest of the application manually or use the Manifest Generation and Editing tool to configure updates for an application. Note that you can open the manifest generated by Visual Studio in the Manifest Generation and Editing tool as well. In fact, administrators can configure the application using this tool after the application has been deployed by using Visual Studio or some other deployment tool. Again, note that the Manifest Generation and Editing tool, and its UI counterpart, comes with the .NET Framework 2.0 SDK.

The update policy of an application is captured in the `deployment` element in the deployment manifest:

```
<deployment install="true" mapFileExtensions="true"
minimumRequiredVersion="1.1.0.0">
    <subscription>
      <update>
        <expiration maximumAge="2" unit="weeks" />
      </update>
    </subscription>
    <deploymentProvider codebase=
"http://sh-9lctkbtqk3uu/HelloFromClickOnce/HelloFromClickOnce.application" />
  </deployment>
```

You should give an application's update configuration some thought. If an application already performs costly operations and is taking considerable time to start, it may not make sense to add to that time by running update checks at start-up. For applications that require finer-grained control over doing updates, application authors can use the ClickOnce APIs to customize installation and updates. We'll talk about the ClickOnce APIs more in this chapter and the next.

Understanding ClickOnce Security

One of the major problems with NTD was that the application was downloaded from the Web and as a result was placed in a very tight security sandbox. It was so tight that the deployment approach was virtually useless for real-world business applications. When Microsoft set out to build ClickOnce, one of the major concerns was a practical solution to addressing security within an application.

By default, applications deployed with ClickOnce are configured with Full Trust permissions. You can verify this by looking at the Project Properties ➤ Security tab, as shown in Figure 7-8. Note that the Enable ClickOnce Security Settings box is checked, along with the This Is a Full Trust Application radio button. Note that if these buttons are not checked, you have not yet published the application; in other words, publishing the application applies these default settings.

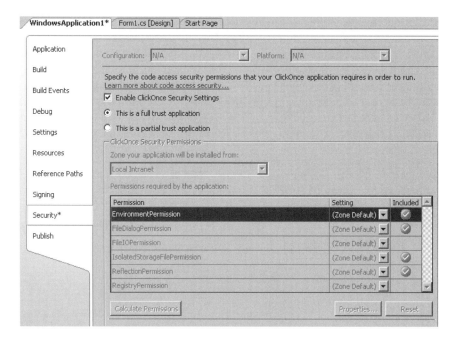

Figure 7-8. *ClickOnce Security tab in Visual Studio 2005*

Even though the application has full rights, it comes at the cost of either providing a trusted publisher certificate from a known certificate authority or requiring your users to click through unfriendly security warnings. The idea behind ClickOnce, however, is to not have users make (possibly wrong) security decisions and to install an application only. You can do this in several ways, and we'll cover how to use a trusted publisher next.

Using Trusted Publishers in ClickOnce

ClickOnce applications use security certificates to identify the identity of an application author (publisher) to the user installing the application. Figure 7-9 depicts the philosophy behind security certificates.

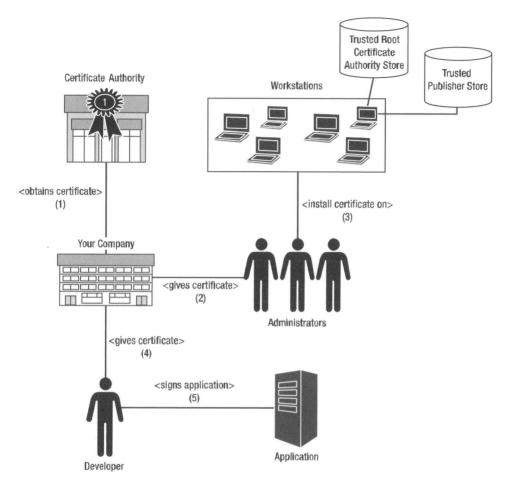

Figure 7-9. *How trusted publishers work*

As shown, a company obtains a certificate from a certificate issuing authority (such as VeriSign) by submitting details about the company. The certificate is then handed off to the company's system administrators to install it on the enterprise workstations. Installation here means placing a copy of the certificate in the Trusted Root Certificate Authority certificate store[3] and the Trusted Publisher certificate store because the certificate authority's identity needs to be stored as well as the publisher who will be publishing applications (the company). Next, the company gives a copy of the certificate to the developer, who signs the applications with the same certificate. When the developer publishes the application, the ClickOnce runtime looks at the certificate attached to the application and sees whether the certificate authority is in the Trusted Root Certificate Authority certificate store and then sees whether the publisher is trusted by looking in the Trusted Publisher certificate store. If all of these checks pass, the user is not prompted, and the application is installed and executed without intervention. We'll now show an example of this in action.

---

3. You can see the installed certificates by selecting Start ➤ Run and executing `certmgr.msc`.

Seeing a Trusted Publisher in Action

To see the trusted publishing side of ClickOnce, create a simple Windows application using Visual Studio 2005. Next, open the Signing tab under the Project Designer (see Figure 7-10).

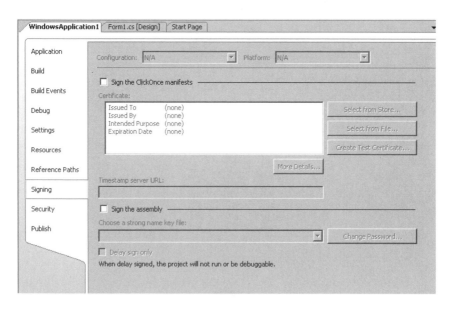

Figure 7-10. *The Signing tab in Visual Studio 2005*

If you have not yet published the application, then by default the Sign the ClickOnce Manifests box is unchecked. If you publish the application and then return to the Signing tab, you'll see the application was signed with an autogenerated certificate during the publishing process. Instead of publishing the application, click Create Test Certificate. Visual Studio displays a password dialog box for you to associate a password with the certificate (see Figure 7-11). Note that the password is optional, so you can just hit OK if you like. However, for real-world applications, your certificates need to have a password associated with them; otherwise, you run the risk of someone getting your certificate and using it to publish applications with your identity. After you create the test certificate, Visual Studio will automatically assign a name to the certificate and place it in your project. Referring to Figure 7-9, you have executed only the first step in that you have obtained a certificate. Now you have to put the certificate in the Trusted Root Certificate Authority certificate store and also identify yourself as a trusted publisher by putting the same certificate in the Trusted Publisher certificate store. To do that, click the More Details button on the Signing tab. Visual Studio displays the Certificate dialog box, which allows you to install the certificate in the two stores. Click the Install Certificate button to be presented with the Certificate Import Wizard. The wizard displays a nice welcome page. The next screen displays two radio buttons; select the Place All Certificates in the Following Stores option, and then click the Browse button. Visual Studio then displays the Select Certificate Store dialog box with a list of certificate stores. First add the certificate to the Trusted Root Certificate Authorities store, and then click OK. The Install Certificate button allows you to install to only a single store at a time, so click More Details again to install the certificate to the Trusted Publisher store (using the same approach).

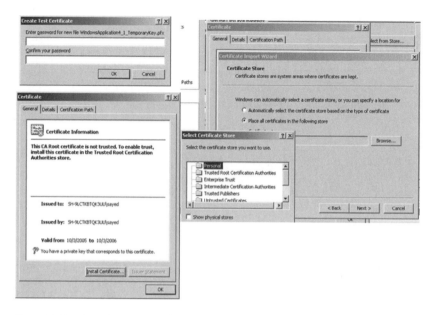

Figure 7-11. *Creating and configuring a trusted publisher*

After installing the certificates in both stores, build the solution, and then publish the application to your local Web server. When the `publish.htm` file opens, click Install to verify that you are not prompted with a security dialog box.

We mentioned earlier that the default trust setting for ClickOnce applications is full trust. Figure 7-8 shows that an application can specify exactly what permissions it needs (partial trust). In the sections that follow, we will discuss partial trust applications. To do that, we'll first provide a quick overview of CAS, which is at the heart of partial trusted assemblies.

Introducing Code Access Security (CAS)

The Windows security model we have used over the years was introduced at a time when computers, software, and users were very different than they are today. For example, then we were building stand-alone applications for an operating system that assumed only one user would be interacting with the machine at a time. Today it's a totally different scenario—software is built for integration and is constructed from components with potentially many users simultaneously interacting with the machine. The security model applied to stand-alone applications of the past is not granular enough to support a component-based development model. The user-based security model gives users permissions, not code. Code gets different permissions depending on the security privileges of the user running the application. This solution is built on an "all-or-nothing" philosophy. With a component-based model, where components are built in-house, purchased and linked in, and possibly downloaded from third-party vendors, you need a more granular security model.

CAS is a component-based security model with the philosophy that if an application uses two assemblies and one of the assemblies is loaded from the application directory and the other is loaded from the Internet, then these two assemblies should be given different security privileges. This is different from the user-based security model of the past. The user-based model said that if two DLLs are loaded into an executable, it doesn't matter where they were loaded from because all that matters is the user running the application. With the addition of CAS, we have the best of both worlds; code can't do something if the user running the code can't, and vice versa.

With that said, the CAS nomenclature is critical to understanding the fundamentals of CAS. In fact, if you have a clear understanding of the terms used with CAS, you'll have a foundational understanding of CAS. Table 7-1 defines the CAS nomenclature.

Table 7-1. *CAS Nomenclature*

Term	Definition
Permission	The authority to do something. For example, this is the authority to read a file, make a network connection, or read the registry. .NET defines 19 permission types (see Figure 7-12).
Permission set	A grouping of arbitrary permissions. .NET defines seven permission sets out of the box (again, see Figure 7-12).
Evidence	Permissions are granted based on evidence. Two types of evidence exist: origin based and content based. With origin-based evidence, where your code comes from determines what permissions your code gets. With content-based evidence, your code content is signed and has a publisher certificate, and that determines what permissions you get.
Code group	Associates evidence with a permission set.
Security policy	Policies define a hierarchy of code groups.

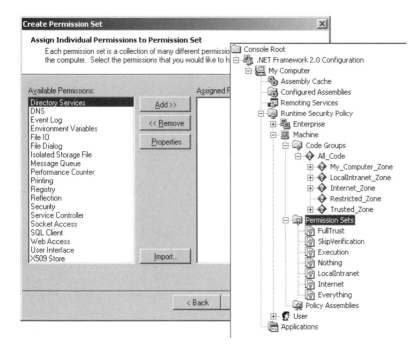

Figure 7-12. *The .NET-defined permissions and permission sets*

With each permission, you have the ability to do something. A permission set contains zero or more permissions and gives you the ability to group permissions. You use evidence to grant permissions. Code groups connect a permission set to evidence, and a security policy is a grouping of code groups. Security policies enable you to create customized levels of security (for example, enterprise, machine, and so on).

CAS is fairly complex, but from a ClickOnce perspective you need to keep several important aspects in mind. First, for an assembly to execute, it must show the appropriate evidence to the CAS security manager. An assembly can do this implicitly or explicitly. Implicit evidence is called *origin-based evidence*, and explicit evidence is *content-based evidence*. Origin-based evidence uses the origin of your assembly to determine what permissions your code gets. For example, if your assembly is downloaded from the Internet versus an intranet, then your assembly will have varying permissions. Content-based evidence is evidence with the assembly (signed with a publisher certificate) that determines the permissions given to the assembly. Another aspect of CAS that is important to ClickOnce is the idea that an application should define, and be granted, only those permissions the author deems necessary to run the application. This is the principle of "run with least privilege."

Thus far, we've talked about full trust applications. You can also configure and deploy a partial trust application with ClickOnce and Visual Studio 2005. In the next section, we'll show how this works, and then we'll return to the idea of full trust versus partial trust later in this chapter.

Introducing Partially Trusted Applications with ClickOnce

As mentioned, the default setting for a ClickOnce application is to run as a full trust application. Generally, it is recommended that you configure the application with the permissions required by the application. This is known as a partially trusted application, and Visual Studio 2005 provides the user interface for you to configure your application with specific permissions (see Figure 7-13).

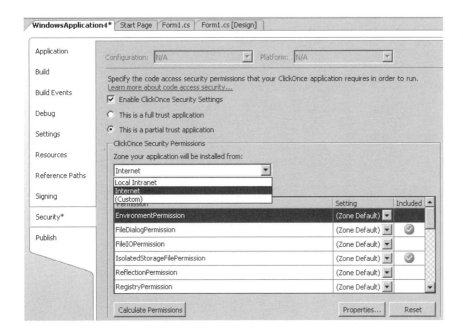

Figure 7-13. *Configuring a partial trust application in Visual Studio 2005*

You configure a partial trust application by selecting the This Is a Partial Trust Application radio button on the Security tab of the Project Designer. By default, there are two defined zones with preconfigured permissions. You can, however, define a new zone if you want by selecting Custom from the drop-down list. Applications that are deployed from the local intranet zone will have more security privileges than those deployed from the Internet zone. When you select a zone from the drop-down list, the included permissions for that zone display a green check mark to the right of the permission grid. Table 7-2 shows the predefined permissions for the local intranet and Internet zones.

Table 7-2. *Available Permissions in the Local Intranet and Internet Zones*

Permission	Description	Local Intranet?	Internet?
EnvironmentPermission	Allows access to environment variables.	Yes	
FileDialogPermission	Allows access to the Open dialog box, Save dialog box, and Open and Save dialog boxes.	Yes	Yes
FileIOPermission	Allows read and write access to files and directories.		
IsolatedStorageFilePermission	Grants isolated storage manipulation. Isolated storage is an application-specific storage area on the file system.	Yes	Yes
ReflectionPermission	Allows reflection on other assemblies.	Yes	
RegistryPermission	Grants access to the Windows registry.		
SecurityPermission	Grants security permissions. For example, this is the ability to skip security verification if you are writing unsafe code.	Yes	Yes
UIPermission	Grants windowing and Clipboard access.	Yes	Yes
KeyContainerPermission	Grants access to key containers. A key container is a place to store public/private keys.		
WebBrowserPermission	Grants access to a Web browser.	Yes	Yes
PrintingPermission	Allows various printing options.	Yes	Yes
DnsPermission	Grants yes- or no-level access to do Domain Name Service (DNS) lookup.	Yes	
SocketPermission	Grants access to manipulate sockets.		

Permission	Description	Local Intranet?	Internet?
WebPermission	Allows access to specific, or all, Web sites.		
EventLogPermission	Grants access to the event log.		
PerformanceCounterPermission	Allows access to performance counters.		
OleDbPermission	Grants access to do OLEDB.		
SqlClientPermission	Allows ADO.NET access to Microsoft SQL Server.		
DataProtectionPermission	Allows access to encrypted data and memory.		
StorePermission	Allows access to stores that contains X.509 certificates.		

The Security tab shown in Figure 7-13 contains a Calculate Permissions button and a Properties button. You can click the Calculate Permissions button to do a static analysis of the security permissions required by the application. *Static analysis* here simply means the permission calculator can determine only those permissions that can be deduced by looking at the references used within the application. If, for example, you load assemblies at runtime without having specific references to these assemblies at compile time, then the security analyzer will not be able to determine the exact set of permissions required by the application. Keep this in mind when you use this feature.

As you're building and debugging your application, it helps if you can test the application with the same security permissions it will be granted when deployed. Visual Studio 2005 has a Debug in Zone feature that kicks in when you select the This Is a Partial Trust Application radio button on the Security tab. The Debug in Zone feature simply places the application within the CAS security sandbox, as defined by the permissions set by the application. If a security exception occurs while debugging, Visual Studio displays a security exception dialog box that allows you to add the required permission directly from the dialog box (see Figure 7-14).

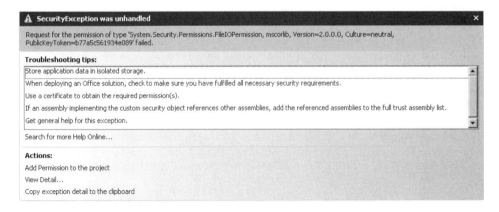

Figure 7-14. *Debug in Zone feature within Visual Studio 2005*

The security exception dialog box shown in Figure 7-14 says that the application requested a permission to do file input/output but was denied because of the security settings of the application. The dialog box also offers some troubleshooting tips, along with a few action links, one of which says Add Permission to the Project. Note that the Debug in Zone feature is not a mandatory feature. You can disable this by clicking the Advanced button in the Security dialog box and then unchecking the Debug This Application with the Selected Permission Set box.

The permission calculator in Visual Studio 2005 actually interfaces with a command-line utility named PermCalc.exe. This utility, as the name suggests, can determine the set of permissions required by any managed assembly (or a list of assemblies). Interesting uses of this tool might include determining permissions required by a ClickOnce add-in assembly. PermCalc.exe can emit an XML file that shows the permissions required by the application.

VB .NET developers have even more to rave about when debugging partial trust applications because VB .NET has a feature called IntelliSense in the Zone. IntelliSense in the Zone looks at the permissions set by the application and the required permissions for methods, properties, and so on, shown in the IntelliSense drop-down list and grays out those that require more privileges than are available to the application, as shown in Figure 7-15.

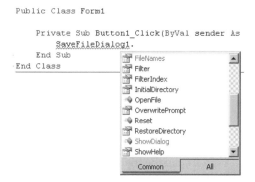

Figure 7-15. *IntelliSense in the Zone feature for VB .NET developers*

The Properties button on the Security tab displays specific details about the selected permission in the permission grid. For example, Figure 7-16 shows the properties for FileDialogPermission.

The Permission Settings dialog allows you to modify the permission settings for a particular permission. For example, by default, applications deployed in the Internet zone can use the file Open dialog box but not the Save dialog box or the Open and Save dialog box. If you modify this setting for the Internet zone, the green arrow to the right of the permission will change to a yellow warning icon to indicate you are asking for more privileges than what are granted for the given zone by default. Note that depending on what permission you choose, the Permission Settings dialog box will change to display the specifics for the permission.

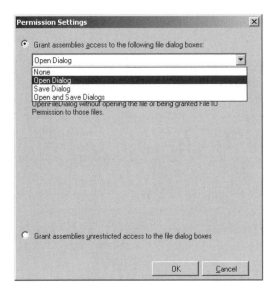

Figure 7-16. *Properties of* `FileDialogPermission`

Full Trust vs. Partial Trust

In the discussion of partial trust applications, we mentioned in passing that in a corporate environment it is recommended that you deploy partial trust applications rather than full trust applications. The obvious questions now is, why would you want to restrict your application and go through the pain of figuring out every little permission you need to run your application? Why not just go with full trust and not risk missing a permission? The answer is simply that if a malicious party overtakes your application, then the malicious party can do only as much damage as your application. Therefore, you should configure your application with as much granularity as possible. For example, if you need access to read a file from a folder and don't require write privileges, then configure the file/folder input/output permissions such that you only read from the folder and file, without write permissions. In other words, be meticulous, and follow the principle of "run with least privilege."

As mentioned, the application manifest contains the application entry point, file dependencies, and so on. This manifest also defines the set of permissions required by the application. In a full trust scenario, the application says it does not have any restrictions. In a partial trust case, each individual permission is declared. Permission requirements fall within the `trustInfo` element. A sample entry for a full trust application is as follows:

```
<trustInfo>
    <security>
        <applicationRequestMinimum>
            <PermissionSet Unrestricted="true" ID="Custom" SameSite="site" />
            <defaultAssemblyRequest permissionSetReference="Custom" />
        </applicationRequestMinimum>
    </security>
</trustInfo>
```

Note that the PermissionSet element has the attribute Unrestricted set to true to indicate full trust. An example of a partial trust trustInfo element is as follows:

```
<trustInfo>
    <security>
      <applicationRequestMinimum>
        <PermissionSet class="System.Security.PermissionSet" version="1"
            ID="Custom" SameSite="site">
          <IPermission class="System.Security.Permissions.FileDialogPermission,
              mscorlib, Version=2.0.0.0, Culture=neutral,
              PublicKeyToken=b77a5c561934e089" version="1" Access="Open" />
          <IPermission class=
           "System.Security.Permissions.IsolatedStorageFilePermission,
              mscorlib, Version=2.0.0.0, Culture=neutral,
              PublicKeyToken=b77a5c561934e089" version="1"
              Allowed="ApplicationIsolationByUser" UserQuota="512000" />
          <IPermission class="System.Security.Permissions.SecurityPermission,
              mscorlib, Version=2.0.0.0, Culture=neutral,
              PublicKeyToken=b77a5c561934e089" version="1"
              Flags="Execution" />
          <IPermission class="System.Security.Permissions.UIPermission,
              mscorlib, Version=2.0.0.0, Culture=neutral,
              PublicKeyToken=b77a5c561934e089" version="1"
              Window="SafeTopLevelWindows" Clipboard="OwnClipboard" />
          <IPermission class="System.Windows.Forms.WebBrowserPermission,
              System, Version=2.0.0.0, Culture=neutral,
              PublicKeyToken=b77a5c561934e089" version="1" Unrestricted="True" />
          <IPermission class="System.Drawing.Printing.PrintingPermission,
              System.Drawing, Version=2.0.0.0, Culture=neutral,
              PublicKeyToken=b03f5f7f11d50a3a" version="1" Level="SafePrinting" />
        </PermissionSet>
        <defaultAssemblyRequest permissionSetReference="Custom" />
      </applicationRequestMinimum>
    </security>
 </trustInfo>
```

Note that with a partial trust application, the Unrestricted attribute is not set. Moreover, each permission is documented clearly.

Available Permissions vs. Actual Permissions

It is important to understand that the permissions defined in the application manifest is what your application is given at runtime, even if you could obtain more privileges (or full trust) via some other form of evidence (for example, a signed publisher certificate or origin-based evidence). This is known as *available* permissions, via evidence, versus *actual* permissions, which are defined in the application manifest. Let's say you deploy a partial trust application from the intranet zone. By default, applications deployed from the intranet zone have the ReflectionPermission permission (see Table 7-2). This means you can use reflection to peek into other assemblies. But because you don't require this permission, you configure the application to exclude this permission. Thus, when your application runs within the CAS security sandbox, your application will not have this permission, even though it could have because of its evidence. That is, even though the evidence your application possesses has more available permissions defined, the actual permissions your application gets are what are defined in the application manifest. Essentially, you can think of an application as being "locked down."

Deploying Prerequisites with ClickOnce

When you get past the Hello World–type applications and have to deploy real-world apps, you will quickly realize that complex systems depend on certain elements that have to exist on the target machine for the application to run. It is not unlikely for an application to depend on a component in the GAC, a Windows service, a registry entry, or a specific user account. It's not unlikely for an application to depend on a database on the client machine or even a specific user or a file or a folder. For a deployment solution to be effective, you need a way to check the prerequisites and make sure they're installed on the target machine. In the following sections, we will discuss bootstrapping a ClickOnce application to install the application prerequisites and to ensure that the prerequisites exist on the client prior to installing the ClickOnce application.

Using the Bootstrapper to Install Prerequisites

When VS 2005 publishes an application, it can also generate a bootstrapper that can install any prerequisites required by the application. The bootstrapper is an unmanaged executable (setup.exe) application that is published next to the deployment manifest. The job of the bootstrapper is to check for a list of prerequisites on the client's machine and if any of the prerequisites are missing, then ensure they are installed prior to running the ClickOnce installation. VS 2005 provides a user interface, via the Project Designer, to configure the bootstrapper with the prerequisites.

You can configure prerequisites by clicking the Prerequisites button on the Publish tab; this opens a Prerequisites dialog box. By default, Visual Studio 2005 creates a bootstrapper that checks for the presence of the .NET Framework 2.0, as shown in Figure 7-17. You can also choose from a list of other commonly required components, and the bootstrapper will ensure that those components are also on the machine prior to running your ClickOnce install.

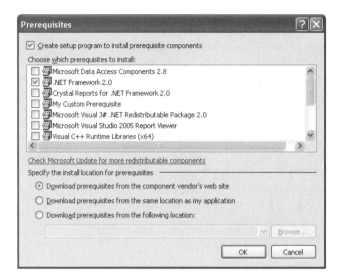

Figure 7-17. *Configuring prerequisites for ClickOnce applications*

You can configure the bootstrapper to install one or more of the components from the list or specify a custom component at a specific location. To configure the bootstrapper to install a custom component, select the Download Prerequisites from the Following Location radio button, and then click the Browse button. This opens a dialog box that allows you to choose a location from the local file system, a local Web server, an FTP site, or a remote Web site, as shown in Figure 7-18.

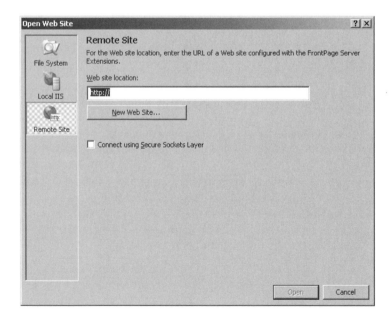

Figure 7-18. *Configuring the bootstrapper to install a component from a specific location, other than the vendor's Web site*

We've already talked about the `publish.htm` page that the Publish Wizard generates, by default, when you publish your application. The default setting also launches this file in the browser to have the user install the application. This is the same file your users can go to in order to install your application. This file has a built-in script that can detect the presence of the .NET Framework 2.0 and lists the required prerequisites, along with a button to download and run the bootstrapper. Figure 7-19 shows a section of the `publish.htm` page that detected that the .NET Framework 2.0 was missing. Note the Install button; users can click this button to install the prerequisites.

Figure 7-19. *The* `publish.htm` *script detects that the .NET Framework 2.0 is not installed on the target machine.*

We'll talk a lot more about the bootstrapper in Chapter 8.

Summary

We covered a lot of ground in this chapter. We started with a discussion of the deployment and application manifest files. The deployment manifest contains details to tell the ClickOnce runtime how to find and update the application. The application manifest contains information specific to a particular version of the application. This manifest file tells the ClickOnce runtime about all the dependencies of the application, the security requirements, the entry point, and so on, of the application.

We also talked about updating ClickOnce applications. We discussed the various alternatives available to creating an update policy. We also talked about ClickOnce security. We showed examples of creating a trusted publisher and talked about full trust applications versus partial trust applications. We concluded with a discussion of the bootstrapper. We talked briefly about how you can use the bootstrapper to ensure that the prerequisites of the application are installed on the target machine prior to running your ClickOnce install.

In the next chapter, you will go deeper into ClickOnce. We'll talk about how you can customize your ClickOnce deployments using the ClickOnce APIs. We'll also talk about customizing the bootstrapper to install custom components.

CHAPTER 8

■■■

The ClickOnce Data Directory and Deploying Prerequisites

All applications need at least one assembly. Most have some support assemblies, and some even have data files (such as additional configuration files, text files, and so on). How does ClickOnce deal with data files? Is there any special treatment of these files? What about a file-based database, for example? For smart client applications, it's not rare to implement offline support in, say, an XML-based database or a Microsoft Access database. And what about migrating this type of database from one version of an application to the next? ClickOnce treats data files differently, and rightfully so. We'll spend the first half of this chapter talking about deploying data files with ClickOnce.

The second half of this chapter continues the discussion of prerequisites from the previous chapter. This chapter dives into the prerequisites and talks about what makes up a prerequisite. We'll talk about two manifest files that define a prerequisite and discuss how you can write a custom prerequisite. We'll also show you how you can get your prerequisite to appear in the Prerequisites dialog box in Visual Studio 2005 so you can just click a checkbox to include it as part of your ClickOnce deployments.

Working with Application Files

Thus far you have learned how to deploy simple applications that have only a single executable. Most applications, however, will also have one or more supporting assemblies, along with various resources (for example, an XML document). In this section, and the next, we will discuss how ClickOnce allows you to deploy these files with your applications.

ClickOnce-deployed applications can have dependencies of all types. You can view the dependencies of your deployment by clicking the Application Files button on the Publish tab in the Project Designer (also referred to as the Project Properties page). Clicking this button displays the Application Files dialog box, which lists all the files that will be deployed with your application (see Figure 8-1).

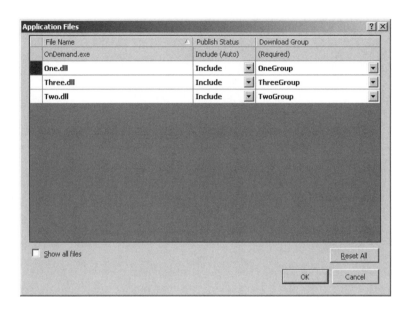

Figure 8-1. *Application Files dialog box*

Note that you can also view the dependencies of your application by looking at the application manifest file.

For simple applications, you don't have to worry about what files are downloaded; Visual Studio and ClickOnce take care of everything for you. Other applications will require special attention, though. For example, consider a large application that is deployed under various licenses: Enterprise, Professional, and Standard. Users of the system can download the application and then enter a license key to activate a particular version. In this scenario, it does not make sense for the user to download the entire application all at once if they need only a subset of the system. It may make more sense for you to partition the application so a user can download each partition on demand. This particular scenario becomes more serious when you consider the options for protecting against software piracy. For example, if you deploy the entire code base of your application to all of your users and rely on a license to determine what modules to enable, hackers can find ways to get around the licensing issues and enable other modules. A better solution is to not deploy the unnecessary modules. ClickOnce offers a facility that can assist with these types of scenarios called *on-demand download*. The idea behind on-demand download is that you create groups of files and then use the ClickOnce APIs to download each group at runtime. This approach offers the benefit of reducing the overall download—the initial download is reduced to what needs to be downloaded to run the application, and if a piece of functionality is not needed, it is not downloaded.

You configure which files get downloaded using the Application Files dialog box. As shown in Figure 8-1, the dialog box displays a grid with three columns: File Name, Publish Status, and Download Group. The File Name column contains the names of the files (with their extensions) on which your application depends. The Publish Status column defines how ClickOnce treats each file during publishing. Valid values for this column are Include (Auto), Include, Prerequisite, Data File, and Exclude. This column works in tandem with the Download Group column. By default, you'll see the values (Required) and (New . . .) in this column.

When you deploy a ClickOnce application, you can control which files get deployed with your application. You can use the publish status of a file in combination with its file group to control if and when the file gets downloaded. By default, application files (assemblies and noncode files with the Build Action option set to Content) are assigned the Include (Auto) publish status and get assigned to the (Required) file group. This indicates that the file is required for the application to run, and thus the file is deployed automatically with the application. You can prevent a file from being downloaded, if your application does not need it, by assigning the Exclude status to the file. If you exclude a file, then it cannot be downloaded (even at runtime). You can assign the Data File status to noncode files. Data files are copied to the ClickOnce data directory, which we'll talk about in the next section. You can include a file for deployment yet prevent its deployment initially by creating a new file group and assigning the Include status to it. This tells ClickOnce that the file should be downloaded with the file group at runtime using the ClickOnce APIs. You can also assign the Prerequisite publish status to files. Files assigned to this value are not deployed and are assumed to be on the client in the GAC. Note that you can assign only assemblies to the Prerequisite status.

Application dependencies are stored in the application manifest when you publish your application. Code dependencies are listed with a dependency element, and noncode dependencies are listed with the file element. The following listing shows several dependency entries from an application manifest file:

```
<dependency>
   <dependentAssembly
      dependencyType="preRequisite"
      allowDelayedBinding="true">
    <assemblyIdentity
       name="Microsoft.Windows.CommonLanguageRuntime"
       version="2.0.50727.0" />
   </dependentAssembly>
 </dependency>
 <dependency>
   <dependentAssembly
      dependencyType="preRequisite"
      allowDelayedBinding="true">
    <assemblyIdentity name="One"
      version="1.0.0.0" publicKeyToken="0A1915B84E9CE3C8"
      language="neutral" processorArchitecture="msil" />
   </dependentAssembly>
 </dependency>
 <dependency>
```

```
<dependentAssembly
    dependencyType="install"
    allowDelayedBinding="true" codebase="Four.dll" size="16384">
  <assemblyIdentity
      name="Four" version="1.0.0.0" language="neutral"
      processorArchitecture="msil" />
  <hash>
    <dsig:Transforms>
      <dsig:Transform
        Algorithm="urn:schemas-microsoft-com:HashTransforms.Identity" />
    </dsig:Transforms>
    <dsig:DigestMethod
        Algorithm="http://www.w3.org/2000/09/xmldsig#sha1" />
    <dsig:DigestValue>
        rf8bbmtjQ58tZSjaHcgQDUeO+74=
    </dsig:DigestValue>
  </hash>
</dependentAssembly>
</dependency>
<dependency optional="true">
  <dependentAssembly
    dependencyType="install" allowDelayedBinding="true"
    codebase="Three.dll" size="16384" group="FGThree">
  <assemblyIdentity name="Three" version="1.0.0.0"
      language="neutral"
      processorArchitecture="msil" />
  <hash>
    <dsig:Transforms>
      <dsig:Transform
        Algorithm="urn:schemas-microsoft-com:HashTransforms.Identity" />
    </dsig:Transforms>
    <dsig:DigestMethod
        Algorithm="http://www.w3.org/2000/09/xmldsig#sha1" />
    <dsig:DigestValue>
        L2Wj4CQlbJ6+G5wsPpFZMXeIYFM=
    </dsig:DigestValue>
  </hash>
</dependentAssembly>
</dependency>
<dependency optional="true">
  <dependentAssembly
      dependencyType="install" allowDelayedBinding="true"
      codebase="Two.dll" size="16384" group="FGTwo">
  <assemblyIdentity name="Two" version="1.0.0.0"
      language="neutral"
      processorArchitecture="msil" />
```

```xml
        <hash>
          <dsig:Transforms>
            <dsig:Transform
              Algorithm="urn:schemas-microsoft-com:HashTransforms.Identity" />
          </dsig:Transforms>
          <dsig:DigestMethod
              Algorithm="http://www.w3.org/2000/09/xmldsig#sha1" />
          <dsig:DigestValue>
            bXWsMx1A9H42VUPZOQNZLQCUfcc=
          </dsig:DigestValue>
        </hash>
      </dependentAssembly>
  </dependency>
  <dependency>
    <dependentAssembly
        dependencyType="install" allowDelayedBinding="true"
        codebase="WindowsApplication16.exe" size="20480">
      <assemblyIdentity
          name="WindowsApplication16" version="1.0.0.0"
          language="neutral" processorArchitecture="msil" />
      <hash>
        <dsig:Transforms>
          <dsig:Transform Algorithm=
          "urn:schemas-microsoft-com:HashTransforms.Identity" />
              </dsig:Transforms>
        <dsig:DigestMethod
        Algorithm="http://www.w3.org/2000/09/xmldsig#sha1" />
        <dsig:DigestValue>
            fPNOFyjxvPAkXXwSAFXbN+uJSug=
        </dsig:DigestValue>
      </hash>
    </dependentAssembly>
  </dependency>
  <file name="TextFile1.txt" size="0">
    <hash>
      <dsig:Transforms>
        <dsig:Transform
        Algorithm="urn:schemas-microsoft-com:HashTransforms.Identity" />
      </dsig:Transforms>
      <dsig:DigestMethod
        Algorithm="http://www.w3.org/2000/09/xmldsig#sha1" />
      <dsig:DigestValue>2jmj7l5rSwOyVb/vlWAYkK/YBwk=</dsig:DigestValue>
    </hash>
  </file>
```

Note that dependencies to components in the GAC[1] have a dependencyType attribute set to preRequisite, and components not in the GAC are set to install. For GAC components, ClickOnce will check the GAC for the specified component and will throw an error if the component is not already installed (see Figure 8-2). For assemblies that have dependencyType set to install, ClickOnce will download and install them. Assemblies that belong to a file group have the group attribute set to the name of the group. Note that when you add an assembly to something other than the default (Required) group, the ClickOnce runtime will not download the assembly at install time, and you have to use the ClickOnce APIs to download the assembly at runtime. Dependencies that have to be downloaded using the ClickOnce APIs have the attribute optional set to true. For code dependencies, the optional attribute appears on the dependency element, and for noncode dependencies, the attribute appears on the file element.

Figure 8-2. *Error message indicating a missing GAC component*

Note also that each dependency has a hash element. The hash element ensures that the dependent file was not tampered with after deployment. For example, say you deploy an application to a Web server and then sometime later someone modifies the file by injecting a virus in the file. If ClickOnce didn't verify the integrity of each file prior to download, it would open the doors to deploying viruses.

Working with Data Files

Client-server applications of the past required a live connection to the server at all times in order to function. Today, we have smart clients, and one of the philosophies behind smart clients is that an application should function even without a connection to the back-end server. To provide offline functionality, smart client applications need a client-side data strategy—a strategy for how to store application state while the application is offline. That is, when the application is online, the data is sent to the server, but when the application is offline, it needs a place to store the data until the connection is restored. Prior to ClickOnce, developers of smart client applications had to determine the best place to store application files (for example, offline support files). Developers often choose to write files within their application folder, which resulted in writing files under the Program Files directory. This manifested in the application needing admin privileges and introduced complexities otherwise not needed. With ClickOnce, you have a unified storage location called the ClickOnce *data directory*.

---

1. You can view the contents of the GAC by going to %windir%\assembly.

To explain how you can use the ClickOnce data directory to store data files, we'll show how to build a simple application that allows a user to enter some text into a text area and then save it for later. The user can shut down the application and later return to continue working. Figure 8-3 shows the user interface of the application. The application is also available via a ClickOnce deployment at `http://sayedhashimi.com/downloads/book/WorkingWithDataApp/publish.htm`.

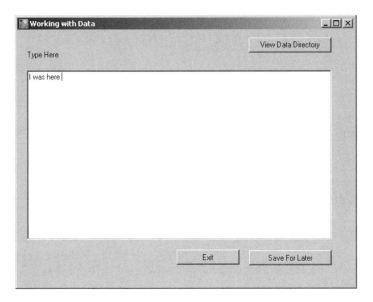

Figure 8-3. *Sample application that demonstrates the use of the ClickOnce data directory*

The main form of the application displays a text box for the user to enter some text and then click Save for Later. The user can then exit the application and return at a later time to continue working. When the user clicks Save for Later, the application gets the path to the ClickOnce data directory and writes a file to that directory. The application can obtain the ClickOnce data directory in several ways:

- Using `AppDomain.CurrentDomain.GetData("DataDirectory")`

- Using `System.Deployment.Application.ApplicationDeployment.CurrentDeployment.DataDirectory`

- Using `Application.LocalUserAppDataPath`

You can see the actual values that these APIs result in by clicking the View Data Directory button in the sample application. Clicking this button opens a modal dialog box that will call these APIs and display the results, as shown in Figure 8-4.

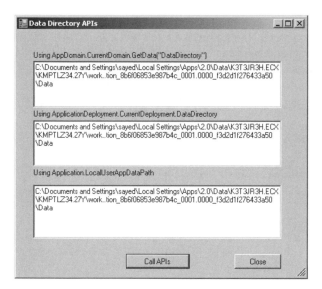

Figure 8-4. *APIs that return the ClickOnce data directory*

Note that all three APIs have the same result. If you installed the application, your results will be different from what is shown in Figure 8-4; ClickOnce puts the data directory somewhere within the deployment folder, and the deployment folder is generated using an unpublished algorithm.

The previous example was fairly convoluted to demonstrate that you can persist application state in the ClickOnce data directory. Persisting application state, saving preferences, and maintaining settings are some uses of the data directory. You'll also sometimes need to deploy files from your solution to the data directory. Files in your deployment marked as Data File are copied to the ClickOnce data directory. The purpose of the data directory is to store state on a user-by-user basis and on an application version level. This means if you have several users working with an application that stores a data file in the data directory, changes made by one user will not be visible to other users on the machine. Moreover, from a smart client perspective, this means if an application stores offline state in the ClickOnce data directory, then the state will need to be synchronized with the back-end database server when the application goes online. Thus, you should treat the data directory as a place to store offline state for an application and remember to synchronize with the back-end database server when the connection is restored. You will also need to remember to clear the state after going online to prevent appending state information from online/offline sessions. Finally, realize that the content of the data directory is meant to be managed by the application, and when the user removes the application, the contents of the data directory for that user are also deleted.

We mentioned earlier that smart client applications support offline capabilities and thus need a strategy to store data on the client machine. You can use several approaches to design a data store. In a simple application, you could use an XML file as a data store. For complex applications, you could use SQL Server Express Edition on the client. Since we are talking about the ClickOnce data directory, we won't talk about SQL Server Express Edition here. Instead, we'll talk about using a Microsoft Access database to store application state. In this section, we'll show how to write a sample application called `ClickOnceAndAccess` where you use the Northwind database in a smart client application. We will answer the following questions with this exercise:

- How do you deploy an Access database with a ClickOnce deployment?

- How do you connect to the database?

- How do you merge data when you update your application?

With a traditional Windows Forms application that is deployed using a setup project, you had the luxury of referencing the database file from anywhere on the user's machine.[2] Using a setup project, you usually don't need a reference to the database in your project. Instead, you would just read the connection string from the application configuration file and use that to connect to the database. With ClickOnce, you do have some restrictions in that you have to include the database in your solution. This is because you need ClickOnce to deploy the database along with the application. This begs the question, how do you connect to the database? From the previous discussion, you know you are going to put the database in the ClickOnce data directory, so to connect to the database, you'll have to dynamically create the connection string at runtime. Finally, the real challenge with using a local database is merging the changes when you do updates.

For example, say you deploy version 1 of an application with version 1 of your database. Your users play with the database, and each user makes additions to, for example, the Customers table. When you publish version 2 of the application, you deploy version 2 of your database too. You can't copy your new database to the client by itself because you will lose all the changes the client made to the older database. So, you'll have to import the data created by the client from the old database to the new database. How do you do that with ClickOnce? It turns out that ClickOnce maintains up to two copies of your application (based on individual users) on the client's machine. When the client installs the second version of the application (with an update), ClickOnce installs the second version of the application on the machine and keeps the old one for rollback purposes.[3] With the new install, ClickOnce creates a folder named `.pre` and puts the data files from the previous version in this folder. The idea is that when your application starts for the first time from an update, you programmatically merge the two databases.

Figure 8-5 shows the user interface of the sample application. Again, you can install the application via ClickOnce by pointing your browser to `http://www.sayedhashimi.com/downloads/book/ClickOnceAndAccessApp/publish.htm`.

---

2. Generally, however, the database was deployed alongside the application, under the `Program Files` directory. Because applications read and write to databases, applications were forced to run with administrator privileges.

3. When you deploy your applications using ClickOnce, you also get a rollback facility. If something goes wrong with an install or your application acts strange after an update, users can restore the previous version of the application via Add Remove Programs.

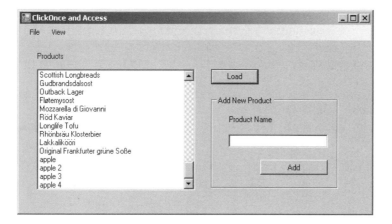

Figure 8-5. *Offline support and ClickOnce sample application UI*

The application shown in Figure 8-5 displays the current set of products in the Northwind database (deployed with the application) and allows users to add new products. The idea is that users add new products, and when an update happens, the application copies the new products from the old database to the new one. You can apply the same principle to handle virtually any kind of change to the database. To that end, refer to the following code that shows how you can implement this functionality:

```
public MainForm()
{
    InitializeComponent();
    if (ApplicationDeployment.CurrentDeployment.IsFirstRun)
    {
    CheckProductsTable();
    }
}
```

As shown in the previous code, when the main form is done initializing its components, the application checks to see whether this is the first time this version of the application is running on the client's machine. If so, the CheckProductsTable() method is called to synchronize the products table, if necessary, which is as follows:

```
private void CheckProductsTable()
{
    string pathToOldDB = GetPathToPreviousDatabase();
    FileInfo fi = new FileInfo(pathToOldDB);
    MessageBox.Show(pathToOldDB);
    if (fi.Exists)
    {
    MessageBox.Show("Old database exists...checking products table");
    // we support changes to the products table only. See whether the table
    // has changed by iterating over the old products and see whether they exist
    // in the new one.
```

```
OleDbConnection oldCon = null;
OleDbConnection newCon = null;
try
{
    MessageBox.Show("connecting to old database");

    oldCon = new OleDbConnection(GetConnectionString(GetPathToPreFolder()));
    oldCon.Open();
    MessageBox.Show("connecting to new database");
    newCon = new OleDbConnection(GetConnectionString());
    newCon.Open();
    if (oldCon == null)
    {
    throw new Exception("failed to get connection to old db");
    }
    if (newCon == null)
    {
    throw new Exception("failed to get connection to new db");
    }
    DataSet oldDs = new DataSet("OldNorthwind");
    DataSet newDs = new DataSet("NewNorthwind");
    OleDbDataAdapter oldDa = new
        OleDbDataAdapter("SELECT * FROM products", oldCon);
    OleDbDataAdapter newDa = new
        OleDbDataAdapter("SELECT * FROM products", newCon);
    oldDa.Fill(oldDs);
    newDa.Fill(newDs);
    // iterate over the old products
    int newProd = 0;
    MessageBox.Show("iterating the rows");
    foreach (DataRow oldDr in oldDs.Tables[0].Rows)
    {
    // see whether the product is in the new products table
    if (!IsRowInNewProductsTable(oldDr, newDs.Tables[0].Rows, newCon))
    {
        MessageBox.Show
            ("have to insert product " + oldDr["ProductName"] as string);
        InsertProduct(newCon, oldDr);
        newProd++;
    }
    }
    MessageBox.Show("Add " + newProd + " to database");
}
catch (Exception ee)
{
    MessageBox.Show(ee.Message);
}
```

```
        finally
        {
            oldCon.Close();
            newCon.Close();
        }
        }
        else
        {
        MessageBox.Show("old db does not exist");
        }
}
```

As mentioned earlier, when ClickOnce installs an update to an application, it copies all the data files from the previous version's data directory into the new version's data directory. Click-Once then performs a check to see whether the data files in the new version's data directory have a hash that is different from the ones in the older version.[4] If so, ClickOnce moves the file from the data folder into the .pre folder within the data directory and then downloads the newer version of the file from the server. The application can then use the files in the .pre folder for migration purposes. Referring to the earlier CheckProductsTable() method example, the method checks to see whether there is a version of the database file in the .pre folder within the data directory. If so, it knows it has to copy new records from the older database into the new one. If it finds that the database file is in the .pre folder, it creates database connections to the two databases, iterates over the rows in the older products table, and checks to see whether that product is in the new products table. If not, the method adds the row to the new products table. For testing purposes, you can download the source code to the application at http://sayedhashimi.com/downloads/book/ClickOnceAndAccessApp/ClickOnceAndAccess.zip.

Applications that use data files that require migration from one version to another will likely require more robust implementations than what we have shown. The approach used in the sample application is to perform a test at application start-up to see whether a new version is running and if so, look for new products to import. This approach certainly works, but for complex applications where many files may be involved with complex migration strategies, a better approach may be necessary. For complex cases, the ClickOnce APIs can prove to be helpful. Although the APIs are somewhat limited, the functionality exposed is generic and can scale for complex solutions.

With this in mind, Figure 8-6 and Figure 8-7 show the UI for the next sample application that demonstrates several of the important methods and properties exposed in the ClickOnce APIs. Specifically, Figure 8-6 shows the Application Info tab.

---

4. ClickOnce actually compares the hash of the data files in both data directories with what is listed for each file in the newer version's application manifest.

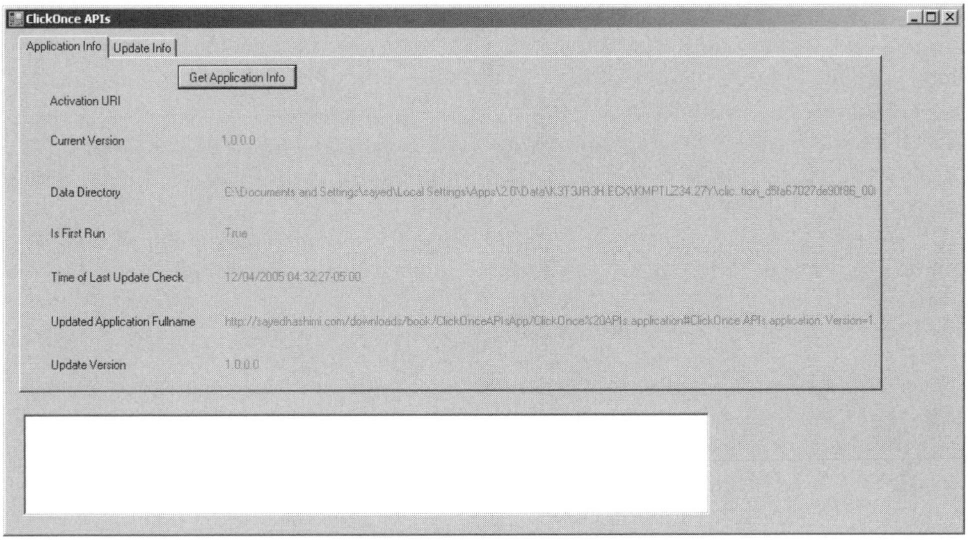

Figure 8-6. *Using the ClickOnce APIs to get application information*

The Application Info tab presents a Get Application Info button. Clicking this button displays deployment details about the application using the ClickOnce APIs.

Figure 8-7 shows the Update Info tab.

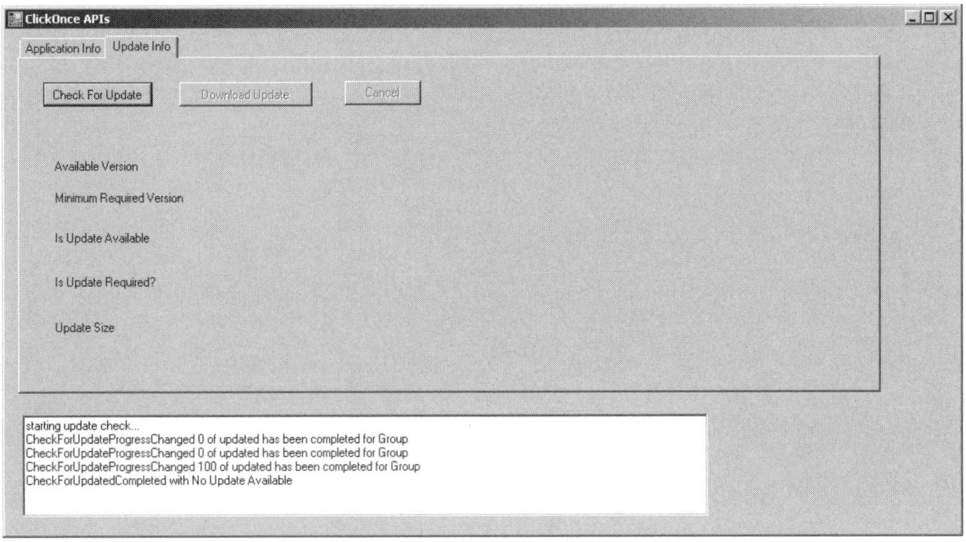

Figure 8-7. *Using the ClickOnce APIs to get update details about an application*

The Update Info tab displays several buttons across the top of the page: Check for Update, Download Update, and Cancel. The Check for Update button is always enabled and can be used to detect updates to the application. Clicking this button performs an asynchronous check for an update and displays update details when an update is available. The Download Update button is enabled only when an update is available. Note that if an update is available, the user can download the update by clicking the Download Update button. The update takes place asynchronously in the background.

The sample application also demonstrates a logging technique that might be useful when getting started using the ClickOnce APIs. The sample application logs important progress events in a text area so the user can view what is happening in the background while the application is updating or the update checks are taking place.

The following code shows the implementation of this application:

```
public MainForm()
{
    InitializeComponent();
    // add event handlers
    ApplicationDeployment appdep = System.Deployment.
        Application.ApplicationDeployment.CurrentDeployment;
    appdep.CheckForUpdateProgressChanged += new
    DeploymentProgressChangedEventHandler(appdep_CheckForUpdateProgressChanged);
    appdep.CheckForUpdateCompleted += new
    CheckForUpdateCompletedEventHandler(appdep_CheckForUpdateCompleted);
    appdep.DownloadFileGroupCompleted += new
    DownloadFileGroupCompletedEventHandler(appdep_DownloadFileGroupCompleted);
    appdep.DownloadFileGroupProgressChanged += new
    DeploymentProgressChangedEventHandler(appdep_DownloadFileGroupProgressChanged);
    appdep.UpdateCompleted += new AsyncCompletedEventHandler
        (appdep_UpdateCompleted);
    appdep.UpdateProgressChanged += new
    DeploymentProgressChangedEventHandler(appdep_UpdateProgressChanged);
}
```

At the heart of the ClickOnce APIs are six events:

- CheckForUpdateCompleted

- CheckForUpdateProgressChanged

- DownloadFileGroupCompleted

- DownloadFileGroupProgressChanged

- UpdateCompleted

- UpdateCompleted

There are three primary "completed" events, and each one has an associated "progress changed" event. For example, there is an UpdateCompleted event and an UpdateProgressChanged event. When an update is fired, you'll have one or more progress events and then a completed event. The sample application registers for all of these events in order to show log messages and to enable/disable user interface controls.

Referring to the earlier data migration sample, rather than perform a check at the start of the application to see whether you have to migrate data, it may make more sense to use these events to handle data migration. For a complex application that, for example, does on-demand downloads of updates, you will find these events very useful. For example, rather than use the built-in self-updating feature of ClickOnce, you could set up a timer to check for application updates. When an update is available, ClickOnce will download it and upon completion kick off data migration. This may seem far-fetched, but for a complex data migration problem this is actually a reasonable solution because checking for and downloading updates using the ClickOnce APIs is extremely easy. For example:

```
private void CheckForUpdateHandler(object sender, EventArgs e)
{
    try
    {
    AddLog("starting update check...");
    ApplicationDeployment appdep = ApplicationDeployment.CurrentDeployment;
    appdep.CheckForUpdateAsync();
    }
    catch (Exception ee)
    {
    MessageBox.Show(ee.Message, "Error", MessageBoxButtons.OK);
    }
}
void appdep_CheckForUpdateCompleted(object sender,
      CheckForUpdateCompletedEventArgs e)
{

    if (e.UpdateAvailable)
    {
    // some logic goes here
    }
}
private void DownloadUpdatesHandler(object sender, EventArgs e)
{
    try
    {
    SetButtonsEnabled(downloadUpdatesBtn,false);
    SetButtonsEnabled(cancelDownloadBtn, true);
    ApplicationDeployment ad =
     System.Deployment.Application.ApplicationDeployment.CurrentDeployment;
    ad.UpdateAsync();
    }
    catch (Exception ee)
    {
    MessageBox.Show(ee.Message,"Error",MessageBoxButtons.OK);
    }
}
void appdep_UpdateCompleted(object sender, AsyncCompletedEventArgs e)
```

```
{
    AddLog("UpdateCompleted");
    SetButtonsEnabled(downloadUpdatesBtn,false);
    SetButtonsEnabled(cancelDownloadBtn, false);
    SetButtonsEnabled(chkForUpdateBtn, true);
}
```

The previous code listing shows how easy it is to use the ClickOnce APIs to check for updates and download one when available. For example, the `CheckForUpdateHandler()` method calls the ClickOnce `CheckForUpdateAsync()` method. When update checking is complete, the ClickOnce runtime notifies the application by firing the `CheckForUpdateCompleted` event with information about a possible update. In this sample, the `appdep_CheckForUpdateCompleted()` event handler is invoked by the ClickOnce runtime with update information. Similarly, when an update is available, the `UpdateAsync()` method is used to download the entire update; the `appdep_UpdateCompleted()` event handler is called when the downloading of the update is finished. Note that you can do all of this using the synchronous APIs as well. For example, this example checked for an update asynchronously using `CheckForUpdateAsync()`. You can do the same synchronously by calling `CheckForUpdate()`.

You can download the source code to this sample from `http://sayedhashimi.com/downloads/book/ClickOnceAPIsApp/ondemandsrc.zip`.

Note that even though the examples in this section talked strictly about storing a file-based database in the ClickOnce data directory, you can store any file type you like. Common uses of the data directory include the following: storing user/application preferences and/or settings, maintaining a persistent cache, maintaining a file-based database, providing offline support, and so on.

Considering Security When Using the ClickOnce Data Directory

In the discussion of the ClickOnce data directory, we avoided talking about security, and for good reason. That's what demos are all about—talk about the good stuff, and don't mention anything else. Well, it turns out that a side effect of using the ClickOnce data directory is that you need unrestricted access to the file system. Why? Well, you don't know the actual path to the data directory so you can't request `FileIOPermission` to that folder. Thus, you need unrestricted access to the file system to ensure access to the data directory.[5]

That's just part of the problem; the other issue deals with using the ClickOnce APIs. As you saw with the sample applications, using the data directory requires that you use the ClickOnce APIs because one of the benefits of the data directory is that you can migrate files from version to version. It turns out that the ClickOnce APIs, for the most part, require full trust—if you deploy a partial trust application that attempts to use the ClickOnce APIs, you'll most likely get security exceptions. We say "likely" because most of the methods (and properties), directly or indirectly, require full trust. You can, however, get by with partial trust for isolated cases. For

---

5. Note that we are talking about CAS here.

example, if you have unrestricted `FileIOPermission` and use the ClickOnce APIs to do only data migration, you can squeeze by without full trust. For general uses of the ClickOnce APIs, however, you need to have full trust. Note that you actually don't need to use the ClickOnce APIs if you need to get access only to the ClickOnce data directory, as shown in Figure 8-4, because the `DataDirectory` property on the `ApplicationDeployment` object is just a wrapper for `AppDomain.CurrentDomain.GetData("DataDirectory")`.

Also realize that if you use ADO.NET to do data migration (as in the sample application), you'll definitely need full trust because the ADO.NET assemblies require it.

Working with Prerequisites

In the previous chapter, we briefly talked about the using the bootstrapper, which is an executable that has two responsibilities:

- Checking for prerequisites on the client machine and installing them if they are missing

- Launching the ClickOnce installer after verifying or installing prerequisites

Since all ClickOnce-deployed applications require the .NET Framework 2.0, the Prerequisites dialog box has the .NET Framework checked by default.[6] Visual Studio actually lists the following prerequisites:

- Microsoft Data Access Components 2.8 (MDAC 2.8)

- The .NET Framework 2.0

- Crystal Reports for .NET Framework 2.0

- Microsoft Visual J# .NET Redistributable Package 2.0

- Microsoft Visual Studio 2005 Report Viewer

- Visual C++ Runtime Libraries (x64)

- Visual C++ Runtime Libraries (x86)

- Windows Installer 2.0

- Windows Installer 3.1

- SQL Server 2005 Express Edition

MDAC 2.8 contains data access components (for example, the OLE DB data provider). The .NET Framework 2.0 is the .NET runtime. Crystal Reports for .NET Framework 2.0 is required if you deploy an application that works with Crystal Reports for Visual Studio. If you deploy an application built with Visual J# 2.0, you'll need Microsoft Visual J# .NET Redistributable Package 2.0 on the client machine. Similarly, you'll need one of the Visual C++ runtime libraries if your application was built with or uses Visual C++. Microsoft Visual Studio 2005 Report Viewer contains the libraries you need on the client machine if your application uses any of the new

---

6. Every ClickOnce-deployed application needs to have the .NET Framework 2.0. Other prerequisites may also be checked, by default, depending on your application type. For example, if you build a Visual J# application, the J# prerequisite package will also be checked.

Report Viewer controls. Prerequisites are packaged as MSI packages. If you have an MSI that requires, for example, Windows Installer 3.1, then you can use the bootstrapper to make sure the specific Windows Installer is on the target machine prior to running your prerequisite. Finally, SQL Server 2005 Express Edition is the next evolution of Microsoft SQL Server Desktop Engine (MSDE).[7] SQL Server 2005 Express Edition is a "free-to-distribute" database engine. In the previous section, we talked about using a Microsoft Access database to implement an offline facility. An Access database can manage offline facilities for most applications, but some smart client applications need the robustness of a full-fledged database on the client.

The previous list shows the common prerequisites. Because every application is unique, your application may have prerequisites that are not covered by the list. If that's the case, you can easily create a prerequisite of your own and have the bootstrapper verify its existence on the client machine prior to running your ClickOnce installer. We'll talk about how you can do that in the "Building a Custom Prerequisite" section. For now, you need to get comfortable with deploying prerequisites: we'll show you how to build an application that uses Visual J#, and we'll show how the prerequisite is installed on the client machine prior to the ClickOnce application.

The sample application that we'll talk about is called WorkingWithPreReqs; you can obtain it via http://www.sayedhashimi.com/downloads/book/WorkingWithPreReqsApp/publish.htm.

When you browse to the publish.htm page of the sample application, you'll see the screen shown in Figure 8-8.

The publish.htm page shown in Figure 8-8 shows two prerequisites required by the application. Note the message just below the list. The message essentially says that if you have these items on the machine, then you can install the application by clicking the Launch link (which points to the deployment manifest). If you don't have the prerequisites, then click the Install button. If you click the Install button, you'll execute the bootstrapper setup.exe file (see the status bar). If you have run through a few ClickOnce deployments, you may have noticed that generally you don't see the .NET Framework prerequisite displayed in the publish.htm page. It turns out that the publish.htm page has a bit of JavaScript in it that can detect the .NET Framework 2.0; however, the other prerequisites are up to the user to determine. By default, when your application lists more than the .NET Framework 2.0 as prerequisites, the publish.htm page displays the entire list of prerequisites in the publish.htm page. If you click the Install button, the setup.exe file is downloaded from the deployment URL, and you can run or save the file (see Figure 8-9).

To install the prerequisites, you can click either Run or Save. If you click Save, you'll have to run the setup.exe file manually. Either way, you have to run the setup.exe file to install the prerequisites.

---

7. Distributing MSDE does have some limitations. See http://msdn.microsoft.com/library/en-us/dnmsde/html/msderoadmap.asp for more details.

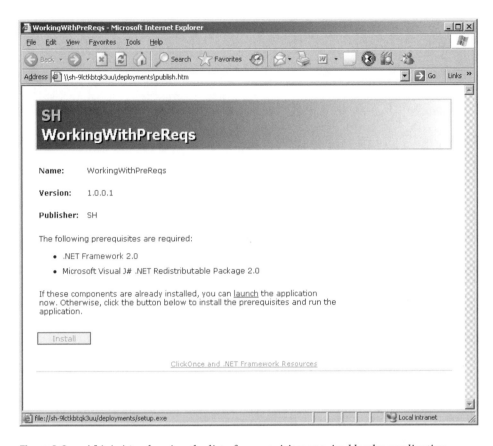

Figure 8-8. `publish.htm` *showing the list of prerequisites required by the application*

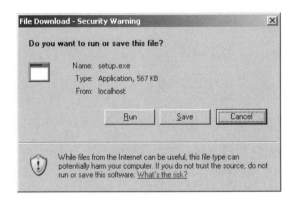

Figure 8-9. *The bootstrapper install dialog box*

PREREQUISITES REQUIRE USERS TO HAVE ADMINISTRATOR PRIVILEGES

One of the issues that we touched on in the previous chapter was that administrator-level permissions are required to run the `setup.exe` file. If a user with nonadmin permissions clicks Run, they will be greeted with an error message. Note that prerequisites have to be installed only once per machine, so in a corporate environment, systems administrators can use admin tools, such as SMS and IntelliMirror, to automate the deployment of prerequisites to workstations prior to users running the ClickOnce deployment.

Administrator privileges are required for several reasons, the primary one being that prerequisites ultimately run MSI packages, and MSI requires admin permissions by default.

When you run `setup.exe`, the bootstrapper iterates over the required prerequisites and checks to see whether the prerequisite is on the machine. If not, it launches the prerequisite installer application. In the sample application, if you do not have the Visual J# 2.0 runtime, then the first screen you'll see is the end user license agreement (EULA) page for the Visual J# 2.0 install. If you click Accept, the prerequisite installer launches an MSI to install the Visual J# runtime.

One of the options that you have when configuring prerequisites using the Prerequisites dialog box in Visual Studio 2005 is to specify from where the prerequisites are going to be downloaded. By default, the Download Prerequisites from the Component Vendor's Web Site radio button is checked. You can also have Visual Studio 2005 copy the prerequisites to your publish location (next to your ClickOnce deployment) and have them downloaded from there. You also have the option of providing a separate location if the component vendor or your deployment location does not work for your deployment scenario. The dialog box shown to the right in Figure 8-10 displays an error message, effectively saying that the prerequisite could not be downloaded. At the bottom of the dialog box, you can see that there was an error downloading from `http://go.microsoft.com/fwlink/?LinkId=37218`.

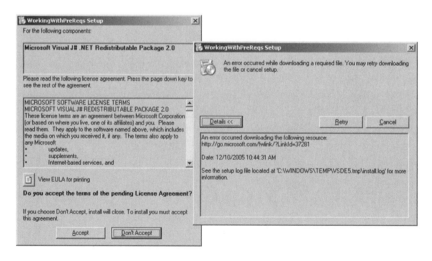

Figure 8-10. *The prerequisite could not be downloaded.*

The link points to the Visual J# Redistributable 2.0, which we had configured to be down-loaded from the Microsoft site. In the case of this sample, we disconnected the Internet connection to demonstrate a failure of a component. To get around the error message, you can reconfigure prerequisite downloads to come from the application deployment location by choos-ing the Download Prerequisites from the Same Location As My Application radio button. Note that Where the Prerequisites Are Downloaded From is a global setting that applies to all prerequi-sites; you cannot have one prerequisite downloaded from the component vendor site and have others downloaded from your site. If you choose to have prerequisites downloaded from your application's deployment location, Visual Studio 2005 copies the prerequisite packages to your deployment folder. It places each of the prerequisites into a separate folder (see Figure 8-11).

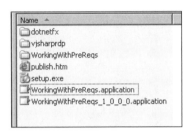

Figure 8-11. *Prerequisites deployed with the application*

Figure 8-11 shows the dotnetfx folder for the .NET Framework 2.0 redistributable and the vjsharprdp folder for the Visual J# redistributable. As mentioned earlier, you can also have pre-requisites downloaded from a custom location. This option makes sense if you deploy more than one application that relies on the same set of prerequisites. You can use this option to circum-vent having multiple copies of the same prerequisite on more than one machine. This option is especially useful if you are deploying custom prerequisites, which we'll talk about shortly.

Understanding the Prerequisite Manifest Files

You saw that if you configure Visual Studio 2005 to download the prerequisites for your appli-cation from the same place as your application, then the prerequisites are copied next to your application. If Visual Studio copies these files to your application's deployment folder, then the prerequisites must exist on the machine somewhere. It turns out that the prerequisite packages that are shown in the Prerequisites dialog box live under %ProgramFiles%\Microsoft Visual Studio 8\SDK\v2.0\BootStrapper\Packages. If you browse to the Packages folder, you'll see the ten prerequisites we listed earlier. If you look inside a few of the prerequisite packages, you'll get an idea of what comprises a prerequisite (see Figure 8-12).

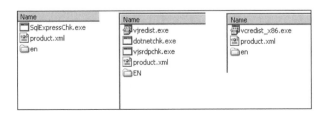

Figure 8-12. *Contents of a few prerequisites*

For Visual Studio 2005 to load prerequisites, you need a way to describe the prerequisite to Visual Studio. Moreover, for the bootstrapper to execute the prerequisite, it has to know what file to execute (for example, `vjredist.exe`). It turns out that prerequisites are composed of not only the binaries that make up the actual prerequisite but also of a few descriptor files (for example, `product.xml`) that describe the prerequisite. Actually, two descriptor files are used: the product manifest and the package manifest. The product manifest describes how to determine the existence of the prerequisite and how to install it if it doesn't exist. The package manifest has to do with culture. This package is specific to a locale, and the information within this manifest paints the prerequisite user interface based on the client's locale settings. The package manifest is named `package.xml` and lives within the culture-specific folder. For example, in Figure 8-12, you can see that all of the prerequisites shown have a folder named en or EN, for English. If you drill down into this folder, you'll find a `package.xml` file in each of them.

An example of a product manifest is as follows:

```xml
<?xml version="1.0" encoding="utf-8" ?>
<Product
  xmlns="http://schemas.microsoft.com/developer/2004/01/bootstrapper"
  ProductCode="Microsoft.Sql.Server.Express.1.0">
    <RelatedProducts>
        <DependsOnProduct Code="Microsoft.Net.Framework.2.0" />
        <DependsOnProduct Code="Microsoft.Windows.Installer.3.1" />
    </RelatedProducts>

    <PackageFiles>
        <PackageFile Name="SqlExpressChk.exe"/>
    </PackageFiles>

    <InstallChecks>
        <ExternalCheck Property="SQLExpressInstalled"
               PackageFile="SqlExpressChk.exe"/>
    </InstallChecks>

</Product>
```

The previous `product.xml` file belongs to the SQL Server 2005 Express Edition prerequisite. The product descriptor shows only three nodes. The root node is the `Product` node. Within the `Product` node, you have nodes named `RelatedProducts`, `PackageFiles`, and `InstallChecks`. The `RelatedProducts` node defines additional products that either are included as part of the defined prerequisite or are products upon which this prerequisite depends. In the previous example, you can see that SQL Server Express Edition depends upon the .NET Framework 2.0 and Windows Installer 3.1. You can also include a product with the prerequisite by using a node named `IncludesProduct`. The `PackageFiles` node defines the files that make up the actual prerequisite. In Figure 8-12, you can see that the SQL Server Express Edition folder contains a file named `SQLExpressChk.exe`. You also see the same file listed within the `PackageFiles` node. The `InstallChecks` node describes how to check for the existence of the prerequisite. In the previous case, the `InstallChecks` node tells the consumer of the manifest file to look for an external property named `SQLExpressInstalled`. There are also several other useful install checks: `AssemblyCheck`, `RegistryCheck`, `FileCheck`, and so on.

The SQL Server Express Edition prerequisite has a nice, short product manifest. It turns out that the Product node actually has two other nodes as well: Command and Schedules. The Command node defines executable commands that implement the tests that are described within the InstallChecks node. The Command node has two child nodes: InstallConditions and ExitCodes. The InstallConditions node describes condition steps in the command. The ExitCodes node defines the list of possible exit codes that an action can return. A sample Command node is as follows:

```
<Command PackageFile="someexe.exe" Arguments=""
    EstimatedInstallSeconds="50" >

  <InstallConditions>
      <FailIf Property="VersionMsi"
          Compare="ValueLessThan"
          Value="3.1"
          String="Invalid Windows Installer Version"/>
  </InstallConditions>

 <ExitCodes>
     <ExitCode Value="0" Result="Success"/>
 </ExitCodes>
</Command>
```

The previous code snippet shows a Command node that has a FailIf condition. Specifically, the FailIf condition is looking for a Windows Installer version that is older than 3.1. If this condition is true, the command fails. Another useful install condition, called BypassIf, can be used to bypass executing a command.

That takes care of the Command node. The Schedules node executes commands based on a schedule. InstallConditions, for example, has a property called Schedule that refers to a defined Schedule node within the Schedules node that defines when the command should execute. An example using Schedules is as follows:

```
<Schedules>
    <Schedule Name="BeforeProductInstall">
        <BeforePackage/>
    </Schedule>
</Schedules>

    <InstallChecks>
      <!-- some conditions -->
    </InstallChecks>

<!-- defines how to invoke the setup for the package -->
<Commands Reboot="Defer">
  <Command PackageFile="somefile.exe"
        EstimatedInstallSeconds="300">
    <InstallConditions>
      <!-- do not install if there is no .NET Framework -->
      <FailIf Property="DotNetInstalled" Schedule="BeforeProductInstall"
```

```
                Compare="ValueEqualTo"
                  Value="0" String="DotNetFxRequired" />
        </InstallConditions>

        <ExitCodes>
            <ExitCode Value="0" Result="Success"/>
            <ExitCode Value="3010" Result="SuccessReboot"/>
        </ExitCodes>

    </Command>
</Commands>
```

The previous code snippet defines a schedule named `BeforeProductInstall`. The schedule is then referenced by the `FailIf` install condition, essentially saying, "Fail if the .NET Framework is not installed."

The following is the package manifest for SQL Server 2005 Express Edition:

```xml
<?xml version="1.0" encoding="utf-8" ?>
<Package
  xmlns="http://schemas.microsoft.com/developer/2004/01/bootstrapper"
  Name="DisplayName"
  Culture="Culture"
  LicenseAgreement="eula.txt"
>

    <PackageFiles CopyAllPackageFiles="false">
        <PackageFile Name="sqlexpr32.exe"
          HomeSite="SqlExprExe"
          PublicKey="public-key-goes-here"
        <PackageFile Name="eula.txt"/>
    </PackageFiles>
    <Commands Reboot="Defer">
        <Command PackageFile="sqlexpr32.exe"
          Arguments='-q /norebootchk /qn
            reboot=ReallySuppress
            addlocal=all
            instancename=SQLEXPRESS
            SQLAUTOSTART=1'
          EstimatedInstalledBytes="225000000"
          EstimatedTempBytes="225000000"
          EstimatedInstallSeconds="420">
        <InstallConditions>
            <BypassIf Property="SQLExpressInstalled"
                Compare="ValueEqualTo" Value="0"/>
            <BypassIf
              Property="VersionNT"
              Compare="VersionGreaterThanOrEqualTo"
              Value="8-1"/>
            <FailIf
```

```xml
            Property="AdminUser"
            Compare="ValueEqualTo"
            Value="false"
            String="AdminRequired"/>
        <FailIf
            Property="Version9x"
            Compare="ValueExists"
            String="InvalidPlatform"/>
        <!-- MORE install conditions HERE-->
    </InstallConditions>
            <ExitCodes>
                <ExitCode Value="0" Result="Success"/>
                <ExitCode Value="1641" Result="SuccessReboot"/>
                <ExitCode Value="3010" Result="SuccessReboot"/>
                <!-- MORE EXIT CODES HERE-->
            </ExitCodes>
        </Command>
        <Command PackageFile="sqlexpr32.exe"
                Arguments='-q /norebootchk /qn reboot=ReallySuppress
                addlocal=all instancename=SQLEXPRESS SQLAUTOSTART=1'
                EstimatedInstalledBytes="225000000"
                EstimatedInstallSeconds="420">
            <InstallConditions>
                <BypassIf
                  Property="SQLExpressInstalled"
                  Compare="ValueEqualTo" Value="0"/>
                <BypassIf Property="VersionNT"
                   Compare="VersionLessThan"
                   Value="8-1"/>
                <FailIf Property="AdminUser"
                   Compare="ValueEqualTo"
                   Value="false"
                   String="AdminRequired"/>
                <!-- MORE CONDITIONS HERE-->
            </InstallConditions>
            <ExitCodes>
                <ExitCode Value="0" Result="Success"/>
                <ExitCode Value="1641" Result="SuccessReboot"/>
                <DefaultExitCode Result="Fail"
                   FormatMessageFromSystem="true"
                   String="GeneralFailure" />
                <!-- MORE EXIT CODES HERE -->
            </ExitCodes>
        </Command>
</Commands>

<Strings>
    <String Name="DisplayName">SQL Server 2005 Express Edition</String>
```

```
        <String Name="Culture">en</String>
        <String Name="AdminRequired">You do not have the permissions</String>
        <!-- MORE STRINGS HERE -->
    </Strings>
</Package>
```

As you probably noticed, the package manifest looks similar to the product manifest. You still see `PackageFiles`, `Commands`, and `InstallConditions`. The difference is that you now have a root node named `Package` and another node named `Strings`. The `Strings` element contains culture-specific resource strings. The `PackageFiles`, `Commands`, and `InstallConditions` nodes are now specific to the particular culture. That is, you now have install conditions.

You may have noticed in the discussion of the product manifest that there was not a `Commands` node in the `product.xml` file for SQL Server Express Edition. You may have even asked yourself, how is this prerequisite going to be installed if there are no commands to execute? Well, the commands that do the install of the prerequisite, in this case, are locale specific.

At this point, you should have a good idea of what the product and package manifests are. The whole idea behind the discussion was to prepare you to create your own custom prerequisites.

Building a Custom Prerequisite

As you have learned, the prerequisites that come with Visual Studio 2005 are stored within the bootstrapper package folder path at `%ProgramFiles%\Microsoft Visual Studio 8\SDK\v2.0\BootStrapper\Packages`. Visual Studio 2005 iterates over the folders in this path and reads the package manifests. From each package manifest it reads the `Name` property of the `Package` node, and then it finds that `String` under the `Strings` node. It uses that string value as the prerequisite name in the Prerequisites dialog box. The goal of the following sections is to show how to create a custom prerequisite, have it appear in the list of prerequisites, and then install it when you install the product. To do this, you'll follow these steps:

1. You'll build a simple Windows Installer that will install something specific on the client machine.

2. You will write a product manifest and then a package manifest.

3. You will then put these items into a folder under `C:\Program Files\Microsoft Visual Studio 8\SDK\v2.0\BootStrapper\Packages`.

4. You'll reference the custom prerequisite in a solution and verify that it worked.

Step 1: Build a Windows Installer

All sorts of prerequisites exist, but the ones you've seen so far are products such as the .NET Framework or SQL Server Express Edition. Your application, however, can have all sorts of dependencies. For example, you might need a file to exist at a particular folder, a registry key, a Windows service, a database, and so on. In this example, we'll keep things simple: you'll create a Windows Installer that writes a registry entry. You'll then write an application that displays the value of the registry entry in a Windows Forms application.

The first step is to create a Windows Installer. Several products can do this, but the easiest is to use Visual Studio 2005 to create the MSI, start Visual Studio 2005, and then open the New

Project dialog box. From the list of project types, choose Other Project Types and then choose Setup and Deployment. From there, create a setup project, and name it `CreateRegKeySetup`. When Visual Studio 2005 creates the project, click the Registry Editor button in the Solution Explorer (see Figure 8-13).

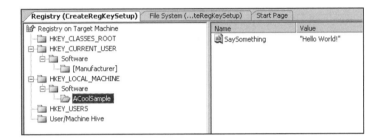

Figure 8-13. *Using the Registry Editor to create a new registry entry*

Clicking the Registry Editor button opens a UI, the Registry Editor, that you can use to create registry entries. Under `HKEY_LOCAL_MACHINE ➤ Software`, create a new key, and name it `ACoolSample`. Select `ACoolSample`, create a string, and give the key/value shown in Figure 8-13. Now build the project by choosing Build ➤ Rebuild All.

With that, you now have an MSI under your build configuration folder. For example, if your build is in Debug mode, you should have an MSI (`CreateRegKeySetup.msi`) under the `Debug` folder. To make sure your MSI creates the required registry key, right-click the project in the Solution Explorer, and choose Install (see Figure 8-14).

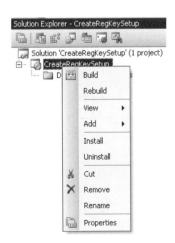

Figure 8-14. *Running the installer*

When you click Install, you should see the Windows Installer. Install the application for everyone, and then verify that the registry key was created. You can do this by typing regedit after selecting Start ➤ Run. After you verify that the installer created the key, delete the key.

Step 2: Write the Manifest Files

At this point, you have an MSI that you can use to create the registry key required by the sample application. You now need to create the product and package manifest files. To do this, create a Windows Forms application in the same solution. You have to package the prerequisite in a folder, so create a folder within this application, and name it MyCustomPreReq. Next create a file named product.xml and then a folder named en. Within en, create a file named package.xml.

Since we've talked at length about the manifest files, you should have no problem entering the following for the product manifest (product.xml):

```
<?xml version="1.0" encoding="utf-8"?>
<Product
    xmlns="http://schemas.microsoft.com/developer/2004/01/bootstrapper"
    ProductCode="ClickOnceAndCustomPreReq">
  <RelatedProducts>
    <DependsOnProduct Code="Microsoft.Net.Framework.2.0"/>
  </RelatedProducts>
  <PackageFiles>
    <PackageFile Name="CreateRegKeySetup.msi"/>
  </PackageFiles>
  <InstallChecks>
    <RegistryCheck Property="ACoolKey"
      Key="HKLM\Software\ACoolSample" Value="SaySomething" />
  </InstallChecks>
  <Commands Reboot="None">
    <Command PackageFile="CreateRegKeySetup.msi" EstimatedInstallSeconds="30">
      <!-- These checks determine whether the package is to be installed -->
      <InstallConditions>
        <BypassIf Property="ACoolKey" Compare="ValueExists"/>
        <!-- Block install if user does not have admin privileges -->
        <FailIf Property="Version9x"
          Compare="ValueExists" String="InvalidPlatform"/>
        <FailIf Property="VersionNT"
          Compare="VersionLessThan" Value="8-0.4" String="InvalidPlatform2K"/>
        <FailIf Property="AdminUser"
          Compare="ValueEqualTo" Value="false" String="AdminRequired"/>
      </InstallConditions>
      <ExitCodes>
        <ExitCode Value="0" Result="Success"/>
        <DefaultExitCode Result="Fail"
          FormatMessageFromSystem="true" String="GeneralFailure"/>
      </ExitCodes>
    </Command>
  </Commands>
</Product>
```

At the top of the manifest you can see that the prerequisite depends on the .NET Framework 2.0. You also see that you have one `PackageFile`, and that's the MSI file you created in the previous step. You have defined a single install check: `RegistryCheck`. You are looking for a key at `HKLM\Software\ACoolSample`, which has a string value named `SaySomething`. The value of the string value `SaySomething` is stored in the property named `ACoolKey`. You have defined one `Command` under the `Commands` node. The command has several `InstallConditions` and `ExitCodes` defined. There are three install conditions, the first of which says that if the property value of `ACoolKey` exists, then bypass the installation of the prerequisite. The three `FailIf` conditions guard against the installation on older versions of Windows and for a nonadmin user. Finally, the `ExitCodes` node lists an exit code for successfully completing the installation and then a default entry for a failure. Note that some commands may require a reboot. In this case, we obviously don't require this, so the `Commands` node has the attribute `Reboot="None"`.

That takes care of the product manifest. You now need to create the package manifest:

```xml
<?xml version="1.0" encoding="utf-8" ?>
<Package xmlns="http://schemas.microsoft.com/developer/2004/01/bootstrapper"
    Name="DisplayName" Culture="Culture" LicenseAgreement="eula.txt">
  <PackageFiles>
    <PackageFile Name="eula.txt"/>
  </PackageFiles>
  <Strings>
    <String Name="DisplayName">My Custom Prerequisite</String>
    <String Name="Culture">en</String>
    <String Name="AdminRequired">Administrator required.</String>
    <String Name="InvalidPlatform">Windows 2000 or later is required.</String>
    <String Name="InvalidPlatform2K">
        Windows 2000 Service Pack 4 or later is required.
    </String>
  </Strings>
</Package>
```

The package manifest for the sample application is also fairly simple. At the top you have the root `Package` node and then a `PackageFiles` node and a `Strings` element. The `PackageFiles` node has only the EULA file and the `Strings` node, which contains culture-specific messages. One of the interesting features in this file is the `Name` attribute on `Package`. Visual Studio 2005 uses this node to determine what gets displayed in the prerequisite list. In this case, you reference the `DisplayName` String, which has the value `My Custom Prerequisite`, which is what you expect to see in the Prerequisites dialog box. Note that the package manifest refers to `eula.txt`. Therefore, create a `eula.txt` file next to the manifest files in the sample application. You'll use all of these files in the next step.

Before you jump to the next step, you need to write some C# code to read the value of the registry key that gets written by the prerequisite. To do that, open `MainForm` in the Windows Forms application you created earlier. Place a button on the form, and double-click the button to access the handler in the code-behind file. Enter the following code to read the registry and display its value:

```csharp
try
{
    using (RegistryKey rg = Registry.LocalMachine)
```

```
        {
            string key = @"Software\ACoolSample";
            RegistryKey myreg = rg.OpenSubKey(key);
            if (myreg == null)
            {
        throw new Exception("Failed to open key [HKLM\\" + key + "]");
            }
            using (myreg)
            {
        string val = myreg.GetValue("SaySomething") as string;
        MessageBox.Show("Read value for SaySomething [" + val + "]");
            }
        }
}
catch (Exception ee)
{
    MessageBox.Show(ee.Message);
}
```

Step 3: Copy Files to the Packages Folder

The next step you need to take is to package the prerequisite and place it in the Packages folder next to the other prerequisites. To do this, take the folder you created within the Windows application named MyCustomPreReq, and copy it to %ProgramFiles%\Microsoft Visual Studio 8\ SDK\v2.0\BootStrapper\Packages. Note that you have not actually copied the MSI into this folder yet. After you copy the folder to the Packages directory, also copy and paste the MSI within your prerequisite folder. Your folder structure should look like Figure 8-15.

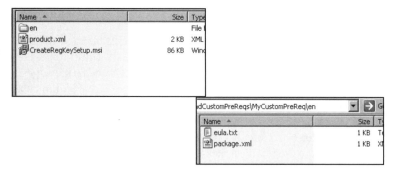

Figure 8-15. *Prerequisite folder contents*

Figure 8-15 shows the contents of the prerequisite folder and shows the en folder to the bottom right. You should have `eula.txt` and `package.xml` within en and the product manifest and the MSI within the root of the prerequisite folder.

Step 4: Use the Custom Prerequisite

At this point, the only step left is to reference the prerequisite and then deploy the application with ClickOnce. To do that, select the Windows Forms application, and then choose Properties. From there, open the Publish tab, and click the Prerequisites button. You should see your custom prerequisite in the list of prerequisites (see Figure 8-16).

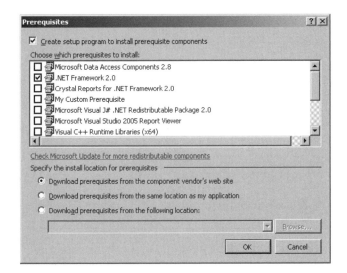

Figure 8-16. *The custom prerequisite within Visual Studio 2005*

Select My Custom Prerequisite from the list, and then publish the application. Note that you'll have to publish the application with full trust. When the application is published and if you have `publish.htm` set to display after a publish, you should see the prerequisite in the list (see Figure 8-17).

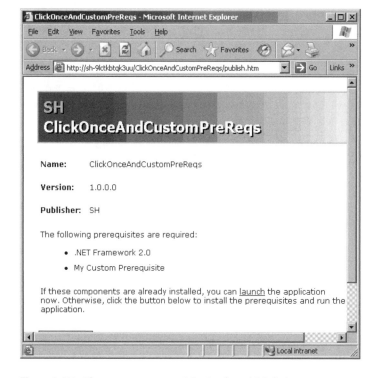

Figure 8-17. *The custom prerequisite in the* publish.htm *page*

You should be able to click the Install button to install the prerequisite and then execute the application (see Figure 8-18). When the application starts, verify that the registry entry was created.

That seems like a lot of work, but after doing it a few times, you'll agree that it is extremely easy to add a custom prerequisite to your ClickOnce deployment. If you followed through the example within Visual Studio 2005, then you now know that Visual Studio has IntelliSense support for the two manifests, which makes creating these two files pretty easy.

You can install this sample application from http://sayedhashimi.com/downloads/book/MyCustomPreReqApp/publish.htm.

You can also get the source from http://sayedhashimi.com/downloads/book/MyCustomPreReqApp/CreateRegKeySetupsrc.zip.

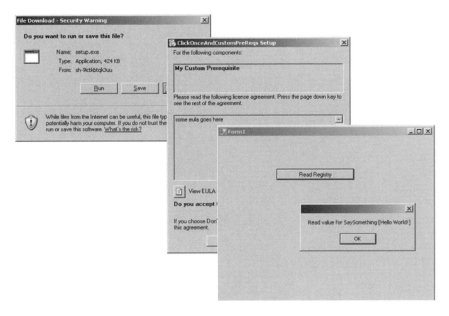

Figure 8-18. *The bootstrapper installing the prerequisite and then running the application*

Summary

In this chapter, we talked at length about using the ClickOnce data directory. You can use the data directory as a place to persist application state, and you can migrate application state from one version to another. We also talked about how you can use the ClickOnce APIs. We identified the various deployment events and described a sample application that showed how you can use these APIs.

The second half of the chapter talked about prerequisites. At the heart of a prerequisite are two manifest files: the product manifest and the package manifest. We described these files and then showed how to create them. We also deployed a custom prerequisite.

In the next chapter, you will look at tools related to deploying with ClickOnce. We'll identify some ClickOnce scenarios and then introduce various tools that can help with the deployment. Specifically, we will cover the Manifest Generation and Editing tool, the Bootstrapper Manifest Generator, MSBuild, and a few practical ClickOnce scenarios.

■■■

ClickOnce Tools and Scenarios

In the previous chapter, we talked about using the ClickOnce data directory and the bootstrapper to install custom prerequisites. In this chapter, we'll pick up where we left off with the bootstrapper by talking about the Bootstrapper Manifest Generator (BMG). This tool, as the name suggests, helps create the manifest files you need to create in order to deploy custom prerequisites. In this chapter, we'll actually talk about several tools in addition to the BMG. Specifically, we'll talk about the Manifest Generation and Editing (MAGE) tool and MSBuild. Toward the end of this chapter, we'll talk about some common ClickOnce scenarios as well. Let's get started with the BMG tool.

Using the Bootstrapper Manifest Generator (BMG)

In the previous chapter, you found that at the core of building a custom prerequisite are two manifest files: the product manifest and the package manifest. When you created these two manifests for your custom prerequisite, you had to build the XML-based manifest files manually. We mentioned that Visual Studio actually helps out quite a bit here by providing IntelliSense support for these files. However, even though Visual Studio has IntelliSense support, manually creating XML files is a bit prone to errors. It would help if you had a UI for this. That's where the BMG comes in.

The BMG has a workspace on Gotdotnet.com where you can see all of the releases of the tool and follow links to install the application via ClickOnce. The current version (1.1.0.1 as of this writing) runs on the final release of the .NET Framework 2.0. The first step to getting the tool on your local machine is to visit the workspace home for the BMG on Gotdotnet.com: `http://www.gotdotnet.com/workspaces/workspace.aspx?id=ddb4f08c-7d7c-4f44-a009-ea19fc812545`. The next step deals with the BMG tool being deployed from an untrusted publisher. As of this writing, the BMG is not signed with a trusted publisher certificate, so to seamlessly install the application, you have to add the deployment site of the application to the trusted sites of Internet Explorer. Once you do this, the application will install quietly and quickly. So, before you install the application, follow these steps:

1. Launch Internet Explorer.

2. Go to Tool ➤ Internet Options.

3. Click the Security tab, and then choose the Trusted Sites icon from the content zone list.

4. With Trusted Sites selected, click the Sites button (see Figure 9-1).

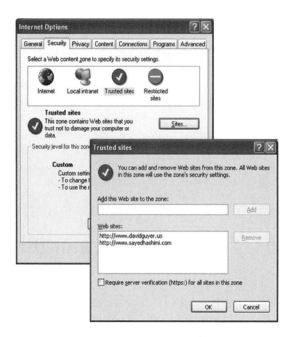

Figure 9-1. *Configuring a trusted site in Internet Explorer*

5. Next, enter **http://www.davidguyer.us** in the top edit box, and then click the Add button. This will add the URL to the Web Sites list shown in Figure 9-1.

6. Uncheck the Require Server Verification (https:) for All Sites in This Zone checkbox.

7. Click OK in the Trusted Sites dialog box and the Internet Options dialog box.

Now you should be able to install the application without problems.

Figure 9-2 shows the application's main window, along with the New Project dialog box. As shown, the application supports two project types: Package Manifest and MSBuild. The Package Manifest option is the facility you are most concerned with because it hides all of the XML in the product and package XML files you saw in the previous chapter. The MSBuild option creates an MSBuild project for a prerequisite package (and will not be discussed in this book).

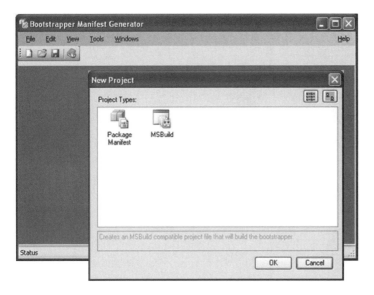

Figure 9-2. *The BMG UI*

In the previous chapter, you created a prerequisite package that checked for a registry entry. Recall that you first created an MSI to write the registry entry and then wrote a prerequisite package that checked for the existence of the registry entry. If the package didn't find the entry, it launched the MSI to install the prerequisite. In this section, you'll create the same prerequisite but use the BMG to do it. To walk along with this exercise, you can download the MSI from the previous example at http://sayedhashimi.com/downloads/book/MyCustomPreReqApp/ mycustomprereq/CreateRegKeySetup.msi.

After you download the MSI, open the BMG, choose File ➤ New, select Package Manifest, and then click OK. This will create a new package manifest project. Next, select the Package node from the tree control. This should display the Package to Install screen. The information typed into this dialog box appears for all localized versions of the package. Enter a project name (such as "Using the BMG"), as shown in Figure 9-3.

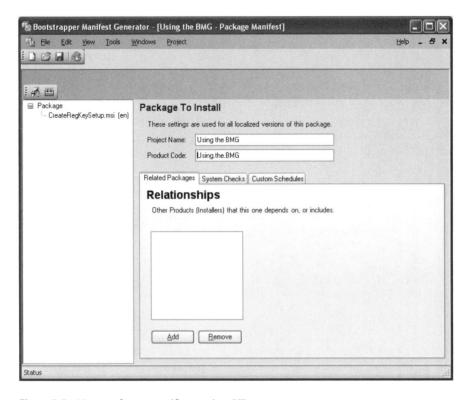

Figure 9-3. *New package manifest project UI*

After you enter a project name, the application automatically generates a product code using the project name. Leave the default product code, right-click the Package node from the tree control, and choose Add Install File. You should see the AddFile dialog box, as shown in Figure 9-4.

Figure 9-4. *The AddFile dialog box*

The AddFile dialog box is for adding the MSI or setup.exe file that will install the prerequisite package. In the example from the previous chapter, you created an MSI that wrote a registry entry. You can download this MSI from http://sayedhashimi.com/downloads/book/MyCustomPreReqApp/

`mycustomprereq/CreateRegKeySetup.msi` if you haven't done so already. In the AddFile dialog box, click the Browse button, and find the MSI. Note that the AddFile dialog box allows you to select a particular language or choose All Languages, if your prerequisite is language neutral. This example supports only the English language, so select Single Language, and make sure English is selected in the drop-down list. Click the OK button. After you add an install file, the application shows an entry for that file under the `Package` node in the tree control. Note that since the prerequisite supports only the English language, the BMG tool displays `(en)` next to the file to indicate that the install file is configured for English.

Select the install file from the tree control. The application will present the Install File screen shown in Figure 9-5.

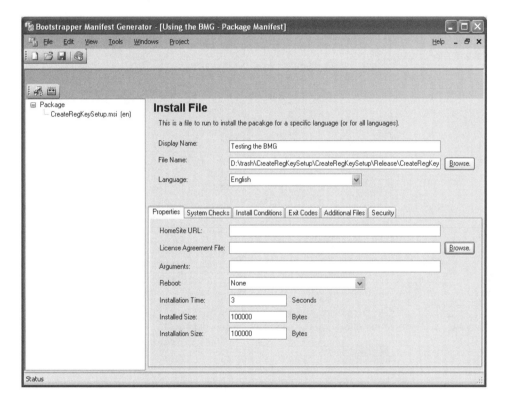

Figure 9-5. *Install File screen*

You can use the Install File screen to configure all aspects of the prerequisite for the given culture. Note that the Install File screen has six tabs: Properties, System Checks, Install Conditions, Exit Codes, Additional Files, and Security. Select the Properties tab (shown in Figure 9-5). The HomeSite URL field represents the location where the package is going to be downloaded from, if it's not included with the installer. The License Agreement File field is a path to the EULA document, the Arguments field is used to pass arguments to the installer, the Reboot field can be used to configure reboot options after the installer completes, the Installation Time field tells the bootstrapper how long the installation might take, the Installed Size field is the total bytes required by the installation, and the Installation Size field is the total size in bytes required by the installer during installation (for example, if the installer has to create temporary files). In this case, the installer did not require a reboot, and the entire package is only about 85KB. Therefore, it might take about three seconds, and its install size and installation requirements are about 100KB.

Next, ensure that the install file you added in the previous section is selected in the tree control, and then click the System Checks tab. The System Checks tab provides UIs for the various checks discussed in the previous chapter (see Figure 9-6).

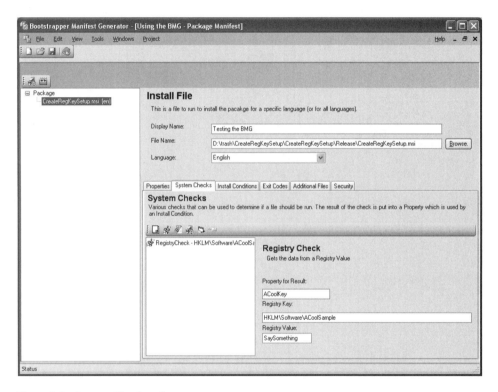

Figure 9-6. *System Checks tab*

You can select the type of check by clicking a toolbar button on the System Checks tab. Each button displays the corresponding screen for the selected check. The application supports the following checks: File Check, Registry Check, Registry File Check, MSI Product Check, External Check, and GAC Check. In this example, you'll check for the existence of a registry key. Specifically, you are interested in the string value of the following: HKEY_LOCAL_MACHINE\SOFTWARE\ACoolSample\ SaySomething. To create this check, click the Registry Check button on the toolbar. In the Registry Check screen, give the Property for Result field the name ACoolKey. Recall that when you did this manually, you created a registry check in the product.xml file that looked like this:

```
<RegistryCheck Property="ACoolKey"
    Key="HKLM\Software\ACoolSample" Value="SaySomething" />
```

ACoolKey creates a property that refers to the registry key HMLM\Software\ACoolSample, which has a string value of SaySomething. To create the same check via the UI, name the property ACoolKey, and use HMLM\Software\ACoolSample for the registry key. To pull the value from the string value SaySomething, use SaySomething for the registry value. Note that when the check is performed by the bootstrapper at install time, the value of the check is put into the property ACoolKey.

Next you need to configure the install conditions for the prerequisite package. Recall that when you did this in the previous chapter, you set up the following install conditions:

```
<InstallConditions>
        <BypassIf Property="ACoolKey" Compare="ValueExists"/>
        <!-- Block install if user does not have admin privileges -->
        <FailIf Property="Version9x" Compare="ValueExists"
String="InvalidPlatform"/>
        <FailIf Property="VersionNT"
      Compare="VersionLessThan" Value="5.0.4" String="InvalidPlatform2K"/>
        <FailIf Property="AdminUser"
      Compare="ValueEqualTo" Value="false" String="AdminRequired"/>
        </InstallConditions>
```

You have four install conditions. You want to bypass installation of the prerequisite package if the registry entry exists and want to fail if you don't have an administrator running the installer or a nonsupported version of the operating system. To configure the same thing using the BMG, select Install Conditions; you should see a screen that looks similar to Figure 9-7.

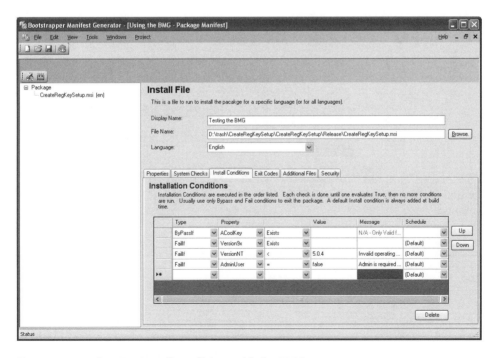

Figure 9-7. *Configuring install conditions with the BMG*

The BMG shines here because it makes configuring installation conditions easy. You select the type of condition, choose from a selected list of properties, select from a list of compare values (such as less than or equal to), provide an optional value (in cases where it makes sense), and then provide a message. Note that the first condition you check is to see whether the registry entry exists. Not surprisingly, when you named the property ACoolKey on the System Checks tab, the property shows up in the drop-down list in the Installation Conditions tab.

Next, you need to configure exit codes for the prerequisite package. Make sure the install file is selected in the tree control, and then choose the Exit Codes tab. Recall that in the previous chapter, you configured the following exit codes:

```
<ExitCodes>
      <ExitCode Value="0" Result="Success"/>
      <DefaultExitCode Result="Fail"
         FormatMessageFromSystem="true" String="GeneralFailure"/>
   </ExitCodes>
```

You configured only a success exit code and a failure exit code. You can do the same using the BMG's Exit Codes tab. As shown in Figure 9-8, you can configure the exit code 0 to indicate a success and then use a default system exit code for failure.

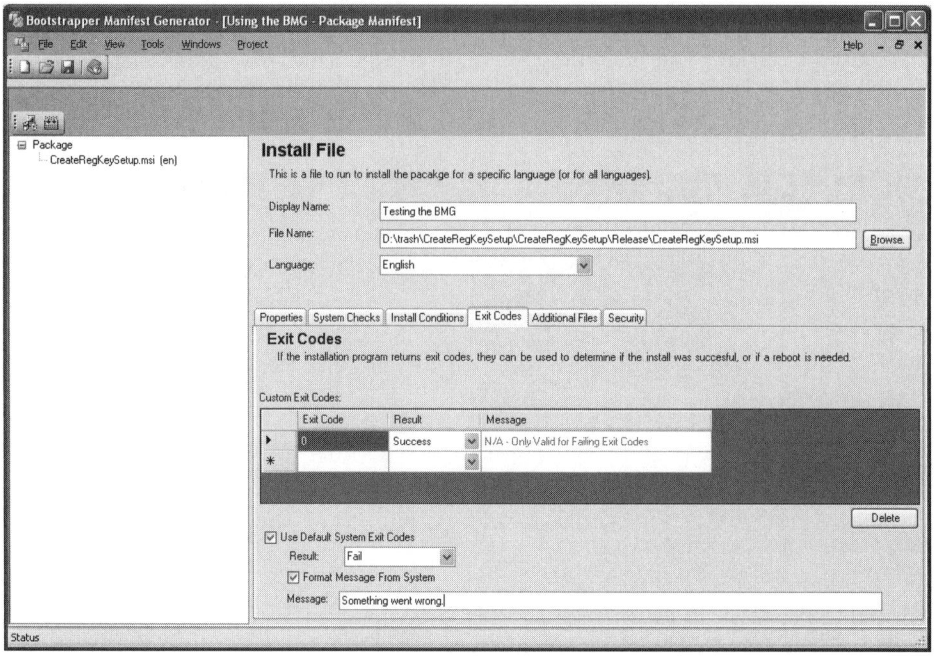

Figure 9-8. *Configuring exit codes with the BMG*

The BMG tool also allows you to add files that may be required by your prerequisite package (such as a CAB file) using the Additional Files tab. You can configure the bootstrapper to run security validations on the install file prior to running the installer. You do this via the Security tab. Figure 9-9 shows both the Additional Files and Security tabs.

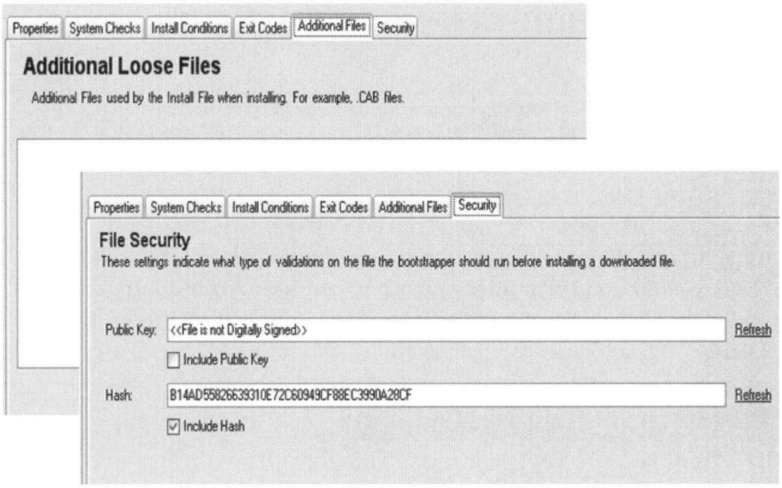

Figure 9-9. *Configuring additional files and security with the BMG*

Since the prerequisite package is not signed, you are not going to require the bootstrapper to perform any validation prior to running the installer. You also don't have any additional files that you need during install, so you are done with configuring the prerequisite package. The last step is to build the package. To do that, click the Build toolbar button above the tree control. This will build the package and copy it to the prerequisite packages folder so that Visual Studio 2005 can display it in the Prerequisites dialog box. (Go to the Project Designer, and then choose the Publish tab. Then click the Prerequisites button.)

The Build Results dialog box displays the contents of a build log file for the BMG (see Figure 9-10). Note that if a build is successful, you'll see the message "Build Succeeded" in the status bar of the Build Results dialog box. Note that there is a link at the top of the dialog labeled Build Output. Clicking this link opens the build output folder, and you can verify that product.xml, package.xml, and the rest of the prerequisite files were created by the BMG tool. You can also verify this by going to the Prerequisites dialog box in Visual Studio 2005.

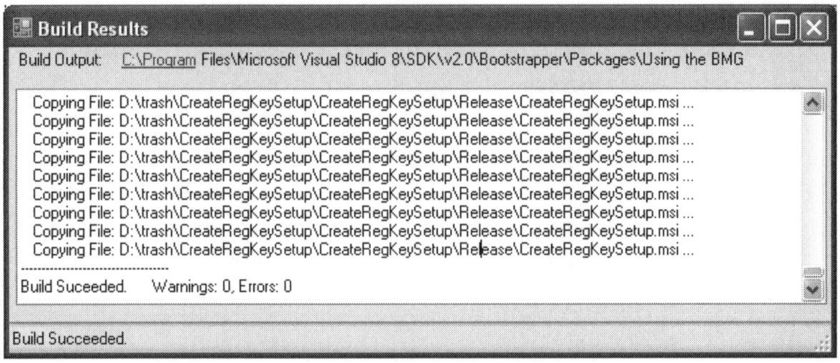

Figure 9-10. *The Build Results dialog box*

Using the Manifest Generation and Editing (MAGE) Tool

The mage.exe tool is a command-line utility that ships with the .NET Framework 2.0 SDK. You can use this tool to generate and modify ClickOnce deployment and application manifests. Moreover, you can use the tool to sign the aforementioned files. Because mage.exe is a command-line utility, the tool can be useful when scripting deployments or when you need a programmatic interface for creating, editing, or signing deployment and/or application manifests. We already mentioned that this tool also has a UI counterpart (mageui.exe) that provides the same facilities via a Windows Forms application (see Figure 9-11).

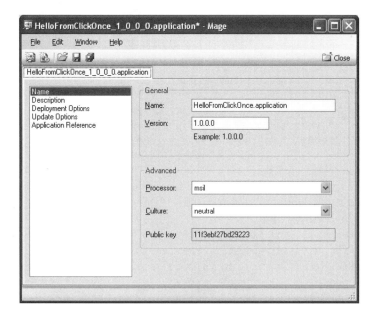

Figure 9-11. mageui.exe

You can launch the UI by double-clicking mageui.exe or by executing mage.exe without any parameters. Both of these applications are stored at %programfiles%\Microsoft Visual Studio 8\SDK\v2.0\Bin.

The first question that comes to mind with regard to the MAGE tool is, why do you need a tool to generate ClickOnce manifest files when Visual Studio 2005 can create the files and publish your application? Even though Visual Studio 2005 can create these files and publish ClickOnce applications, sometimes you'll have to manually create and modify them. Prior to diving into using the MAGE tools, it will help if we discuss a few scenarios where this tool is useful.

MAGE Scenario: ClickOnce Application Has to Be Deployed to More Than One Server

Applications often have to be deployed to more than one server. In this scenario, an application is developed and then has to move through one or more environments prior to arriving at the production server, as depicted in Figure 9-12.

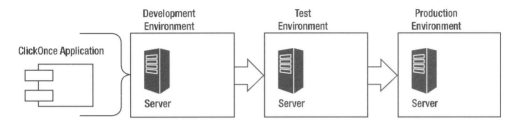

Figure 9-12. *Deploying a ClickOnce application to more than one environment*

An application starts out in the development environment. In this environment, developers use Visual Studio 2005 to publish the application while building the application. After development is complete, however, the deployment team takes over and is responsible for moving the application through several other environments (to ensure quality) prior to publishing the application to the production environment. Generally, the application goes through at least a testing environment prior to going to production; however, larger organizations have a performance-testing environment, among others. When the deployment team gets the application, the team is responsible for creating the ClickOnce manifest files for each environment. To build these manifest files, deployment engineers can use the MAGE tools. As an application moves from the test environment to the production environment, the ClickOnce manifest files have to be modified and re-signed. You can use the MAGE tool to do this.

MAGE Scenario: The Producer of the Application Doesn't Know Where the Application Will Be Hosted for Deployment

Software companies don't always know where an application is going to be hosted. For example, a software company builds a ClickOnce application that provides problem-tracking functionality. One of the companies that purchased the software wants to deploy the software to their internal users who do not have an Internet connection; however, they have a connection to the internal network (see Figure 9-13).

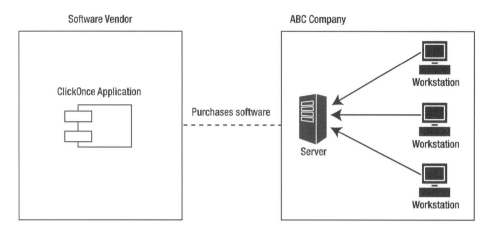

Figure 9-13. *The software vendor ships the application to the purchaser, and the purchaser deploys the application to its internal server.*

In this scenario, the software vendor can create the deployment and application manifest files, but they will have to be modified once the deployment server and update server are known. Note that you are assuming that it is not practical for the software vendor to preconfigure the manifest files for the purchaser of the software because servers often move or have to be renamed, so the software purchaser will need to take responsibility for maintaining the manifest files.

In this scenario, the software vendor can produce and distribute a ClickOnce deployable application. The software purchaser can take the ClickOnce deployment, modify the manifest files, and re-sign them using the MAGE tool.

MAGE Scenario: ClickOnce Application Has to Delay-Sign Assemblies

The assemblies shipped with the .NET Framework are strong-named, signed assemblies. The CLR verifies the integrity of signed assemblies prior to loading. If an assembly is tampered with, the CLR doesn't load it. Because of this, some organizations heavily guard the private key used to sign assemblies. If they didn't and someone with bad intentions obtained the private key, they could sign the assembly and perform malicious activities. For example, if someone got a hold of the private key used to sign the .NET Framework system assemblies (for example, System.dll), they could copy their own version of an assembly and do virtually whatever they liked.

Because organizations heavily guard their private keys, developers don't have access to the private key. This poses the question, if the private key is not exposed to developers to sign assemblies with, how do they build strong-named assemblies? Well, the .NET Framework supports the concept of *delay-signing* assemblies. Delay-signing assemblies allows developers to tell the CLR not to verify the integrity of an assembly. You can do this by following these steps:

1. Use the public key to sign the assembly. The public key is usually in the form of an `*.snk` file. You can create this file using the signing tool, `sn.exe`, that ships with the .NET Framework SDK. The signing tool comes with the .NET Framework SDK and is located at `%programfiles%\Microsoft Visual Studio .NET 2003\SDK\v1.1\Bin`.

2. Apply the strong-named key file to the assembly by adding `AssemblyKeyFileAttribute` to `AssemblyInfo.cs`:

   `[assembly:AssemblyKeyFileAttribute("myapp.snk")]`

3. Set the delay-signing attribute to `true`:

   `[assembly:AssemblyDelaySignAttribute(true)]`

4. Register the assembly for verification skipping using the signing tool:

   `sn.exe -Vr myapp.dll`

Delay-signing assemblies should happen only during development. The idea is to skip verification during development and then properly sign the assemblies prior to deployment. The problem with delay-signing assemblies and Visual Studio publishing is that after you do a build of your application, you have to take the generated assemblies and have them signed using the private key. If the assemblies are modified, the ClickOnce manifests (at least the application manifest) have to be re-signed, so you can't publish an application that is delay-signed using Visual Studio 2005. Instead, you'll have to use the MAGE tool or a similar tool.

MAGE Scenario: ClickOnce Application Assemblies Need to Be Obfuscated

Historically it has been difficult to reverse-engineer the binaries of an application to a form that can be easily understood. With languages such as Java, C#, and others, reverse-engineering has become easy. These languages are compiled to an intermediate form (Java goes to bytecode and C#, and all supported .NET languages go to MSIL), which makes them easy to decompile. More and more, organizations are looking for approaches to prevent the decompilation of their software. Preventing someone from reverse-engineering binaries (whether bytecode, MSIL, or even native machine code[1]) is nearly impossible. Because of this, organizations interested in protecting themselves against decompilation use obfuscation. *Obfuscation* takes the intermediate form and changes it, such that when decompiled, it becomes difficult to understand.

So, what does this have to do with ClickOnce and the MAGE tool? Well, if you have to obfuscate your software, you'll have to either create the ClickOnce manifest manually or edit the Visual Studio–generated manifest files. The reason for this is that obfuscation is applied to the assemblies. After you compile your application, you obfuscate and then publish. Visual Studio 2005 doesn't support plugging in obfuscation to this process. As a result, after you obfuscate your assemblies, you have to re-sign manifest files created by Visual Studio. The MAGE tool can help with this.

---

1. Cifuentes, Cristina, and K. John Gough. "Decompilation of Binary Programs." *Software: Practice and Experience* (July 1995): 811–829.

Creating the ClickOnce Manifest Files with the MAGE Tool

By now you should understand the usefulness of the MAGE utility. In this section, you'll learn more about the MAGE tool by walking through the steps required to create the application and deployment manifests with the MAGE tool. You'll use the GUI version of the MAGE tool (`mageui.exe`) rather than the command-line version.

To start, open Visual Studio 2005, and create a new Windows Forms application named `ClickOnceWithMage`. When you create a Windows Forms application, Visual Studio 2005 creates a form for you named `Form1`. Open `Form1.cs`, and rename this form to `MainForm`. Do this by right-clicking the name of the class and then choosing Refactor ➤ Rename. Visual Studio will open the Rename dialog box. Name the form `MainForm`, make sure the Preview Reference Changes checkbox is checked, and then click OK.

When you click OK, Visual Studio's Preview Changes – Rename dialog box opens (see Figure 9-14). Review the changes, and then click Apply.

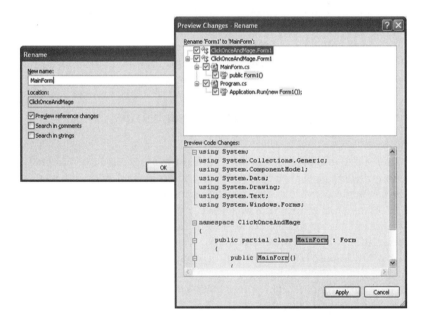

Figure 9-14. *Using Visual Studio 2005's refactor facilities to rename a class*

Next, open `MainForm` in design view, drag a button from the Toolbox, and drop it on the form. Finally, build the application in Release mode.

To create a ClickOnce deployment using the MAGE tool, you have to collect the application files and then create the deployment and application manifests. Open the folder where you stored the application, and then open the `bin\Release` folder. Notice that Visual Studio 2005 has created an executable named `ClickOnceAndMage.exe` along with two other files,

ClickOnceAndMage.pdb and ClickOnceAndMage.vshost.exe. The first file is obviously the application executable, but what are the other two? These two files are new to Visual Studio and are used for debugging purposes. The *.vshost.exe file, in particular, is interesting. Read more about this file at http://msdn2.microsoft.com/en-us/library/ms185331.aspx.

To deploy this application, first create a new folder named MageDeployments. In this file, copy ClickOnceAndMage.exe. Next, go to Start ➤ All Programs ➤ Microsoft .NET Framework SDK 2.0 ➤ SDK Command Prompt. Now type mageui.exe, and press Enter. You should see the MAGE GUI shown in Figure 9-15.

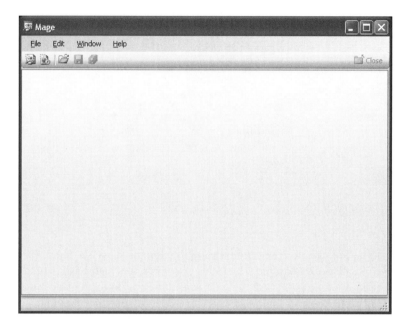

Figure 9-15. *The Mage window*

The Mage window has a toolbar that allows you to create a new application manifest, create a new deployment manifest, open existing manifest files, and save modified manifests. You'll start by creating the application manifest.

Creating the Application Manifest

You have to create the application manifest first because the deployment manifest has a reference to the application manifest. The leftmost button on the toolbar creates a new application manifest. Figure 9-16 shows the new application manifest UI panes.

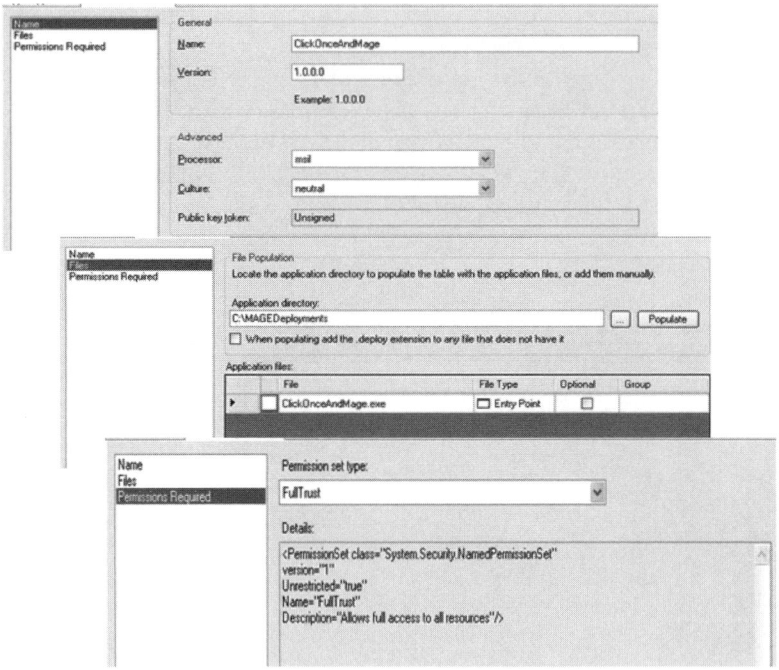

Figure 9-16. *The UIs used to create/edit application manifest files*

Three configuration panes are used to create/edit the application manifest file. These UI panes are Name, Files, and Permissions Required. The Name pane captures high-level details about the application. The interesting panes are the next two. The Files pane identifies the files that make up the application. Because an application can consist of any number of files and file types, the Files pane is designed so that you specify the application directory and click the Populate button to specify the files that make up the application. When you click Populate, the application creates an entry for each file in the Application Files grid. You can use this grid to create optional files and file groups, just like you can when using Visual Studio 2005. The Permissions Required pane allows you to set the CAS security requirements for the application. The drop-down list shown in Figure 9-16 allows you to choose FullTrust, LocalIntranet, Internet, or Custom. FullTrust, LocalIntranet, and Internet are preconfigured with specific permission set/permissions. If you want to specify your own permission set/permissions, you can choose Custom, and then the pane will allow you to enter your own permission requirements.

After you fill in these details, you can save the application manifest. When you click the Save toolbar button or choose the File ➤ Save or File ➤ Save All menu item, the application displays the Signing Options dialog box (see Figure 9-17).

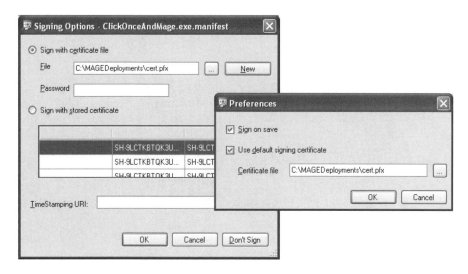

Figure 9-17. *Signing the manifest files*

The Signing Options dialog box allows you to sign with an existing certificate or create a new one.

Figure 9-17 also shows the Preferences dialog box that you open by selecting File ➤ Preferences. This dialog box configures two global signing options. You can tell the application to sign the manifest file(s) upon saving and also define a default certificate file to use for signing files.

This completes the discussion concerning the creation of the application manifest file. We'll now talk about the deployment manifest.

Creating the Deployment Manifest

To create a deployment manifest, click the New Deployment Manifest toolbar button. Figure 9-18 shows the new deployment manifest UI panes.

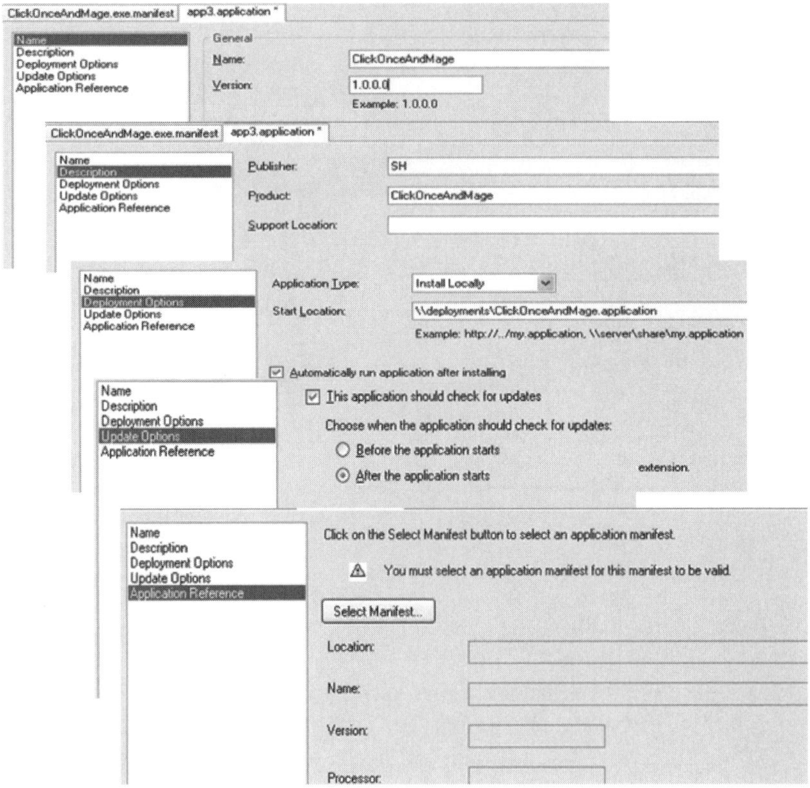

Figure 9-18. *UIs used to create/edit the deployment manifest*

The Name and Description panes are self-explanatory. The Deployment Options pane has several interesting features. The first is that you can configure the application type or deployment mode of the application. Recall that you can deploy a ClickOnce application as an offline or online application. An offline application is set to an application type of Install Locally, and online applications are set to Online Only. The second interesting feature on this pane is that you use the Start Location text box to specify where the application is going to be launched from (that is, the ultimate location of the deployment manifest). The Start Location setting is equivalent to the Publish Location setting in the Publish tab of the Project Designer in Visual Studio 2005. The Update Options pane defines how the application will be updated, if at all. Note that this pane captures the same information that the Updates dialog box captures in Visual Studio 2005. The Application Reference dialog box associates the deployment manifest to the application manifest. The Select Manifest button allows you to browse to and select a .manifest file. After you fill out all the panes associated with the deployment manifest and select an application manifest, you can save the deployment manifest.

This concludes the discussion of the MAGE application. We'll now discuss how you can use MSBuild and ClickOnce to make your deployments easier.

Using MSBuild with ClickOnce

In the previous section, we talked about the MAGE tool. We discussed the GUI version of the tool; however, we mentioned that the tool also has a command-line interface. The command-line interface is useful for situations where you need to script the creation of the ClickOnce manifest files. So when would you need to script the creation of manifest files? Scripting might be helpful in several situations; the primary reason is to automate the entire build and deployment of an application. For example, it's not uncommon for deployment engineers to script the entire build and publish process. Specifically, the steps might be something like the following:

1. Get the latest version of an application from the source control system.

2. Build the application.

3. Create the ClickOnce manifests.

4. Publish the application.

With the MAGE tool, you can do step 3, but the other steps have to be scripted using some other technique. That's where MSBuild comes in—you can use MSBuild to create a fully customized ClickOnce deployment. To see how, you'll build a simple Windows Forms application and create the ClickOnce deployment using MSBuild.

Creating the ClickOnce Deployment Using MSBuild

Thus far, you have published ClickOnce applications using Visual Studio 2005 and the MAGE tool. Now you'll see how to do the same using MSBuild. You know from the earlier chapters that you can write an MSBuild script from scratch and execute it. To keep things simple, this example will use the project file generated by Visual Studio 2005. To use MSBuild to create the ClickOnce deployment, you'll need to perform three steps:

1. Create a Windows Forms application.

2. Set properties on the Publish, Security, and Signing tabs under the Project Designer.

3. Execute the `publish` target using MSBuild.

The first step is obvious, but what about the second step? That too is a requirement because you have to modify the project file with elements such as the following:

- The publish URL

- Application update configuration

- Security requirements

- Signing details

- Application prerequisites

You can guess some of these (via default values) but not others. For example, how will MSBuild know where you want to publish the application? Thus, after you create an application, you need to modify the ClickOnce-related tabs with enough information so that the `publish` target can execute without errors. To do that, you need to provide at least the following:

1. Provide the `publish` URL in the Publish tab.

2. Set the application CAS security requirement in the Security tab.

3. Check the Sign the ClickOnce Manifest checkbox on the Signing tab.

After you create a Windows application and set the ClickOnce properties, you can use MSBuild to create the ClickOnce deployment. That's the easy part—it takes only one command:

```
msbuild yoursolutionfile.sln /target:publish
```

This command tells MSBuild to execute the `publish` target on the given solution. The output of the command is a ClickOnce deployment in the working build configuration (such as `Debug`). If your build configuration is set to `Debug`, then you'll have a `yourprojectname.publish` folder within the `bin\debug\` folder. The contents of the folder will look familiar (see Figure 9-19).

Figure 9-19. *An MSBuild-generated ClickOnce deployment*

Figure 9-19 shows you how simple it is to create a ClickOnce deployment using MSBuild. Note that in this example, you used Visual Studio 2005 to add the ClickOnce properties to the project file. Having Visual Studio 2005 is obviously not a requirement—you can modify the project file using any text editor. All you need to know is where and how the ClickOnce properties are stored in the project file. To build a ClickOnce deployment using MSBuild, all you need to do is the following:

1. Create a signing certificate (optionally using the signing tool, `sn.exe`, that ships with the .NET Framework SDK)—this is the certificate that will be used to sign the Click-Once manifest files.

2. Add the ClickOnce properties to the project file. Do this by adding properties to the first property group defined in the project file. For example, the following code lists some of the ClickOnce properties stored in a typical project file:

```
<PropertyGroup>
    <PublishUrl>c:\deployments\</PublishUrl>
```

```
   <Install>true</Install>
   <InstallFrom>Unc</InstallFrom>
   <UpdateEnabled>true</UpdateEnabled>
   <UpdateMode>Foreground</UpdateMode>
   <UpdateInterval>7</UpdateInterval>
   <UpdateIntervalUnits>Days</UpdateIntervalUnits>
   <UpdatePeriodically>false</UpdatePeriodically>
   <UpdateRequired>false</UpdateRequired>
   <MapFileExtensions>true</MapFileExtensions>
   <InstallUrl>\\products\deployments\</InstallUrl>
   <BootstrapperEnabled>true</BootstrapperEnabled>
   <SignManifests>true</SignManifests>
   <GenerateManifests>true</GenerateManifests>
   <ManifestKeyFile>WindowsApplication10_TemporaryKey.pfx</ManifestKeyFile>
 </PropertyGroup>
<ManifestKeyFile>WindowsApplication10_TemporaryKey.pfx</ManifestKeyFile>
```

3. Execute the `publish` target on the project file.

The previous steps show how easy it is to use MSBuild to create a ClickOnce deployment. The valuable lesson to take away from this discussion is that there is a predefined target named `publish`. Moreover, you can customize and automate the ClickOnce deployments using all of the facilities of MSBuild.

You'll now explore how to use MSBuild to automate the generation of a ClickOnce deployment.

Using MSBuild and ClickOnce As Part of a Build Process

Thus far, you've seen that you can use Visual Studio, the MAGE tool, and MSBuild to create a ClickOnce deployment. With Visual Studio and the MAGE tool, you utilize a user interface where you supply parameters and then click a button to have the implementation generate the ClickOnce manifests. With MSBuild, you saw that you can execute the `publish` target to generate a ClickOnce deployment. All of these methods serve their purpose; however, one area that is not addressed by the previous methods is generating a ClickOnce deployment as part of a build and deployment process. Figure 9-20 depicts a typical build and deployment process.

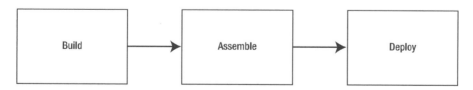

Figure 9-20. *A typical build and deployment process*

Figure 9-20 shows that a typical build and deployment process has three phases: build, assemble, and deploy. In the build phase, a script (for example, an MSBuild-based script) is executed to create binaries from the source code. In the assemble phase, the generated assemblies are assembled into one or more applications (for example, a smart client or a web application). In the deploy phase, the assembled applications are deployed to one or more servers.

Each of the three phases has specific input from the previous phase and generates output, which is used in the next phase. Figure 9-21 shows the input and output of the three phases.

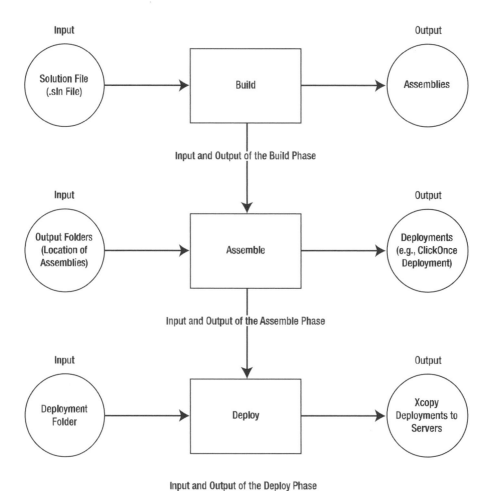

Figure 9-21. *The input and output of the three phases of a build process*

A build and deployment process generally consists of build, assemble, and deploy phases. The build phase takes the source artifacts and generates assemblies. Typically, you either use the Visual Studio solution file or enumerate the project files. The assemble phase uses the output assemblies from the build phase. The assemble phase is responsible for assembling a deployable application from the generated assemblies. After the assemble phase creates deployable applications, the deploy phase does the actual deployment to servers.

The build and deployment process is generally an automated process. To realize the benefits of an automated build and deployment process, you have to write an MSBuild script that automatically generates a ClickOnce deployment. For example, if your solution has a smart client along with a Web application in the assemble phase, you need to automate the process of generating the ClickOnce deployment from a list of assemblies. MSBuild defines three tasks you can use to generate a ClickOnce deployment. The ClickOnce-related tasks include `GenerateApplicationManifest`, `GenerateDeploymentManifest`, and `GenerateBootstrapper`. The `GenerateApplicationManifest` task and the `GenerateDeploymentManifest` task generate the ClickOnce application and deployment manifests, respectively. The `GenerateBootstrapper` task generates a bootstrapper. We'll now show how you can automate the generation of a ClickOnce deployment using these tasks.

In this exercise, you'll use MSBuild to create a ClickOnce deployment. The goal of this exercise is to write an application that has one DLL and one EXE and then write an MSBuild script to create a ClickOnce deployment. You can download the application for this exercise from `http://sayedhashimi.com/downloads/book/AutomatedDeployment.zip`.

The application is a Visual Studio 2005 Windows Forms application consisting of three files: an EXE file (`.exe`), a support assembly (`SupportAssembly.dll`), and a configuration file. Figure 9-22 shows the UI for the application.

Figure 9-22. *The user interface of the Windows Forms application*

The application has one form, which has a button on it. When the user clicks the button, the application calls a method in a class stored in the supporting assembly to get a string. The string is then displayed in a label on the form.

To create an MSBuild script, you need to build the application and then take the EXE, the config file, and the DLL and place them in a directory. This step simulates the build phase of an automated build process. In this phase, build the application, and take the two assemblies and the config file and put them in a folder. The MSBuild script will take the files from this folder and will create a ClickOnce deployment from it. This is the assemble phase of an automated build and deployment process. To follow along, create the following folder structure: `c:\hold\release`. Now put the three files in the `release` folder.

Now that you have the application files where you want them, you can start to build the input for the MSBuild script. As we said earlier, all of the ClickOnce deployments you've done so far have been done using Visual Studio 2005, the MAGE tool, or the `publish` target with MSBuild. Using these techniques, you used UIs to configure the ClickOnce deployment. Automating this process requires that you input all the ClickOnce parameters into the script.

What kind of input do you need? For example, you need to know the update policy of the application. You need to know the location of the certificate used to sign the ClickOnce manifests, the version of the application, and so on. The following list outlines the order:

1. The update URL (has to be HTTP or UNC)

2. The deployment mode of the application (online/offline)

3. The path to a certificate file

4. The application's update policy

5. The name of the application name and its version

6. A flag to indicate whether to use the .deploy file extension

7. The path to the assembly folder

8. The path to the output folder

The update URL defines where clients will be sent for updates. The online/offline property tells ClickOnce whether the application will be installed as an online application or an offline application. ClickOnce manifest files have to be signed, so you need to know how to get to the certificate file. The application name and version are self-explanatory. ClickOnce deployments have three registered file extensions (.deploy, .application, or .manifest). The .application and .manifest extensions are for the deployment and application manifest, respectively. The .deploy extension is for all the files that make up the application. This flag tells the build script whether to apply this file extension to all the files. Note that ClickOnce uses this file extension to circumvent potential problems that often arise because of Web servers configured not to serve specific file extensions (such as .exe).[2] The assembly folder tells the script where to find the files that need to be part of the ClickOnce deployment. The output directory property tells the script where to put the ClickOnce deployment after it generates it.

Now let's start the MSBuild script. You'll start by defining the properties you need for your ClickOnce deployment:

```
<PropertyGroup>
<UpdateUrl>
  http://localhost/AutomaticDeployTakeOne/AutomaticDeployTakeOne.application
</UpdateUrl>
  <CertificateThumbprint>
   <!-- PUT CERT THUMBPRINT HERE-->
  </CertificateThumbprint>
  <ApplicationVersion>1.0.0.0</ApplicationVersion>
  <UseDeployExt>true</UseDeployExt>
  <ApplicationPublisher>Sayed Y. Hashimi</ApplicationPublisher>
  <ApplicationSupportUrl>http://localhost/</ApplicationSupportUrl>
  <EntryPointAssembly>AutomaticDeployTakeOne.exe</EntryPointAssembly>
  <BinFolder>C:\hold\release\</BinFolder>
  <RootOutputFolder>c:\inetpub\wwwroot\AutomaticDeployTakeOne\</RootOutputFolder>
```

---

2. For more about the .deploy file extension, see http://msdn2.microsoft.com/en-us/library/ms165433.aspx.

```
    <ApplicationName>AutomaticDeployTakeOne</ApplicationName>
    <ConfigFile>AutomaticDeployTakeOne.exe.config</ConfigFile>
    <LooseFiles></LooseFiles>
    <ApplicationDescription>
        Automating ClickOnce Deployment Generation
    </ApplicationDescription>
 </PropertyGroup>
```

We hinted at most of the properties earlier; however, a few require special attention. The
`CertificateThumbprint` property contains the thumbprint of the certificate that will be used to
sign the ClickOnce manifest files. You can obtain the thumbprint of a certificate by looking at
the certificate in `certmgr.exe`. The `certmgr.exe` application displays the installed certificates
(for the logged-in user). If you have the .NET Framework SDK installed, open a Visual Studio
command prompt, and enter `certmgr.exe`.

To obtain the thumbprint of a certificate, select a certificate, click the View button, and
then select the Details tab, as shown in Figure 9-23. From the Details tab, scroll down until the
Thumbprint field is visible. Choose Thumbprint, select the contents from the text box, and press
Ctrl+C to copy the thumbprint. You can then paste the thumbprint in your build script.

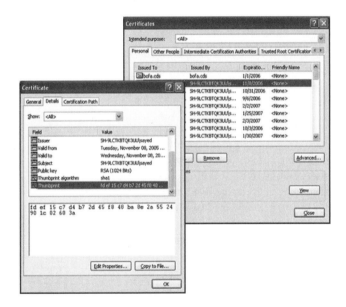

Figure 9-23. *The* `certmgr.exe` *user interface*

Now that you have defined your properties, you need to define a few MSBuild items that
will capture the files that make up the application. These items, along with the properties, will
be used as input to the ClickOnce-related MSBuild tasks:

```
<EntryPoint Include="$(BinFolder)$(EntryPointAssembly)">
    <AssemblyType>Managed</AssemblyType>
    <DependencyType>Install</DependencyType>
</EntryPoint>
```

```
  <Dependency Include="$(BinFolder)*.dll">
    <AssemblyType>Managed</AssemblyType>
    <DependencyType>Install</DependencyType>
  </Dependency>

  <ConfigFile Include="$(BinFolder)$(ConfigFile)" />
```

```
</ItemGroup>
```

The previous snippet shows three items: EntryPoint, Dependency, and ConfigFile. The EntryPoint item defines the EntryPoint assembly (that is, the EXE that contains the Main method). The Dependency item refers to the support assembly (SupportAssembly.dll), and the ConfigFile item points to the application configuration file.

Now let's see the task that generates the application manifest:

```
<GenerateApplicationManifest
      AssemblyName="$(EntryPointAssembly)"
      AssemblyVersion="$(ApplicationVersion)"
      ConfigFile="@(ConfigFile)"
      Dependencies="@(Dependency)"
      Description="$(ApplicationDescription)"
      EntryPoint="@(EntryPoint)"
      OutputManifest="$(RootOutputFolder)$(ApplicationName).exe.manifest">
      <Output ItemName="ApplicationManifest"
            TaskParameter="OutputManifest"/>
  </GenerateApplicationManifest>
```

The GenerateApplicationManifest task outputs a ClickOnce application manifest. The OutputManifest property of the task defines the location where the manifest is generated. In this example, you have followed the naming convention used by Visual Studio 2005. Namely, you have used the <application name>.exe.manifest naming convention. The EntryPoint property points to the application executable, and the Dependencies property points to the collection of dependent assemblies. The ConfigFile property defines the application configuration file. The rest of the properties are self-explanatory.

Now let's see how you can generate the deployment manifest:

```
<GenerateDeploymentManifest EntryPoint="@(ApplicationManifest)"
      OutputManifest="$(RootOutputFolder)$(ApplicationName).application"
      AssemblyVersion="$(ApplicationVersion)"
      Install="true"
      DeploymentUrl="$(UpdateUrl)"
      UpdateEnabled="true"
      Product="AutomaticDeployTakeOne"
      Publisher="$(ApplicationPublisher)"
      SupportUrl="$(ApplicationSupportUrl)"
      MapFileExtensions="$(UseDeployExt)">
      <Output
          ItemName="DeployManifest"
          TaskParameter="OutputManifest" />
  </GenerateDeploymentManifest>
```

The `GenerateDeploymentManifest` task generates a ClickOnce deployment manifest. As expected, the deployment manifest defines properties that capture the update policy of the application and the location where updates are obtained. The `MapFileExtensions` property is a flag that tells the tasks whether to use the `.deploy` file extension. Similar to `GenerateApplicationManifest`, this task defines an `OutputManifest` property that tells the task where to generate the deployment manifest and what to name the file. Note that the deployment manifest has to have a reference to the application manifest. You specify the application manifest using the `EntryPoint` attribute on the `GenerateDeploymentManifest` task. In the previous example, you are using the usual convention of naming deployment manifests with the `.application` extension.

Earlier we talked about signing manifests. After you define the task that generates the application or deployment manifest, you can use the `SignManifest` task to sign the manifest with a certificate:

```
<SignFile
    CertificateThumbprint="$(CertificateThumbprint)"
    SigningTarget="@(DeployManifest)"/>
```

The `SignFile` task takes a certificate thumbprint and a manifest file and signs the manifest with the certificate.

The MSBuild script for this example is included with the solution, and both are packaged in a file at `http://sayedhashimi.com/downloads/book/AutomatedDeployment.zip`. Note that for the script to work, you'll need to paste in a certificate thumbprint into the script.

Looking at Some Common ClickOnce Scenarios

We'll now talk about some common scenarios with regard to ClickOnce deployments.

Passing Parameters to a ClickOnce Application

ClickOnce supports a mechanism where you can pass the ClickOnce-deployed application parameters. By default, this option is not enabled when you configure an application for deployment using Visual Studio 2005. To enable arguments to be passed to your application, go to Project Properties ➤ Publish, and click the Options button. In the Publish Options dialog box, check the Allow URL Parameters to Be Passed to Application option. To pass parameters, you can then construct the URL to your deployment manifest with URL parameters such as `http://localhost/ClickOnceURLParams/ClickOnceURLParams.application?username=sayed&password=mypass`.

You can retrieve URL parameters by using the `HttpUtility` class in the `System.Web` assembly. The following code snippet demonstrates this:

```
private void DisplayURLParameters()
{
    try
    {
        Uri appUri = System.Deployment.Application.ApplicationDeployment.
        CurrentDeployment.ActivationUri;
        if (appUri != null)
        {
```

```
                NameValueCollection parms =
                HttpUtility.ParseQueryString(appUri.AbsoluteUri);
                if (parms != null)
                {
                    paramCountLbl.Text = parms.Count.ToString();
                    usernameLbl.Text = parms[0];
                    pwdLbl.Text = parms[1];
                }
                else
                {
                    MessageBox.Show("no parameters passed to application");
                }
            }
        }
        catch (Exception ee)
        {
            MessageBox.Show(ee.Message);
        }
    }
```

The DisplayURLParameters method gets the URI to the application using the ActivationUri property. The method uses the static ParseQueryString method to parse the query string. You can download the sample application from http://www.sayedhashimi.com/downloads/ClickOnceURLParams.zip.

The MAGE tool can also create a ClickOnce deployment to support passing URL parameters (similar to Visual Studio 2005). If you are generating a ClickOnce deployment using MSBuild, then you'll need to set the TrustUrlParameters property to true when you create your GenerateDeploymentManifest task. This property is set to false by default.

Note that there is a caveat to passing URL parameters to a ClickOnce-deployed application: ClickOnce does not support passing URL parameters to the application if the application is activated from the Start menu shortcut. In other words, you have to activate the application using a URL. If the user starts the application by going to the Start menu, you will not get the URL parameters. The URL parameter-passing feature works really well with online applications. Recall that online applications don't get Start menu shortcuts (or an entry in Add/Remove Programs) and are always activated via the URL. With offline applications, the URL parameter passing works particularly well in situations where the application is passed in a username and password (and possibly other parameter) on the URL to bypass the user having to log in.

Installing the Publisher Certificate Programmatically with a Prerequisite

Chapter 7 discussed using trusted publishers with ClickOnce. We said that when your application's deployment manifest is downloaded to the client, the ClickOnce runtime sees whether the publisher certificate of the application is in the Trusted Publisher store for the logged-in user. If the trusted publisher certificate is found, then it verifies that the certificate authority that issued the certificate is in the Root Certificate Authority store. If both of these conditions pass, then ClickOnce does not display the Unknown Publisher security dialog box to the user.

In Chapter 7 we showed that you can manually take a certificate and install it in the two certificate stores using Visual Studio 2005. In an enterprise environment, it's not possible to get to all of the clients and do this step. Generally, you do this using a network setup package (such as Tivoli or SMS) prior to users installing the application. If this is possible in your environment, then this option is preferable. If not, you can install the certificate that your application is signed with to the two stores using a custom prerequisite. The idea here is to write a small MSI that uses a custom installer action to put the certificate into the desired stores. Here is a custom installer action class that does this:

```
using System;
using System.Collections.Generic;
using System.ComponentModel;
using System.Configuration.Install;
using System.Security.Cryptography.X509Certificates;
using System.Reflection;

namespace Installers
{
    [RunInstaller(true)]
    public partial class CertInstaller : Installer
    {
        // the certificate is packaged as
        // part of this assembly. The following path refers
        // to the certificate using a fully qualified name.
        private static readonly String CERTIFICATE_PATH
            = "Installers.deploycert.cer";

        public CertInstaller()
        {
            InitializeComponent();
        }
        public override void Install(System.Collections.IDictionary stateSaver)
        {
            base.Install(stateSaver);
            // we have to put the certificate in two stores:
            // the Trusted Root Certification Authorities store and
            // the Trusted Publisher store.

            Stream certStream = null;
            X509Store rootStore = null, publisherStore = null;
            try
            {
                // get a reference to the root store
                rootStore = new X509Store("Root", StoreLocation.LocalMachine);

                if (rootStore != null)
                {
                    // open it with write access
```

```
                    rootStore.Open(OpenFlags.ReadWrite);
                    // get a reference to the Trusted Publisher store
                    publisherStore
        = new X509Store("TrustedPublisher", StoreLocation.LocalMachine);

                    if (publisherStore != null)
                    {
                        // open it with write access
                        publisherStore.Open(OpenFlags.ReadWrite);
                        // get the certificate. Note that the certificate
                        // is an embedded resource in this assembly.
                        Assembly asm = Assembly.GetAssembly(this.GetType());
                        if (asm != null)
                        {
                            certStream = asm.GetManifestResourceStream
                          (CertInstaller.CERTIFICATE_PATH);

                            if (certStream != null)
                            {
                                // read the certificate
                                BinaryReader reader = new BinaryReader(certStream);
                                byte[] certData = reader.
                                  ReadBytes((int)certStream.Length);
                                // create a certificate object
                                X509Certificate2 cert =
                                    new X509Certificate2(certData);
                                if (cert != null)
                                {
                                    // add it to the root store
                                    rootStore.Add(cert);
                                    // add it to the Trusted Publisher store
                                    publisherStore.Add(cert);
                                }
                            }
                        }
                    }
                }
            }
            finally
            {
                if (rootStore != null)
                {
                    rootStore.Close();
                }
                if (publisherStore != null)
                {
                    publisherStore.Close();
                }
```

```
            if (certStream != null)
            {
                certStream.Close();
            }

        }
    }
  }
}
```

This installer class overrides the `Install` method of the base class to install the certificate to the two stores. As shown, the method gets references to the Root Certificate Authority store and the Trusted Publisher store (using the `X509Store` class) and then adds the certificate (an instance of the `X509Certificate2` class) to each store. Note that if the certificate already exists in these stores, calling the add method again doesn't create a duplicate.

Creating File Type Associations for ClickOnce Deployments

Windows Forms applications often work with various file formats. For example, an application that creates picture albums or allows for picture manipulation likely supports the Joint Photographic Experts Group (JPEG) file format and the Graphics Interchange Format (GIF). Similarly, it's not rare for an application to produce/consume a proprietary file format. When this is the case, it helps if the deployment technology supports registering the various file types during the initial install of the application. Unfortunately, ClickOnce does not support file type registration out of the box. You can solve this problem in a couple of ways, however. The first, and recommended, approach is to use a custom prerequisite that does the registration for you. The second option is to take advantage of the following well-known facts:

- After ClickOnce installs an application, it immediately launches it.

- The ClickOnce APIs provides a way for you to detect whether the application is running for the first time.

You can use the `IsFirstRun` property on the `ApplicationDeployment` object to determine whether the application is running for the first time:

```
if (System.Deployment.Application.
        ApplicationDeployment.
            CurrentDeployment.IsFirstRun)
{
    // do file registration here
}
```

If `IsFirstRun` returns `true`, then register the file types that your application works with.

This approach is not recommended, however, because it creates an additional problem for you when the application needs to be removed from the machine. That is, when the application is uninstalled, how do you unregister the file associations? ClickOnce doesn't provide a mechanism for you to plug into the install, so creating file associations in this manner ends up with a dirty uninstall scenario. Therefore, it is recommended that you stick with using a custom prerequisite.

Both of these approaches have a compromise. Using a prerequisite package, for example, requires the user installing the application to have administrator privileges (this is a Windows Installer requirement). The second option requires full trust because, at the least, you need to query the `IsFirstRun` property, which demands full trust.

Creating a Desktop Icon for a ClickOnce-Deployed Application

ClickOnce does not support creating desktop icons. If this is a requirement, you can take advantage of the same principles we talked about earlier. That is, you can either opt to use a prerequisite package or use the ClickOnce APIs. Again, consider the side effects before jumping in.

Requiring a Prerequisite After the Initial Install

We've talked at length about deploying prerequisites with ClickOnce applications. You know that when an application is installed for the first time, the user can run a bootstrapper package that can check for and install the application's prerequisite list. This works great for the initial install, but what happens if an application develops a prerequisite in a later version? That is, what happens if you deploy version 1.0 and then in version 2.0 you need an additional prerequisite? For most applications, users will likely activate a ClickOnce application either by going to the Start menu shortcut or by clicking a link that points to the deployment manifest. In these scenarios, you'll have to account for how the user needs to be instructed to download and install the new prerequisite. You have a couple of options.

Option 1: Use a Customized Launch Page and Have Users Always Launch the Application by Running the Bootstrapper Package

The general procedure of deploying a ClickOnce application is to write the application, create its prerequisites, and then publish the application to, for example, a Web server. Users are then sent a link to the deployment manifest or a launch page for the application. For example, this can be something similar to the `publish.htm` page that Visual Studio 2005 generates. Most organizations generally customize the launch page and send users the link to this page rather than distributing the link to the deployment manifest. The launch page serves several purposes:

- It can be used to give users an overview of the application.

- It tells users about the prerequisites of the application and how to run the bootstrapper that can install them, prior to running the application.

- It gives users information about future versions and possibly helpful hints.

- It offers security warnings.

Having a launch page like this not only provides the previous benefits, but you can use it to instruct users to click a link that always kicks off the boostrapper rather than a link that runs the deployment manifest. This ensures that if an additional prerequisite is added to an update, the prerequisite will be installed prior to running the application.

Option 2: Deploy an Update to Notify Users to Install the Prerequisite

It may not be desirable to have users always come to the launch page to run your application, especially with applications that support offline capabilities where users always launch the application from the Start menu shortcut. In these scenarios you can take a different approach. You can deploy a tiny update to your application, ahead of the actual update, to simply instruct users of the prerequisite for the next version. For example, you could create a What's Coming dialog box and have instructions for users to go to the launch page to run the bootstrapper setup package. This option is attractive because you can do sophisticated checks to ensure that all of your users have run the bootstrapper package. For example, you deploy an update with the What's Coming dialog box. This dialog box provides an overview of what is coming in the next version and provides a link for more information about the next version. The link points to the launch page. When the user browses to the launch page, you can run server-side code to record that the user read the page and if the user clicks a button or a link to run the bootstrapper to install the prerequisite, you can then run server-side code to record that the user ran the setup package. Moreover, in your application you can check to see whether the prerequisite has been installed and then decide to continue to show the What's Coming dialog box or not. Once you think all (or most) users have installed the prerequisite, you can then deploy the real update.

Option 3: Wait Until the Prerequisite Is Used and Then Show the User a Message After an Exception

Checking for prerequisites can be as simple as running a piece of code that uses the prerequisites within a `try`/`catch` block. If you get an exception, you can direct the user to the launch page, discussed in the "Option 1" scenario, and have them run the bootstrapper package.

Again, all of the options have pros and cons and thus require considerable attention to ensure that users receive a seamless update experience (if possible).

Deploying a ClickOnce Application from a CD/DVD

With ClickOnce, you can perform the initial install of your application using removable media (such as a CD or DVD) while providing updates from a Web server or file server. When would you want to do this? ClickOnce provides this feature to support the following deployment scenarios:

- You have a large project, and it is unreasonable for your users to suffer through the initial install of the application.

- You have a medium/large deployment, but your user base has a slow network connection.

- Your users have no network connection or their network connection is not stable (they don't have connectivity all the time).

As you can see, in all these cases it would be nice if you could put your ClickOnce deployment on a CD/DVD and at the same time take advantage of automatic updates provided by ClickOnce. ClickOnce supports this by allowing application publishers to specify an update location (a file share/Web server). Here are the steps to produce an application that can be installed from a CD/DVD and updated from a network share/Web server:

1. Create a new folder at `c:\testpublish\`.

2. Create a new Windows Forms application in Visual Studio 2005.

3. Open the Project Designer, and go to the Publish tab.

4. Set the Publish Location to `c:\testpublish\`.

5. Click the Publish Wizard button.

6. Choose Next in the first dialog box. In the How Will Users Install the Application dialog box, choose From a CD-ROM or DVD-ROM. Press Next.

7. In the Where Will the Application Check for Updates dialog box, either enter a network share or create a virtual directory under a Web site that you have used to deploy Click-Once applications. ClickOnce will use this URL to detect and download updates.

8. In the Ready to Publish dialog box, choose Finish.

Visual Studio will then publish the application to `c:\testpublish\`. You can then take the application and burn it onto a CD/DVD. Take the CD/DVD to another machine and run the `setup.exe` bootstrapper to install the application. Note that because the entire application is copied to the CD/DVD, your users don't need a network connection to install the application. To get updates, however, a network connection is a necessity.

If you want to test how an update will work, then after you install the application, publish an update to your update folder and then start the application.

Summary

In this chapter, we discussed three important tools related to ClickOnce. We talked about the Bootstrapper Manifest Generator (BMG), the Manifest Generation and Editing (MAGE) tool, and MSBuild. All of the discussions in this chapter related to practical problems. For example, we showed how you can use the BMG tool to quickly create the product and package XML files needed to create custom prerequisites. The discussions about the MAGE tools gave four practical scenarios where the MAGE tool can be useful, and the discussion of MSBuild showed how to automate the generation of a ClickOnce deployment. All of these tools will be useful as you work with ClickOnce. The last portion of this chapter talked about some practical ClickOnce scenarios.

Index

You Need the Companion eBook

Your purchase of this book entitles you to its companion eBook for only $10.

We believe this Apress title will prove so indispensable that you'll want to carry it with you everywhere, which is why we are offering the companion eBook for $10 to customers who purchase this book now. Convenient and fully searchable, the eBook version of any content-rich, page-heavy Apress book makes a valuable addition to your programming library. You can easily find, copy, and apply code—and then perform examples by quickly toggling between instructions and the application. Even simultaneously tackling a donut, diet soda, and complex code becomes simplified with hands-free eBooks!

Once you purchase this book, getting the $10 companion eBook is simple:

❶ Visit **www.apress.com/promo/tendollars/**.

❷ Complete a basic registration form to receive a randomly generated question about this title.

❸ Answer the question correctly in 60 seconds and you will receive a promotional code to redeem for the $10 eBook.

2560 Ninth Street • Suite 219 • Berkeley, CA 94710

eBookshop

Offer valid through 11/06.